NEW YORK REVIEW BOOKS
CLASSICS

LETTERS

SUMMER 1926

BORIS PASTERNAK (1890–1960), the son of a distinguished
painter, was born in Moscow and made his reputation as a
poet with his first collection, *My Sister, Life*, written in 1917.
Silenced by the Soviet authorities for much of his career, in 1957
Pasternak permitted the publication abroad of his novel *Doctor
Zhivago*. He was forced by his government to decline the 1958
Nobel Prize for Literature.

MARINA TSVETAYEVA (1892–1941), whose father was a
classicist and whose mother was a pianist, was born in Moscow
and published her first book of poems at seventeen. Tsvetayeva
left Russia in 1922 with her two children and her husband, Sergei
Efron, who fought against the Red Army in the 1918–1921 Civil
War but was later to become a Soviet spy. Often living from hand
to mouth, the family remained abroad until 1939. Two years later,
after the execution of her husband and the arrest of her daughter,
Tsvetayeva committed suicide. Along with numerous lyrics, her
works include several extraordinary long poems, among them *The
Poem of the End*, *The Poem of the Mountain*, and *The Ratcatcher*.

RAINER MARIA RILKE (1875–1926) was born in Prague, the
child of a military officer who worked for the railways. His major
books include *The Book of Hours*, inspired by a trip to Russia,
the two volumes of *New Poems*, *The Duino Elegies*, and *Sonnets
to Orpheus*.

SUSAN SONTAG has written novels, stories, essays, and plays;
written and directed films; and worked as a theater director in the
United States and Europe. In 2001 she was awarded the Jerusalem
Prize. Her most recent book is *In America*, a novel which won the
National Book Award for Fiction in 2000.

LETTERS

SUMMER 1926

BORIS PASTERNAK

MARINA TSVETAYEVA

RAINER MARIA RILKE

Edited by
YEVGENY PASTERNAK
YELENA PASTERNAK
KONSTANTIN M. AZADOVSKY

Translated by
MARGARET WETTLIN
WALTER ARNDT
JAMEY GAMBRELL

Preface by
SUSAN SONTAG

NEW YORK REVIEW BOOKS

New York

This is a New York Review Book
Published by The New York Review of Books
435 Hudson Street, New York, NY 10014
www.nyrb.com

Library of Congress Cataloging-in-Publication Data
Pasternak, Boris Leonidovich, 1890–1960.
  [Correspondence. English. Selections]
  Letters, summer 1926 : Boris Leonidovich Pasternak, Marina Tsvetayeva,
Rainer Maria Rilke / translated by Margaret Wettlin, Walter Arndt, Jamey
Gambrell ; edited by Yegevny Pasternak, Yelena Pasternak, Konstantin M.
Azadovsky ; preface by Susan Sontag.
    p. cm.
Previously published in German in 1983 under the title: Rainer Maria
Rilke, Marina Zwetajewa, Boris Pasternak.
  ISBN 0-940322-71-4 (alk. paper)
  1. Pasternak, Boris Leonidovich, 1890–1960—Correspondence. 2.
TSvetaeva, Marina, 1892–1941—Correspondence. 3. Rilke, Rainer Maria,
1875–1926—Correspondence. 4. Authors, German—20th
century—Correspondence. 5. Authors, Russian—20th
century—Correspondence. I. TSvetaeva, Marina, 1892–1941. II. Rilke,
Rainer Maria, 1875–1926. III. Pasternak, E. B. (Evgenii Borisovich),
1923– IV. Pasternak, E. V. V. Azadovskii, K. (Konstantin) VI. Title.
  PG3476.P27 Z48 2001
  891.71'42—dc21   2001001874

ISBN 978-0-940322-71-4

Book design by Lizzie Scott
Printed in the United States of America on acid-free paper.
10 9 8 7

To the memory of Alexandra Ryabinina

CONTENTS

CONTENTS

PREFACE: 1926 . . .

WHAT IS happening in 1926, when the three poets are writing to one another?

On May 12, Shostakovich's Symphony No. 1 in F Minor is heard for the first time, performed by the Leningrad Philharmony; the composer is nineteen years old.

On June 10, the elderly Catalan architect Antonio Gaudí, on the walk he takes every day from the construction site of the Cathedral of the Sagrada Familia to a church in the same neighborhood in Barcelona for vespers, is hit by a trolley, lies unattended on the street (because, it's said, nobody recognizes him), and dies.

On August 6, Gertrude Ederle, nineteen years old, American, swims from Cap Griz-Nez, France, to Kingsdown, England, in fourteen hours and thirty-one minutes, becoming the first woman to swim the English Channel and the first woman competing in a major sport to best the male record-holder.

On August 23, the movie idol Rudolph Valentino dies of endocarditis and septicemia in a hospital in New York.

On September 3, a steel Broadcasting Tower (Funkturm), 138 meters high with restaurant and panorama platform, is inaugurated in Berlin.

Some books: Volume Two of Hitler's *Mein Kampf*, Hart Crane's *White Buildings*, A. A. Milne's *Winnie the Pooh*, Viktor Shklovsky's *Third Factory*, Louis Aragon's *Le Paysan de Paris*, D. H. Lawrence's *The Plumed Serpent*, Hemingway's *The Sun Also Rises*, Agatha Christie's *The Murder of Roger Ackroyd*, T. E. Lawrence's *The Seven Pillars of Wisdom*.

A few films: Fritz Lang's *Metropolis*, Vsevolod Pudovkin's *Mother*, Jean Renoir's *Nana*, Herbert Brenon's *Beau Geste*.

Two plays: Bertolt Brecht's *Mann ist Mann* and Jean Cocteau's *Orphée*.

On December 6, Walter Benjamin arrives for a two-month stay in Moscow. He does not meet the thirty-six-year-old Boris Pasternak.

Pasternak has not seen Marina Tsvetayeva for four years. Since she left Russia in 1922, they have become each other's most cherished interlocutor and Pasternak, tacitly acknowledging Tsvetayeva as the greater poet, has made her his first reader.

Tsvetayeva, who is thirty-four, is living in penury with her husband and two children in Paris.

Rilke, who is fifty-one, is dying of leukemia in a sanatorium in Switzerland.

Letters: Summer 1926 is a portrait of the sacred delirium of art. There are three participants: a god and two worshipers, who are also worshipers of each other (and who we, the readers of their letters, know to be future gods).

A pair of young Russian poets, who have exchanged years of fervent letters about work and life, enter into correspondence with a great German poet who, for both, is poetry incarnate. These three-way love letters—and they are that—are an incomparable dramatization of ardor about poetry and about the life of the spirit.

They portray a domain of reckless feeling and purity of aspiration which it would be our loss to dismiss as "romantic."

The literatures written in German and in Russian have been particularly devoted to spiritual exaltation. Tsvetayeva and Pasternak know German, and Rilke has studied and attained a passable mastery of Russian—all three suffused by the dreams of literary divinity promulgated in these languages. The Russians, lovers of German poetry and music since childhood (the mothers of both were pianists), expect the greatest poet of the age to be someone writing in the language of Goethe and Hölderlin. And the German-language poet has had as a formative early love and mentor a writer, born in St. Petersburg, with whom he traveled twice to Russia, ever since which he has considered that country his true, spiritual homeland.

On the second of these trips, in 1900, Pasternak actually saw and probably was presented to the young Rilke.

Pasternak's father, the celebrated painter, was an esteemed acquaintance; Boris, the future poet, was ten years old. It is with the sacred memory of Rilke boarding a train with his lover Lou Andreas-Salomé—they remain, reverently, unnamed —that Pasternak begins *Safe Conduct* (1931), his supreme achievement in prose.

Tsvetayeva, of course, has never set eyes on Rilke.

All three poets are agitated by seemingly incompatible needs: for the most absolute solitude and for the most intense communion with another like-minded spirit. "My voice can ring out pure and clear only when absolutely solitary," Pasternak tells his father in a letter. Ardor inflected by intransigence drives all of Tsvetayeva's writings. In "Art in the Light of Conscience" (1932), she writes:

> The poet can have only one prayer: not to understand the unacceptable—let me not understand, so that I may not be seduced . . . let me not hear, so that I may not answer . . . The poet's only prayer is a prayer for deafness.

And the signature two-step of Rilke's life, as we know from his letters to a variety of correspondents, mostly women, is flight from intimacy and a bid for unconditional sympathy and understanding.

Although the younger poets announce themselves as acolytes, the letters quickly become an exchange of equals, a competition of affinities. To those familiar with the main branches of Rilke's grandiose, often stately correspondence it may come as a surprise to find him responding in almost the same eager, jubilant tones as his two Russian admirers. But never has he had interlocutors of this caliber. The sovereign, didactic Rilke we know from the *Letters to a Young Poet*, written between 1903 and 1908, has disappeared. Here is only angelic conversation. Nothing to teach. Nothing to learn.

Opera is the only medium now in which it is still acceptable to rhapsodize. The duo that concludes Richard Strauss's *Ariadne auf Naxos*, whose libretto is by one of Rilke's contemporaries, Hugo von Hofmannsthal, offers a comparable effusiveness. We are surely more comfortable with the paean to love as rebirth and self-transformation sung by Ariadne and Bacchus than with the upsurges of amorous feeling declared by the three poets.

And these letters are not concluding duos. They are duos trying, and eventually failing, to be trios. What kind of possession of each other do the poets expect? How consuming and how exclusive is this kind of love?

The correspondence has begun, with Pasternak's father as the intermediary, between Rilke and Pasternak. Then Pasternak suggests to Rilke that he write to Tsvetayeva, and the situation becomes a correspondence *à trois*. Last to enter the lists, Tsvetayeva quickly becomes the igniting force, so powerful, so outrageous are her need, her boldness, her emotional nakedness. Tsvetayeva is the relentless one, outgalloping first Pasternak, then Rilke. Pasternak, who no longer knows what to demand of Rilke, retreats (and Tsvetayeva also calls a halt to *their* correspondence); Tsvetayeva can envisage an erotic, engulfing tie. Imploring Rilke to consent to a meeting, she succeeds only in driving him away. Rilke, in his turn, falls silent. (His last letter to her is on August 19.)

The flow of rhetoric reaches the precipice of the sublime, and topples over into hysteria, anguish, dread.

But, curiously, death seems quite unreal. How astonished and shattered the Russians are when this "phenomenon of nature" (so they thought of Rilke) is in *some* sense no more. Silence should be full. Silence which now has the name of death seems too great a diminishment.

So the correspondence has to continue.

Tsvetayeva writes a letter to Rilke a few days after being told he has died at the end of December, and addresses a long prose ode to him ("Your Death") the following year. The manuscript of *Safe Conduct*, which Pasternak completes almost five years after Rilke's death, ends with a letter to Rilke. ("If you were alive, this is the letter I would send you today.") Leading the reader through a labyrinth of elliptical memoiristic prose to the core of the poet's inwardness, *Safe Conduct* is written under the sign of Rilke and, if only unconsciously, in competition with Rilke, being an attempt to match if not surpass *The Notebooks of Malte Laurids Brigge* (1910), Rilke's supreme achievement in prose.

Early in *Safe Conduct*, Pasternak speaks of living on and for those occasions when "a complete feeling burst into space with the whole extent of space before it." Never has a brief for the powers of lyric poetry been made so brilliantly, so rapturously, as in these letters. Poetry cannot be abandoned or renounced, once you are "the lyre's thrall," Tsvetayeva instructs Pasternak in a letter of July 1925. "With poetry, dear friend, as with love; no separation until it drops you."

Or until death intervenes. Tsvetayeva and Pasternak haven't suspected that Rilke was seriously ill. Learning that he has died, the two poets are incredulous: it seems, cosmically speaking, unjust. And fifteen years later Pasternak would be surprised and remorseful when he received the news of Tsvetayeva's suicide in August 1941. He hadn't, he admitted, grasped the inevitability of the doom that awaited her if she decided to return to the Soviet Union with her family, as she did in 1939.

Separation had made everything replete. What would Rilke and Tsvetayeva have said to each other had they actually met? We know what Pasternak *didn't* say to Tsvetayeva when they were briefly reunited after thirteen years, in June 1935, on the day he arrived in Paris in the nightmarish role of official Soviet delegate to the International Writers Congress for the Defense of Culture: he didn't warn her not to come back, not to think of coming back, to Moscow.

Maybe the ecstasies channeled into this correspondence could only have been voiced in separateness, and in response to the ways in which they failed one another. (As the greatest writers invariably demand too much of, and are failed by, readers.) Nothing can dim the incandescence of those exchanges over a few months in 1926 when they were hurling themselves at one another, making their impossible, glorious demands. Today, when "all is drowning in Pharisaism"—the phrase is Pasternak's—their ardors and their tenacities feel like raft, beacon, beach.

—SUSAN SONTAG

FOREWORD TO
THE SECOND EDITION

THE YEAR 2001 marks the seventy-fifth anniversary of the death of the great German poet Rainer Maria Rilke. This book, which we first compiled twenty-five years ago, concerns 1926, the last year of his life. It contains his brief correspondence with the poets Marina Tsvetayeva and Boris Pasternak, who were drawn to the elder poet by their love and admiration for his great poetic gift.

The body of the correspondence, which we unexpectedly received a quarter of a century ago, was accompanied in the first edition by commentary on the circumstances that brought these three great poets together and on their relationships with one another. The book was translated into many languages. For the Russian edition, which became possible only in the early 1990s, the commentary was significantly expanded by new documents. A second, enlarged Russian edition appeared last year.

In addition to the letters to and from Rilke, this book contains part of the 1926 correspondence of Pasternak and Tsvetayeva. The full extent of the Russian poets' correspondence, which continued over the course of many years, is not yet known. The primary collection of Tsvetayeva manuscripts was deposited at the State Archives of Literature and Art in Moscow by her daughter, Ariadna Efron, and was closed for twenty-five years. Last year the archive was opened. Elena Korkina, the scholar preparing the archives for publication, estimates that she will be able to begin work on the Pasternak letters no sooner than several years from now.

On October 12, 1941, during the alarming days of the German attack on Moscow and the evacuation, Pasternak gave the originals of Tsvetayeva's letters for safekeeping to her admirers Ekaterina Krasheninnikova and Olga Setnitskaya. He had just met with Marina Tsvetayeva's son, Georgy (Mur), who had returned from Elabuga with news of the days preceding his mother's suicide. Two days later Pasternak himself was evacuated from Moscow with a group of writers and joined his family.

On receiving the Tsvetayeva papers, the young women made copies of the poems and some of the letters and wrote a description of the correspondence. In 1944–45, with Pasternak's permission, they took a number of letters to be copied to the poet and collector Aleksei Kruchyonykh, who planned to include them in the archive he was compiling. In the course of this transfer, the letters were lost. Drafts of these letters were, however, preserved in notebooks in the Tsvetayeva archives, and we have drawn on some of these in this new edition.

The May 11, 1927, letter from Tsvetayeva to Pasternak included in the epilogue was discovered only two years ago in a manuscript version of Krasheninnikova's copy of October 19, 1941. Illegible words and omissions have been filled in according to context, and they are given in brackets. The letter, written over a year after Rilke's death, discusses a possible meeting between Tsvetayeva and Pasternak. In the spring of 1926, they had planned to visit Rilke together in Muzot; now they dreamed of visiting his grave in Rarogne, the grave to which "the path will not be overgrown," as Tsvetayeva wrote Pasternak's father in 1928.

We can only surmise how Tsvetayeva's passionate soul-baring was received, since we do not have access to Pasternak's reply. But judging by the fact that Pasternak immediately wrote Raisa Lomonosova that he had rejected the idea of a trip abroad, we can assume that Tsvetayeva's plea did not have the desired effect.

The unexpected appearance of this long-lost letter leads us to believe that others will undoubtedly emerge once the full contents of the relevant archives have been made available. We hope that at some point another more complete edition of this book will be possible, one that will broaden and deepen our understanding of this extraordinary poetic encounter.

—THE EDITORS
MARCH 12, 2001

A NOTE ON THE ENGLISH EDITION

ALL THE letters in this correspondence except those from Rilke and those to Rilke from Pasternak and Tsvetayeva were originally written in Russian, and have been translated by Margaret Wettlin. She has also translated the introduction to this volume, the editorial remarks within individual chapters, and many of the notes that appear at the foot of the pages and at the back of the book. Letters from Rilke and letters to Rilke from Pasternak and Tsvetayeva, written in German, have been translated by Walter Arndt, who has also added elucidatory footnotes on his translation. He has in addition translated and annotated the Russian, German, and French poetry appearing in this volume.

Notes helpful to an understanding of the correspondence (identifications of persons and places, for example) have been placed at the foot of the pages and are indicated in the text by asterisks and other standard symbols. Superscript numbers in the text (mostly in the introduction) refer the reader to the bibliographic notes at the end of the book, which will prove useful to those wishing to consult original sources. In preparing this edition for an English-speaking audience, the publisher has added many explanatory footnotes not contained in either the original Russian manuscript or the published German translation; by the same token, the publisher has abridged or dropped notes that were not absolutely essential for an appreciation of the correspondence, many of these notes referring to material not available in English translation. The interested reader is referred to Rilke-Zwetajewa-Pasternak, *Briefwechsel* (Frankfurt am Main: Insel Verlag, 1983).

The publisher is grateful to Konstantin and Emilia Hramov for the many helpful suggestions they made after reading the portion of this volume that was translated from Russian, and to Walter Arndt for his review of the whole manuscript. Walter Arndt gratefully acknowledges the valuable help of his colleague Lev Losev on some points of Orthodox liturgy and on some breathtaking artifacts of Tsvetayeva's highly personal syntax that figure in Tsvetayeva's "A New Year's."

A NOTE ON THE
SECOND ENGLISH EDITION

This edition contains a revised and substantially enlarged version of the epilogue, which corresponds largely to the new Russian version published by the editors in 2000. It also includes Tsvetayeva's two essays on Rilke, which were published in the Russian émigré press during her lifetime.

All revisions and additions to the epilogue, including, most notably, Tsvetayeva's May 11, 1927, letter to Pasternak and the poems "Signs," were translated by Jamey Gambrell, as were Tsvetayeva's essays on Rilke, "Your Death" and "A Few of Rainer Maria Rilke's Letters." These essays first appeared in English in, respectively, *Partisan Review*, No. 2, 1987, and *Antaeus*, Spring 1987. The translator wishes to express her gratitude to Alexander Sumerkin for help in elucidating the more daunting passages of Tsvetayeva's prose.

LETTERS

SUMMER 1926

INTRODUCTION

1

LETTERS: SUMMER 1926 gathers together material that is tragic and sublime: the four-month correspondence of three European poets, brought to an end by the illness and death of the eldest, Rainer Maria Rilke (1875–1926). The letters brilliantly concentrate and refract the entire correspondence of the two other poets, Marina Tsvetayeva (1892–1941) and Boris Pasternak (1890–1960), a correspondence which extended over many years and much of which cannot be published until the next century.

The editors felt obliged to prepare all the Pasternak-Tsvetayeva-Rilke letters for publication after the release of Tsvetayeva's letters to Rilke by the Manuscript Department of the Swiss National Library in Berne in January 1977, when Tsvetayeva's fifty-year ban on their publication expired. Soon afterward *Zeitschrift für slavische Philologie* printed Tsvetayeva's letters, but this violated the wishes of the author and, more important, profaned the substance of the letters. For at various times Tsvetayeva had insisted that the correspondence could and should be published *as a whole*

> in fifty years, when all this is over, *completely* over, and our bodies have rotted, and the ink has faded, when the receiver has gone to join the sender (I—the first letter to be delivered!), when Rilke's letters will be simply Rilke letters—not to me—to everybody—when I myself will merge with all things and—oh, this is the main thing!— when I will have no need of Rilke's letters because all of

Rilke will then be mine. They must not be published without asking. Without asking means—ahead of time. As long as the receiver is here and the sender is there, no answer can be given. His answer to my asking will be the date. Will that do? Thank you. It will not be sooner than—God knows when. . . .

The seven letters lying in my box (doing exactly what he is doing—not he, but his body—like the letters —not thoughts, but the body of thoughts)—those seven letters lying in my box along with pictures of him and that last Elegy, I give to future generations—give them now, not in the future. When they are born they will receive these letters. When they are born I will have passed away. That will be the day of the resurrection of his thoughts in the flesh. Let them sleep until Judgment Day, a day not of Fear but of Light. Thus, dutiful and jealous, I neither betray nor hide them.[1]

Tsvetayeva's actions confirm her intentions. In 1939 she returned to the Soviet Union from Western Europe, only to be evacuated from Moscow to the city of Yelabuga at the outbreak of Soviet–German fighting in 1941; it was here that, on August 31, 1941, she took her own life. But on leaving Moscow she had removed from her papers a packet containing Rilke's letters and photographs, books he had inscribed to her, and eleven letters from Boris Pasternak. She went to the State Publishing House, whose Department of Literature of National Republics of the USSR had supplied her with translating work (her only source of income), and entrusted the packet to the department's editor-in-chief, Alexandra Ryabinina. Tsvetayeva must have been particularly concerned about the fate of these letters: copies carefully traced in her own hand remained among her personal papers, but apparently she felt that the originals required a more secure place.

Shortly after her return to the Soviet Union Tsvetayeva

had been brought to Ryabinina by Pasternak himself, who had on more than one occasion been aided by Ryabinina. Tsvetayeva saw Ryabinina as someone she could trust implicitly, and she was not to be disappointed. After jealously preserving the papers for many years, Ryabinina turned them over to Pasternak's heirs in 1975, explaining that she did this to enable the remarkable correspondence to be published before long. On the packet, in Tsvetayeva's hand, was written: "Rilke and Pasternak 1926."

During World War II virtually all of Tsvetayeva's letters to Pasternak were lost, in circumstances related in Pasternak's autobiographical article "People and Circumstances."[2] But before this loss occurred, copies had been made of twenty of them,[3] and four originals had been saved. Furthermore, Tsvetayeva had the habit of drafting her letters in a notebook; since this notebook has survived, the text of the letters she sent Pasternak in the summer of 1926 can be verified. Thus we have at our disposal all that Tsvetayeva intended when she said she would neither betray nor hide the letters but preserve them until such time as she considered proper.

The editors would like to thank all those who aided them in their work, especially Anastasia Ivanovna Tsvetayeva, Anna Alexandrovna Saakyants, Yelena Baurdzhanovna Korkina, Lydia Pasternak Slater, Josepha Baier, Christoph Sieber-Rilke, and Joachim Storck.

2

Unlike a correspondence that covers an extended period, this exchange of letters covers but a single moment. In one bright flash we glimpse a scene of startling concentration, more vivid in detail than if the picture were exposed to prolonged light. One has to read and reread, to ask questions and seek answers in the works, the biographies, the circumstances relating to a different reality—a tragically interrupted historical reality. Boris Pasternak wrote that historical changes affected every aspect of their lives, that "even the language in which people once spoke disappeared." For that reason, "rejecting much, rejecting things that are risky and extreme, rejecting the peculiarities of the art of the earlier time," he makes it his purpose to "present in a modern translation, in the more ordinary, commonplace, and tranquil language now prevailing, at least part of the former world, and this the most precious part"—that which has throughout the ages been distinguished by the Gospel theme of "the thermal, spectral, organic perception of life."[4] It is of this that Pasternak spoke when he wrote to Tsvetayeva, in a letter of April 20, 1926, that he would remain in Moscow one more year for the sake of his work: "One year—this is my time limit and I will observe it. I am speaking *only* about work, about fortifying myself, about continuing efforts aimed at *restoring* to history a generation that seems to have dropped out of it, the generation to which *you and I belong*."

This introduction will attempt to throw light on details that remain in shadow, and to provide an account of the circumstances that shaped the correspondence.

3

Each of the three correspondents occupies an independent place in European literature and has created his or her own poetic world. In contrast to innovators of the avant-garde, they changed nothing that was tried and true: they did not find the destruction of the old essential or even justifiable. The new emerged because direct imitation does not allow for the preservation of lofty traditions; only inspiration—freshness, originality, the artist's personal vision—can add to the wealth of mankind's spiritual legacy. Tradition, as Pasternak wrote, lies at the heart of an artist's work, and faithfulness to tradition is precisely what promises him distinctiveness, the unexampled originality of his personal experience.

Presumably this was Rilke's attitude toward German romanticism, which, both directly and in the refracted light of Russian symbolism, became the spiritual cradle of Pasternak and Tsvetayeva. Unlike those who followed the beaten path of fashionable literary schools and trends, they both "withdrew from the world at an early age," repelled by "reigning modes" (Pasternak's letter to Tsvetayeva of March 25, 1926).

For Pasternak and Tsvetayeva, Rilke was the incarnation of poetry and the spiritual life, a model to be worshipfully followed. His German lyric poetry especially attracted the Russian poets because it allowed them to make use of his experience in a highly original way, without a shade of imitation. Tsvetayeva defines this relationship with the word *nachdichten*: "Today I would like Rilke to speak—through me. In everyday language this is called translation. (How much better the Germans put it—*nachdichten*! Following in the poet's footsteps, to lay again the path he has already laid. Let *nach* mean follow, but *dichten** always has new meaning. *Nachdichten*—laying anew a path, all traces of which are instantaneously grown over.) But 'translate' has another meaning: to translate not only *into* (into Russian, for example) but also *to* (to the opposite bank of the river). I will translate Rilke into Russian and he, in time, will translate me to the other world."[5]

Pasternak, too, wrote of the use he made of Rilke's creative experience: "I always believed that in my own efforts, in all of my work, I did nothing but translate or write variations on his themes, adding nothing to his world, always sailing in his waters."[6]

For Tsvetayeva and Pasternak, Rilke's poetry was the high-

---

*Sing? Relate? Fancy? Create? In Russian—no word for it. [M. Ts.]

est proof that in this divided and distorted world there exist
real and immutable values not to be measured by pragmatic
standards.

4

The intense interest Rilke took in the fate of Pasternak and
Tsvetayeva during that last year of his life had its roots in
memories, carefully nurtured and treasured, of visits he made
to Russia in 1899 and 1900.

Rilke, who was quite a young man when he visited Russia,
remained her loyal and ardent admirer until his death. Everything associated with Russia was for him filled with deep
spiritual meaning. "He loved Russia as I love Germany, not
bound by ties of blood but in the free passion of a spirit,"
wrote Tsvetayeva of Rilke.[7] Rilke himself spoke of this again
and again: "Among the great and mysterious assurances up-
holding my life is the fact that Russia is my native land"
(1903).[8] "What do I owe Russia? She made me what I am, of
her my inner self was born; there is the homeland of my in-
stinctual being, every kind of spiritual origin" (1920).[9] "Russia became in a certain sense the basis of my perceptions and
experience," he confessed to his "young friend" not long before his death.[10] And in a letter to the French writer and translator Maurice Betz, Rilke called his meeting with Russia the
decisive event of his life.[11]

Rilke's two trips to Russia, his determined efforts to learn
the Russian language, to become familiar with Russian history, art, and literature, his making the acquaintance of eminent Russian writers and artists—all this testifies to the
strength of the country's attraction for him.

In that neoromantic period the late nineteenth century,
Western Europe was discovering, through Dostoyevsky and
Tolstoy, a little-known land inhabited by what many consid-

ered a special people, chosen by God, which had yet to make its contribution to history. Western Europeans believed that their own civilization, sunk in rationalism and atheism, had run its course and was fast declining, while Russia, a youthful land, had not exhausted its fund of primordial faith and could expect a great spiritual blossoming. Seen in such a light, patriarchal Russia was the antipode of the bourgeois West.

This attitude was confirmed in Rilke by his friend Lou Andreas-Salomé, whom the young poet first met in Munich in the spring of 1897. At the time, Andreas-Salomé was well known in German modernist circles. She wrote critical and philosophical articles for leading German periodicals and was also trying her hand at fiction. In 1894 she published a book about her friendship with Nietzsche (1882–83).

Andreas-Salomé was born and raised in St. Petersburg, the daughter of a general stationed in Russia. At the age of nineteen she left Russia for Zurich, then, in 1887, married the well-known orientalist Friedrich Carl Andreas. Although she lived permanently in Germany after that, she never severed her spiritual ties with Russia. Almost every year she visited her mother in St. Petersburg, and from 1897 on she kept turning to Russian themes in her writing. She tried to contribute to the St. Petersburg journal *Severny vestnik*, the first Russian periodical to publish the works of Russian and West European symbolists. It was she who introduced Rilke to the critic Akim Volynsky.

For the young Rilke, then avidly seeking his path in art, meeting Lou Andreas-Salomé was an event of enormous significance. She interested him in Russian culture and the Russian language, and helped him begin preparing for Russia. The Russian writer Sofia Schill (pseudonym Sergei Orlovsky), who met Rilke and Andreas-Salomé in the winter of 1899–1900 in Berlin, shortly after their first visit to Russia, says in her unpublished memoirs: "... actually it was Luisa Gustavovna [Lou] who displayed such a warm and lively interest in

our country; under her influence Rainer Osipovich began
studying Russian writers." In another passage from her memoirs, Schill observes that the young Rilke "found support in
the exemplary life of his friend Andreas-Salomé. Her influence on the young poet was unmistakable."[12]

On April 27, 1899, Rilke, accompanied by Andreas-Salomé
and her husband, arrived in Moscow for the first time. The
travelers put up at the Grand Hotel, near the Kremlin. From
their hotel windows they looked out at the Iversk Gates and
the shrine of Our Lady of Iversk. It was Holy Week and a
crowd of worshipers surrounded the shrine. Church bells
were ringing, services were being held in churches and cathedrals. The sensitive, impressionable Rilke was carried away
by the scene. Twenty-five years later, in a conversation with
the Polish writer and translator Witold Hulewicz, Rilke described his first hours in Russia:

> Tired as I was, I set out, after a short rest, to see the
> town.
> Out of the twilight mist rose the contours of the
> cathedral, with two little silver chapels on either side of
> it and pilgrims resting on the steps, waiting for the
> doors to be opened. This spectacle, so extraordinary for
> me, shook me to the depths of my soul. For the first
> time in my life I was overcome by an indescribable
> emotion, as if I had found my native land. . . .[13]

A week later, on May 2, Rilke and his companions went to
St. Petersburg. Here he spent almost a month and a half that
were filled, as he wrote his mother, "with people and pictures." But he also spent a good deal of time alone, taking
special interest in Russian paintings, including icons, and reflecting deeply on "things Russian," in his effort to plumb
the meaning of what he saw in this new land.

The impressions Rilke received in his first weeks in Russia

confirmed his preconceived idea of it as a wholly unique country. "The poet's image of Russia was of a land of pro-phetic dreams and patriarchal traditions as contrasted with the industrial West," wrote Sofia Schill.[14] Here, he believed, he had found all that he had so desperately been seeking. He saw a fabulous country living in perfect harmony with na-ture, free from the lies of civilization, inhabited by a people who had not exhausted their rich spiritual powers. "It would be hard to describe how new this land is, how it speaks of the future, as though its palaces and churches were yet to be," Rilke wrote to the poet Hugo Salus on March 18, 1899.[15] On the following day, in a letter to the writer Franziska von Reventlow, he said: "Day after day it fills one with a strange feeling to be among people so full of reverence and piety, and I profoundly rejoice in this experience."[16]

During a stay in Italy in 1898, the year before he went to Russia, Rilke had developed his philosophical conception of the artist, the creator, who makes God as Michelangelo did by carving him out of stone, who discovers him in all things and makes him visible. In his "Florentine Diary" Rilke defines the artist as a religious man, solitary and withdrawn from the world in order to concentrate on the inner life. It seemed to Rilke that in Russia his ideals merged with reality, that the Russian was an artist. "In your country," he wrote to his Rus-sian friend Yelena Voronina (Kazitsina) on July 27, 1899, "every-one is a thinker, a philosopher—a poet, I might even say."[17]

Rilke's sojourn in Russia helped him to recover the inner wholeness he had lost in the explorations of his youth, and to regain confidence in himself. In the summer of 1899 he felt certain that he was a poet and was finally convinced of his calling. He believed that "everything Russian" was the "best description" of his thoughts and feelings. "My art has be-come stronger and richer by the addition of immeasurable new territory," he wrote Voronina, "and I return to my native land at the head of a long caravan of shining treasure."[18]

When he got back to Germany he threw himself heart and soul into the study of Russian and everything associated with Russia. Rilke told Voronina in a letter of July 27 that he was spending time "in the company of a Russian grammar," and with such success that he was on the point of reading Pushkin and Lermontov in the original. "Lately," he went on to say, "I have done a great deal of other reading: Tolstoy (I was especially impressed by his little sketch 'Lucerne') and Dostoyevsky, whose *Brothers Karamazov* I am still reading. Dostoyevsky has completely charmed me with his *White Nights*—how delightful they are! As for Garshin,* I have begun to fall under his spell, too."[19]

The views Rilke adopted under the influence of his Russian impressions found their way into his poems, prose, articles, and letters from the second half of 1899. Most of the poems written in September and October are included in the first part of *The Book of Hours: The Book of the Monastic Life*. In their first version these poems were called prayers, and the text that linked them was supposedly written by a monk who was an icon painter. In November 1899 Rilke wrote a cycle of short stories published the following year under the title *The Book of God and Other Things*. Three of them were dedicated to Russia: "How Old Timothy Sang, Dying...," "Song of Truth," and "How Betrayal Came to Russia." His article "Russian Art," which was written at this time and contained his general conception of Russia, is illustrated with paintings by Viktor Vasnetsov, whose work, in Rilke's opinion, best expressed the national spirit.

Early in 1900 Rilke made his first translations from the Russian, the most important of which was Anton Chekhov's *The Sea Gull*, though this was unfortunately lost and no trace of it has come down to us. Thanks to his correspondence with Sofia Schill, Rilke was introduced to the work of the

---

*Vsevolod Garshin (1855–88): Russian author of novellas.

Russian peasant poet Spiridon Drozhzhin, a few of whose poems he translated into German.

Then Rilke and Andreas-Salomé prepared to make a second, longer visit to Russia. In a letter of February 5, 1900, to Leonid Pasternak, the father of Boris Pasternak, Rilke wrote:

> Now first of all I must tell you that Russia, as I predicted to you, meant much more to me than a mere chance event. Ever since last August I have devoted myself almost exclusively to studying Russian art, Russian history and culture, and—I mustn't omit this— your wonderful, peerless Russian language. Although I cannot speak it as yet, I can without much effort read your great poets (and how great they are!). I also understand most of what I hear spoken. What a pleasure it is to read the verse of Lermontov or the prose of Tolstoy in the original! What sheer delight! The immediate consequence of my efforts is that I feel an uncommon longing to go to Moscow and, if nothing unforeseen occurs, will join you there on April 1 (Russian calendar), this time to spend more time with your circle of friends, and spend it as one initiated and informed.[20]

The instant Andreas-Salomé and Rilke arrived back in Moscow, on May 9, 1900, they plunged into its varied and unique life. Sofia Schill, who often saw them, described their stay in Moscow:

> Luisa Gustavovna, large and somewhat heavy, in *reform* clothes* of her own making and of an odd color; beside her a thin young man of middle height wearing a queer felt hat and a jacket covered with pockets. Rainer Osipovich was as fair of skin as a girl; his nose and oval

---

*A manifestation of a movement at the time toward "natural" food and dress.

face were elongated; his large pale eyes gazed with the clarity of an infant's upon these strange scenes. Nothing could have become him more than his little brown goatee.

This pair wandered about Moscow, the Arbat,* up and down alleys and side streets, holding hands like children, causing passers-by to smile and cast backward glances. But this did not disturb them.

Often they had tea in taverns frequented by day laborers so as to hear their speech and talk to them. They spent their mornings in art galleries and museums. They attended church services. They joined the crowds at the Sukharev and Smolensk markets. They discovered the most remote corners of the city, unabashed by our dirt, rudeness, or hovels. Wherever they went they talked to the people, and according to their own testimony they were met everywhere with frankness, friendliness, and a desire to please. They were bent on discovering *the true face of Russia*. The further their explorations took them from the world of Europe and literature, the better they liked it. They made little use of the letters of introduction I gave them to my literary acquaintances. On the other hand, they were vastly interested in the people who attended my classes at the Prechistensky Workers' School. On several occasions I held tea parties for them at which my foreign guests listened to what our weavers and typesetters had to say.... I found it fascinating to be present at meetings where our peasant workers spoke with representatives of Europe's most refined culture. They were less interested in Russian workers' first attempts to enter the political arena than in their daily lives, their village background, their wholesome roots: "the plowman's

---

*One of Moscow's main streets.

soul has not yet been completely destroyed by the city and by living in workingmen's barracks." That is why they were particularly drawn to my peasant friend from Smolensk *guberniya* [province], now working as a warehouse attendant at the Kotov Textile Factory near Moscow. This man told them of the ecstasy he experienced when he was out alone tilling the fields in early morning, the air sharp and fresh, the spring sky filled with the singing of larks, the grass sparkling with dew.[21]

On the evening of May 30, Lou Andreas-Salomé and Rilke set out on a long journey through Russia. Their first stop was at Yasnaya Polyana, Tolstoy's country estate south of Moscow. Their experiences on this journey are best recorded in the letters they sent Sofia Schill. On June 2, Rilke gave her a colorful and detailed description of their second encounter with Tolstoy. Then, from Yasnaya Polyana, they took the train to Kiev, where they stayed some two weeks visiting the cathedrals of Sophia and Vladimir and the Kiev-Pechersky Monastery. After Kiev they went by steamer on the Dnieper to Kremenchug, crossed the entire Ukraine, and spent a few days in Poltava. Once more they traveled by train, passing through Kharkov and Voronezh on their way to the city of Saratov. There they boarded the river steamer *Alexander Nevsky* for a weeklong cruise up the Volga, stopping at all the large towns. The Volga scenery made a deep impression on Rilke, and the memory of it returned to him again and again in later years. "All that I had seen up to then," he wrote on July 31, 1900, "was but a picture of country, river, world. Here was the real thing in natural size. I felt as if I had watched the Creation; few words for all that is, things made on God the Father's scale."[22]

The boat trip ended on July 2 at Yaroslavl. Rilke and Andreas-Salomé spent three days in the village of Kresty-Bogorodskoye, about three miles from Yaroslavl. "I spent three days in a little hut, living like a peasant among peasants," Rilke wrote to his mother. "I slept without sheets and shared with my hosts the humble meals that they fitted into their hard labor now and then. The weather was fine, so this primitive life had much beauty in it. . . ."[23]

From July 6 to 17 Rilke and Lou Andreas-Salomé stopped in Moscow, staying at the New Moscow Inn. On July 18 they went to the village of Nizovka in Tver *guberniya*, where for almost a week they were Drozhzhin's guests. "Thanks to his great hospitality we feel very much at ease," Rilke wrote Sofia Schill from Nizovka.[24] Their visit with Drozhzhin only deepened both travelers' love and adoration for the simple folk. "Such poetry and tranquillity attend these people's life of labor, such spiritual force, such spiritual power, that one is astonished and can only repeat Tolstoy's words: 'Go to the people and learn from them!'" (Letter from Lou Andreas-Salomé to Sofia Schill from Nizovka, July 20, 1900.)[25]

The travelers returned to St. Petersburg at the end of July, stopping on the way for three days in Novgorod. Andreas-Salomé then set out to visit her relatives on the Finnish coast, leaving Rilke alone in the city to study in the public library and at the Museum of Alexander III (now called the Russian Museum). His main interest was still in Russian art, especially the "World of Art" trend, whose searchings in many ways paralleled those of avant-garde German painters.

It was during this period that he made the acquaintance of the painter and art critic Alexander Benois, a founder of, and a main contributor to, the magazine *Mir iskusstva* (World of Art). Their first meeting, on August 17 at the dacha in Peterhof, just outside of St. Petersburg, where Benois was then staying, initiated a lively correspondence and collaboration (1900–2).

On August 22, 1900, Rilke and Lou Andreas-Salomé left St. Petersburg. Thus ended Rilke's second and last trip to Russia.

5

On his return to Germany, Rilke lived for some time in a painters' colony in the North German village of Worpswede. The young poet became deeply attached to Heinrich Vogeler, the most outstanding representative of the group, to the painter Paula Becker-Modersohn, and to the sculptress Clara Westhoff, a talented pupil of Rodin's who in March 1901 became Rilke's wife. Recalling Rilke's arrival in Worpswede in the summer of 1900, Heinrich Vogeler wrote: "He was at the time deeply influenced by the Russian character as described by Dostoyevsky. The catacombs of the Kiev churches had further strengthened his leanings toward mysticism. He had also visited Tolstoy. Many of his impressions were reflected in his art, much in the same way as Bohemian cut glass reflects the real world, with manifold variations enriching it and reproducing its form and color."[26]

Rilke talked a good deal to his friends in Worpswede about Russia and her artistic life, hoping to interest them in Russian art. Acting as a link between Russian and German artists, he attempted to organize an exhibition of contemporary Russian art in Berlin.

From 1900 to 1902, Rilke read a great deal in Russian, going beyond fiction and art criticism. He read Nikolai Chernyshevsky's *What Is to Be Done?*, Pyotr Kropotkin's *Memoirs of a Revolutionist*, Gogol's essay on the Middle Ages. Of the latter he wrote (in Russian) to Alexander Benois on February 9, 1901: "I am reading Gogol and cannot tear myself away. What a man! His essay 'The Middle Ages' is wholly delightful!"[27]

Among the translations from the Russian Rilke made in 1900–2 was a fragment of Dostoyevsky's *Poor People* (considered lost) and "Pilgrims," a story by Vasily Yanchevetsky, a writer he had met in St. Petersburg in August 1900.

What he had seen and experienced in the summer of 1900 is reflected in the second part of *The Book of Hours*, written in September 1901 and subtitled *On Pilgrimage*. The background to almost every poem in this cycle is the vast expanse of Russia, her cities and steppelands, her pilgrims making their way to places of worship from towns as far away "as Tashkent and Tiflis." Rilke's love for Russia "had found sanctuary" in this book, as he wrote Leonid Pasternak in December 1906, when he sent him a copy.

About a year after his second visit to Russia Rilke wrote an essay called "Basic Trends in Modern Russian Art," in which he makes clear his view of its history and its future. At the end of 1900 Rilke had written six poems in Russian (two others were written in April 1901). One cannot help agreeing with the opinion of Lou Andreas-Salomé (to whom the poems were dedicated and presented) that "though the grammar is pretty awful, they still somehow are mysteriously poetic."[28] Rilke had begun writing in Russian as early as the summer of 1900 (letters to Drozhzhin and Sofia Schill). By late in that year he wrote Russian fluently. Rilke's letter in Russian to Leonid Pasternak earned Pasternak's boundless admiration. In his reply of January 2, 1901, Pasternak said: "I couldn't believe my eyes! To have learned such a difficult language in one year, and so thoroughly as to be able to correspond in it! This is a feat so remarkable that I am still astounded; I show it to all my friends and they are as astounded as I am! Honor and glory to you!"[29]

In late 1901 and early 1902 Rilke found himself in strained circumstances. His marriage to Clara Westhoff, the birth of a daughter, the acquiring of a home—all this demanded a steady income. At first he tried to find employment as an art reviewer for a German periodical, but this came to nothing. Gradually the idea of going to live in Russia took root in his mind, an idea first expressed in a New Year's greeting to Benois in December 1901. On January 9, 1902, he wrote Leonid Pasternak: "If only I could find some modest situation in Moscow that would give me a marginal income and allow me to go on with my work peacefully and without mundane worries, I would come and live in your country without a moment's hesitation! As it is, I miss Russia greatly and long to be there." Two days later, in a letter to his friend Nicolai Tolstoy, Rilke exclaimed: "It becomes more and more clear to me that Russia is my native land—all others are alien to me."[30]

Eventually, Rilke decided to take some practical steps. With his letter of March 5, 1902, to Benois he enclosed a long letter to Alexei Suvorin, an eminent Russian publisher and publicist, in which he described his visits, his impressions, and his love for Russia. Hoping for Suvorin's support, Rilke offered to work for *Novoye vremya*—one of Russia's biggest newspapers at the beginning of the century, owned by Suvorin —and elaborated his reasons for deciding to take his family to Russia.

"My wife," wrote Rilke, "doesn't know Russia; but I have told her so much about it that she is ready to leave her native land, which has become as alien to her as to me, and join me in making the move to your country—which is my own country spiritually. Ah, if only it turned out that we could live there for good! I believe this is possible—possible because I love your country, love its people, its suffering, and its greatness; love is the power and the ally of God."[31]

Suvorin never answered this letter from an unknown German writer, and as it happened, Rilke soon abandoned the idea of going to live in Russia: on August 27, 1902, he went to Paris to write a book about Rodin. Nevertheless, his spiritual ties with Russia never weakened. In his letters to Lou Andreas-Salomé and his Russian friends, the theme of Russia and his nostalgic mood are ever-present. "When I was in Paris," he wrote Lou Andreas-Salomé on August 15, 1903, "I seemed to be inexpressibly closer to Russia; and yet I feel that even here in Rome, as I contemplate the things of antiquity, I am preparing myself for things Russian, and for a return to them one day."[32]

As he roamed through the countries of Western Europe he was always meeting Russian artists, writers, actors; he was always adding new friends to his old ones. On April 12, 1907, Rilke met Maxim Gorky on the island of Capri, an event he was to write about in several letters. Rilke's attitude toward the famous Russian writer was ambivalent: although Gorky, as a man of the people who became a great artist, wholly conformed to Rilke's image of the Russian character, his socialist views and his sociopolitical activities intimidated Rilke and made him distrust the Russian writer.

The Russian theme did not stop turning up in Rilke's poetry after 1902. We find it in the cycle "The Czars" from *The Book of Images*, completed in Paris in 1906, in the poem "Night Ride" from *New Poems* (August 1907), and, finally, in the "Russian" sonnet, the twentieth in Part I of his *Sonnets to Orpheus* (February 1922). The soul of Russia breathes in each of these works. His novel *The Notebooks of Malte Laurids Brigge* is filled with Russian reminiscences. In fact, Rilke originally planned the book to culminate in the chapter on Tolstoy.

Rilke's spiritual development underwent significant changes over the years. Even so, in his basic ideas on life and art the mature Rilke of the *Duino Elegies* and *Sonnets to Orpheus* differs little from the author of *The Book of Hours*. With all his former vehemence he condemns the lack of spirituality and compassion in a modern world saturated with bourgeois values and relationships (see, for example, the third book of *The Book of Hours* and *The Notebooks of Malte Laurids Brigge*). His rejection of a world divorced from God and Nature is as basic to his later outlook as it was to his earlier view. This finds fullest expression in his call for an intense inner life, both spiritual and emotional, an effort best furthered by solitary living, of which he always dreamed. Accordingly, in his intimate and confessional letter to Suvorin, Rilke speaks of himself as lonely and unwanted in his native land, of longing to lead a serious, solitary existence, out of which would emerge deep and tranquil poetry. Rilke realized his ideal of being an artist-recluse by moving, in 1921, into the ancient Swiss castle of Muzot. There he spent the last five years of his life, and there it was that fame and glory caught up with him—"the quintessence of all misconceptions that collect around a new name."[33]

The number of Rilke's readers and admirers grew quickly in postwar Europe, as his name became a symbol: a poet sequestering himself in a medieval tower from all world events, from war, revolution, inflation, misery, and ruin, became to many the very personification of poetry, deepening of perception, and genuine creativity. People of different ages and callings, deeply dissatisfied with the place accorded things of the spirit in the modern world, turned to Rilke and his works, finding in them an antidote for their epoch.

Marina Tsvetayeva wrote of him:

Rilke is neither the mission nor the mirror of our times; he is their counterpoise. War, slaughterhouses, flesh shredded by discord—and Rilke. The earth will be forgiven for our times for the sake of Rilke, who lived in them. He could have been born only in our times because he is their opposite, because he is essential, because he is an antidote. That is what makes him our contemporary. The times did not commission him, they brought him forth. . . . Rilke is as ineluctably necessary to our times as a priest is to the battlefield: to be for these and for those, for them and for us: to pray—for the enlightenment of the still living and at the parting from the fallen.[34]

From January to August 1925 Rilke was again living in Paris. He showed the same lively interest in all things Russian that he had shown twenty-five years earlier, making new acquaintanceships and reviving old ones. Probably, as he looked back upon his life in anticipation of his fiftieth birthday,

Rilke felt as never before the strength of his spiritual ties with Russia, "that fabled land." Once more he began reading Russian literature systematically, and he met with the eminent poet and prose writer Ivan Bunin—"an exceedingly pleasing figure," as Rilke observed in a letter to L. P. Struve. He was especially taken by Bunin's story "Mitya's Love."

In Paris Rilke enjoyed attending the puppet theater directed by Yulia Sazonova (Slonimskaya), and there he renewed his acquaintance with Yelena Voronina, but this encounter brought disappointment to both of them. He wrote his friend Nanny Wunderly-Volkart, on March 3, 1925:

> Little by little I have been able to find most of the Russians I knew earlier.... Poor Yelena Voronina, whom I lost sight of twenty-six years ago because she did not care to tell me her new name after her marriage, which took place after I left St. Petersburg.... She is living here now with her husband, living among the émigrés, in poverty (she, for whom wealth had been a natural condition from the day of her birth!)—old, destitute, miserable, and, like all the Russians here, without hope for the future....[35]

Among the plans Rilke nurtured in his last days was that of writing a book about his Russian travels. He wanted to give new life to his memories, and thus the letter from Boris Pasternak, and the ensuing correspondence with Marina Tsvetayeva, came to him as a very pleasant surprise.

6

Although coincidences often play a major role in people's lives, scholarly works usually minimize their importance. In this case, however, coincidence cannot be ignored.

On first arriving in Moscow in 1899, Rilke had called on a young professor at the School of Painting, Sculpture, and Architecture named Leonid Pasternak.

"On a beautiful spring day with the sun pouring its ecstasy over all things after a long hard winter," recalls Leonid Pasternak, "I found a young man standing before me in my studio—a very young man, fair-haired and delicate-looking, wearing a dark green Tyrolese cape. In his hand he held letters of introduction from my friends in Germany, asking me to help him in word and deed to see our country and meet its people. If I am not mistaken, they also asked me to arrange for him to meet Leo Tolstoy."[36]

This request was not hard to grant, since Leonid Pasternak saw Tolstoy frequently at the time: he was illustrating Tolstoy's novel *Resurrection*, which had been appearing in installments in the St. Petersburg magazine *Niva* since March 1899. On that very day Pasternak must have told Tolstoy about the guests from Germany, for on the evening of the next day, April 28, Rilke, Andreas-Salomé, and her husband visited Tolstoy at his home in the Khamovniki district of Moscow.

Leonid Pasternak also introduced him to the well-known Russian sculptor Paolo (Pavel) Trubetskoy, who since 1897 had also been teaching at the School of Painting, Sculpture, and Architecture. Trubetskoy had made a bust of Tolstoy and two statuettes, one of which, *Tolstoy on Horseback*, won the Grand Prix at the World Exposition in Paris in 1900.

On leaving Moscow at the end of his first visit, Rilke wrote Leonid Pasternak: "Let me thank you once more for your friendly welcome and the help you so readily offered us. It was in your company that I spent the best, the most rewarding hours of my stay in Moscow."

A year later, chance brought Rilke and Leonid Pasternak together at a railroad station. Rilke was setting out to see Tolstoy at Yasnaya Polyana, not knowing for certain whether

Tolstoy was there. Pasternak, who was taking his family to Odessa, came to his aid by sending a telegram to Tolstoy. He wrote of this meeting: "Another curious coincidence was that my son Boris, then a ten-year-old schoolboy waiting with me for the train to leave, saw my young German friend for the first and last time in his life. Little did he or I dream that the great German poet was to wield such an influence over him in the future, and that Boris in his turn, through his translations, was to bring Rilke's poetry to Russia's new literary circles."[37]

Boris Pasternak himself described this memorable encounter, thirty years later, in his autobiographical work *Safe Conduct*, dedicated to Rilke:

> On a hot summer day our express was about to leave Moscow's Kursk Station. Just then someone in a dark Tyrolese cape approached our train window from the outside. A tall woman accompanied him. Father began talking to them about something that aroused the same warm interest in all three, but from time to time the woman exchanged brief remarks with Mother in Russian; the man spoke only German, and though I knew the language well, I had never heard it spoken as he spoke it. On our way, as we approached Tula, this same couple visited us in our compartment. They said that the express stopped at Kozlovka-Zaseka only on request and they were not sure that the head conductor would inform the engineer in time for them to get off at this stop. . . . They then took leave of us and went back to their car. . . . The faces and the incident were forgotten, presumably forever.[38]

During his first visit to Italy, in 1904, Leonid Pasternak ran into Rilke on the streets of Rome. Rilke invited Pasternak to call on him and meet his young wife, Clara. "Unforgettable are the hours we spent conversing with them," Leonid Pasternak wrote. "Once again the main topic of conversation, outside of art, was Rilke's beloved Russia and Russian literature, of which he had made a serious study. With what knowledge and enthusiasm did he speak of the beauties of old Russian poetry, of *The Lay of Igor's Host*, which he had read in the original."[39] (Rilke had not only read this classic of old Russian literature but even translated it into German.)

The intervals between these meetings were bridged by letters and an exchange of books.[40]

In December 1925, Western Europe joined in celebrating Rilke's fiftieth birthday. Among the many greetings he received was a heartfelt one from Leonid Pasternak, who had been living with his wife and daughters in Berlin since 1921. In this letter Pasternak refers to still another encounter, their last, in a train in Switzerland.

The poet's reply to this greeting from his old friend, dated March 14, 1926, was the indirect cause of the correspondence between Rilke, Boris Pasternak, and Marina Tsvetayeva that soon began.

7

Marina Tsvetayeva and Boris Pasternak were both from Moscow, both children of professors, both of roughly the same age. Their fathers came to Moscow from the provinces and, by virtue of their outstanding abilities, gained success and social position. The mothers of both were gifted pianists, pupils of Anton Rubinstein, though their careers as performers are not to be compared: Marina's mother (née Meyn) was forbidden by her father to play in public, whereas Rosa Pasternak (née Kaufman) won a European name for herself in her youth and became a professor at the Petersburg Conservatory. Yet, when they got married, both women gave up all thought of a professional career, to devote their talents to their children and families.

The frequent trips which the Tsvetayev family made to Germany (1904–5) owing to the mother's ill health, trips that gave Marina an intimate knowledge of German *Pensionen*, might be paralleled with the Pasternaks' yearlong sojourn in Berlin in 1906 and young Boris Pasternak's studies at Marburg University during the summer semester of 1912.

Yet these similar childhood and adolescent experiences left entirely different imprints. Boris Pasternak emerged with a distaste for, and an inner struggle against, the romantic license and suicidal propensity associated with romanticism, and in the end he overcame them. Marina Tsvetayeva, on the contrary, regarded these qualities as basic to her life and art, and accordingly leaned upon them, cultivated them.

By the outbreak of World War I Tsvetayeva's talent was recognized by contemporary Russian poets of such authority as Valery Bryusov and Maximilian Voloshin, and she was gaining a name for herself in Moscow's artistic circles. Before long she looked upon poetry as her destiny and mission. But it was not until the summer of 1913 that Pasternak, who had given more than ten years of his life to the study of musical composition and philosophy, began to write poems for his first youthful collection—an immature work for whose publication he was later to reproach himself.

Pasternak's early books of poetry were published as part of a futurist publishing venture and betrayed the effects of his dependence on a group, a trend. In the work and life of Rainer Maria Rilke, Pasternak found support and approval in his search for freedom and independence. Soon after he returned from Germany in 1907 he made the acquaintance of Rilke's first collections—*In Celebration of Myself*, *The Book of Hours*, and *The Book of Images*—which had been presented to his father with inscriptions by the author. He was struck by their depth and seriousness, examples for which he remained

grateful the rest of his life. In Pasternak's university notebooks we find, interspersed with his lecture notes, his first attempts to translate Rilke.

Pasternak was not exaggerating when he said that Rilke
laid the foundations for his spiritual development. The basis
of Pasternak's early rejection of romanticism was his striving
toward perfection as a means of reshaping life. As early as
1910 he included the superb Danish prose stylist Jens Peter
Jacobsen among his favorite authors, a novelist who had
meant a great deal to Rilke, too. Prose became the musical and
harmonic basis of his poetry. All the rest of his life he tried to
impart the essence, the substance, with such concentrated vi-
tality that the artistic form emerged naturally, as in a living
organism. The life of the artist is a kind of ascetic novitiate,
and the artist's labors must be devoted to the task of giving
verbal expression to an image of the world suffused with the
joy of living, and with a feeling of kinship with all things.
This becomes all the more necessary in time of tragedy and
privation. Pasternak considered his first success in this respect the volume *My Sister, Life*, written in 1917.

At the time of World War I and the Russian Revolution,
Tsvetayeva and Pasternak were barely acquainted. According
to Tsvetayeva:

Three or four brief meetings. Almost without words,
because I never want anything new. Heard him once
giving readings with some other poets in the Polytech-
nical Museum. He spoke tonelessly and had forgotten
most of the poems. His awkwardness on the stage reminded me of Blok.* He gave the impression of painful
concentration, one wanted to push him—like a cart that
is stuck—"Go on, go on!"—and since not a single word
came across (a kind of mumbling, like a bear stretching

*Alexander Blok (1880–1921), the great Russian symbolist poet.

itself) one couldn't help thinking impatiently, "Good Lord, why torture yourself and others like this?"[41]

Pasternak also remembered how taciturn their first meetings had been: "At a public poetry reading at the beginning of the revolution she was one of the poets I heard recite their works. Then, during one of the winters of War Communism,* I went to see her on some matter or other. I said nothing in particular, nor did she. Somehow Tsvetayeva didn't impress me."[42]

In May 1922, after a long separation, Tsvetayeva rejoined her husband, Sergei Efron, who was then in Berlin. When Pasternak read her collection *Versts*, published in 1921, he immediately wrote her a letter full of admiration. Thirty-five years later he recalled this in his autobiography:

> One had to read *into* her poetry. When I did this I was astounded by its immense strength and purity. Nothing comparable was being done at the time. Let me put it briefly: accepting the risk, I dare to assert that, with the exception of Annensky† and Blok and, with a few reservations, Andrei Bely,‡ the early Tsvetayeva was what all the other symbolists longed to be and were incapable of being. While they floundered in a sea of contrived schemes and lifeless archaisms, Tsvetayeva soared easily above the difficulties of creative work, achieving her tasks with superb ease and dazzling technique.
>
> In the spring of 1922, by which time she was already abroad, I bought her little volume called *Versts*. I was immediately struck by the lyrical power of her form, born of her life's blood, strong-chested, fiercely com-

---

*The Bolsheviks' stringent economic policy from 1918 to 1920.

†Innokenty Annensky (1856–1909): Russian poet, dramatist, essayist, translator, and classical scholar.

‡Russian symbolist novelist and poet (1880–1934).

pressed and condensed, not depending on individual lines, but captivating the attention by preserving the logical development of her stanzas without any interruption of rhythm. These qualities were close to my heart, perhaps because of the similar influences we had both been exposed to, or similar motivations in the forming of our characters, the similar role of the family and music, the similarity of the sources from which our aims and choices sprang. I wrote to her in Prague a rapturous letter full of amazement that I had so long passed over her, failed to appreciate her. She answered my letter. We began to correspond, most frequently in the mid-twenties, when her *Craft* was published, and a little later when copies of her larger works—the striking, sweeping, innovative "Poem of the End," "Poem of the Mountain," and "The Pied Piper"—circulated in Moscow. We became friends.[43]

In 1975, in the journal *Zvezda*, Tsvetayeva's daughter, Ariadna Efron, wrote brilliantly and concisely about the friendship, collaboration, and genuine love between the two writers, as expressed in the poems, prose, and critical notes they sent to each other, and especially in their extraordinary letters. In her will she stipulated that most of this correspondence not be published until the next century. Its eventual publication will be an invaluable contribution to Russian literature and its history.

Ariadna Efron writes that the Tsvetayeva-Pasternak correspondence extended from 1922 to 1935, reaching its peak in the twenties, then gradually falling off. The two poets never met during this period; although they often planned a meeting, it was invariably postponed for one reason or another.

In the early twenties Pasternak was destitute; he had

no means of supporting his family. At the same time, he was becoming more and more convinced of the insignificance of all he had written since *My Sister, Life* and *Themes and Variations* (1917–18). He came to doubt that the writing of lyrical poetry was justified in the times in which he lived, and he began to feel that such an occupation was both useless and unethical, that wars and revolutions required historians or writers of epics. Interestingly, a similar feeling inspired Tsvetayeva to write essays such as "Art in the Light of Conscience."

Pasternak recalled that, around this time, when he asked a delegation of German proletarian expressionist poets about Rilke, they had not even heard of him. One, more informed than his colleagues, said, "*Rilke? Er ist ja so gut wie tot!*"* And it was at this very time that Rilke's *Duino Elegies* and *Sonnets to Orpheus* were published—his best work, the very poems that earned him immortality. There was indeed good cause for despair.

Pasternak shared his doubts with Tsvetayeva, and she was delighted to be his confidante: "Boris, this is the first really *human* letter from you (the rest are *Geisterbriefe*†) and I am flattered, rewarded, borne aloft," she wrote on July 19, 1925. "You found me worthy of reading your intimate notes." In this same letter Tsvetayeva foretold where his mood was leading him: "I can't understand you. Stop writing poetry? And then what? Jump off the bridge into the Moscow River? With poetry, dear friend, as with love: no separation until it drops *you*. You are the lyre's thrall."

From then on Tsvetayeva's understanding and support were vitally important to Pasternak. That summer, with her approval and encouragement, he began the poem *The Year 1905*. It was difficult for him to switch from lyric to epic po-

---

*Rilke? Why, he's as good as dead.

†Ghost letters.

etry, but since he nurtured the idea of writing a long novel in prose, he forced himself to regard this as necessary training.

In early August 1925, Tsvetayeva passed on to Pasternak rumors that Rilke had died. His reply, of August 16, asked her to verify the rumors and tell him the circumstances of Rilke's death. So distraught was he that in a letter to his sister Josephine he mentioned that he had premonitions of his own imminent death.

It was not only his long separation from his parents and sisters (resident in Germany since 1921) that led Pasternak to apply for permission to go abroad with his family, but also his longing to meet Tsvetayeva. He had a growing awareness of the importance of *The Year 1905*, *Lieutenant Schmidt*, and *Spektorsky*, major poems written while he was in constant contact with Tsvetayeva, his first reader and critic. He believed that she alone could fully appraise the tasks he set himself, his method of solving them, and his success in doing so. Tsvetayeva wrote of this to Leonid Pasternak on February 5, 1928:

> Boris is marvelous! And how little he is understood, even by those who love him! "His feeling for words . . . ," "Words as an end in themselves . . . ," "The independent life of words . . ."—when all his work, every single line, is a fight for *essence*, when he cares not a fig for anything *but* essence (of course, as a poet, it is through words that he frees himself). "Difficult form" indeed! Not difficult form but difficult essence! His hastily written letters are not a bit "easier" than his verse. Don't you agree? I can see from his last letters that he is lonely in art. Most of the praise he receives refers to the *theme* of *1905*—he is receiving certificates of honor, so to speak, for his being a good boy.

Pasternak finished *The Year 1905* in the spring of 1926, still battling his sense of hopelessness and crisis. He was helped to a recognition that he could go on living—and even make happy plans for the future—by reading Tsvetayeva's "Poem of the End" and by learning that Rilke was alive and knew of him and his work.

8

For Pasternak Rilke offered the example of a poet who had disengaged himself from German romanticism for the sake of European unity and the movement toward realism in contemporary art. Tsvetayeva considered Rilke the personification of the poetic spirit, but he also embodied the romanticized Germany she loved so dearly.

"Rilke was my last Germany. My beloved language, my beloved land...just what Russia was for him (the Volga world)," wrote Tsvetayeva.[44] She called Germany "my passion, my native land, the cradle of my soul."[45]

Tsvetayeva's mother had inculcated in her daughters a love of Germany and a thorough knowledge of its language when they were still children. In her memoirs Anastasia Tsvetayeva, Marina's sister, writes: "My mother, who was deeply attached to her father, told us about traveling abroad with him, about their journeys down the Rhine, that legendary river flowing between high banks, about ancient castles on promontories, about the Lorelei, where the nymph sang. We learned about her from Heine's famous poem. The green and foaming Rhine became a part of our lives."[46]

In the autumn of 1904, at the age of twelve, Marina saw Germany with her own eyes when her parents transferred her and Anastasia from Lausanne, where they had been studying in a Catholic boarding school, to Freiburg. They spent the winter there, in the Brinck Boarding School, while their mother followed her doctor's recommendation and took the mountain air of the Black Forest for her consumption. Impressions of this winter are reflected in Marina's adolescent poems, later included in her first book, *Evening Album* (1910). Apparently it was on this visit that she made her first serious acquaintance with German literature: Anastasia recalls that in Freiburg Marina "threw herself into reading German books with complete absorption."[47]

In letters and in a questionnaire she sent to Pasternak (see Chapter 2), Tsvetayeva referred to German as second only to Russian as her favorite language, and alluded to her constant reading of favorite German authors, especially Goethe.

Tsvetayeva probably read Rilke's *Book of Hours* in 1912–13, when that volume came as a revelation to Moscow intellectuals. In a letter to Rilke of May 12, 1926, Tsvetayeva wrote: "The Beyond (not the religious one, more nearly the geographic one) you know better than the Here, this side, you know it topographically, with all its mountains and islands and castles.

"A topography of the soul—that's what you are. And with your *Book* (oh, it was not a book after all, it was becoming a book!) *of Poverty, Pilgrimage, and Death* you have done more for God than all the philosophers and priests taken together."

Tsvetayeva began her dialogue with Rilke by saying, "You are the very incarnation of poetry." For Tsvetayeva, Rilke was a poet of the first order, an artist creating things immortal. In her very first words to Rilke she hastened to distinguish him from the contemporary world she hated ("Your name does not rhyme with our time—stems from earlier or later—has always been"). Time and again she asserted that Rilke was the incarnation of poetry, as in her letter to Anna Tesková of January 15, 1927: "The German Orpheus, that is, Orpheus who *this time* has made his appearance in Germany. Not *Dichter** (Rilke)—*Geist der Dichtung*."[†48] And in a letter

---

*A poet.

†The spirit of poetry.

to Charles Vildrae written in 1930: "... you and I are bound by ties of kinship: you love Russia and Pasternak—and especially Rilke, who is not a poet but *poetry itself*."[49]

Tsvetayeva's conviction that poetry is the timeless, immortal, transcendent spirit made manifest in the temporal realm by its "bearers"—poets—was expressed in her first letter to Rilke; she also spoke of it in her essay "A Poet on Criticism" and elaborated it in the analysis of *Sonnets to Orpheus* contained in her letter of May 12, 1926, to Rilke. This conception of poetry was so congenial to him that he instantly recognized their spiritual affinity.

The idea of the immortality of the soul caught in a cycle of births and deaths was adopted by the romantics from the Orphic school. Orpheus, the school's poet and prophet, was Rilke's and Tsvetayeva's chosen hero. The concept gained many followers. Pasternak spoke of it in his *Safe Conduct*:

"It was a concept of life as the life of the poet. It came to us from the symbolists, who took it from the romantics, especially the German romantics.... In its symbolism, that is, in all that imaginatively touches upon the Orphic and Christian schools in their presentation of a standard of life for which the poet pays with his life, the romantic conception is irresistibly attractive and incontrovertible."[50]

The young Pasternak could not remain indifferent to the beauty and brilliance of this view, and, as he confessed, he was only one of many. Later he completely liberated himself from it by concentrating on his craft and deliberately refusing to poeticize.

As he matured, he adopted another concept, which he uncovered in the spring of 1913 in "Symbolism and Immortality" and summarized nearly fifty years later in his autobiographical essay "People and Circumstances."

Pasternak considered that "when any man dies there remains some of that undying subjectivity which was part of him when alive and which constitutes his contribution to

human existence." He believed that this deathless subjectivity, which is separate from the individual, "this patch, this
fragment of the universal soul common to all mankind, rep-
resents a timeless cycle of action and is the principal matter
of art." In other words, "while the artist, like everyone else,
is mortal, the joy of existence that he experiences is deathless
and, with some approximation of his personal and immediate experience, can be experienced by others centuries later
through his works."[51] Pasternak spoke in a letter to Rilke
about the poet "who is himself always the essence of poetry,
called though he may be by different names at different times."

The four lines of poetry Rilke wrote on the flyleaf of the
copy of the *Duino Elegies* he presented to Tsvetayeva at
Pasternak's request may be seen as a paraphrase of these
words:

> We touch each other. How? With wings that beat,
> With very distance touch each other's ken.
> *One* poet only lives, and now and then
> Who bore him, and who bears him now, will meet.

The poet lives not today but always, not in history but in
time, not in the moment but in infinity. The eternal kinship
of poets in time—that is the theme of the quatrain, and in
this light must be understood its concluding words, about the
individual bearing the burden of the poetic gift, about the
"poet" in the "man."

These four lines were the prologue to Rilke's ensuing correspondence with Tsvetayeva. She took up the idea and further developed the image. In her first letter to him she spoke
of Rilke the man and Rilke the spirit, "who is still greater
than the poet." In other words, she clearly delineated two aspects of his life: the real, everyday aspect, subject to time, and
the spiritual, metaphysical aspect, beyond time. The theme
"man and poet" was continued in her letters of May 12 and

13, with the image of Saint George mounted on a horse, the subject of a cycle of poems she had written earlier (included in the volume *Craft*), symbolizing the indivisibility of man and poet, with one (the man) "bearing" the other (the poet).

Elaborating the idea that Rilke was not a poet but poetry itself, Tsvetayeva said in her first letter: "You are a phenomenon of nature"; then: "You are the fifth element incarnate*: poetry itself or (still too little) that whence poetry comes to be and which is greater than it (you)." She wrote the same to Pasternak in an early letter to him (February 11, 1923): "You are a phenomenon of nature." These words are basic to an understanding of Tsvetayeva's conception of poetry and life.

Tsvetayeva's spiritual nature was formed at the turn of the century. In her own way she adopted the views and outlook of that neoromantic epoch: the pathos of revolt against God, against rationalism, the acceptance of the romantic cult of the "soul." Critics writing of Tsvetayeva spoke of her "Dionysian leanings." Tsvetayeva, like Rilke, often employed the concept of "Nature" in the spirit of the times, which attributed special powers to it, deified it, spiritualized it, especially in the last decade of the nineteenth century. Accordingly, the human spirit, an integral part of Nature, is of prime importance. Tsvetayeva assumed that spirit and Nature merge and are at times interchangeable. "Nothing touches me but Nature, i.e., the soul; and the soul, i.e., Nature," she wrote to Tesková on December 12, 1927.[52] Nature—sentient nature, to be exact—was for Tsvetayeva the source of all life, poetry, and creative energy. "The poet *is* nature and not a contemplation of it," she declared categorically in one of her letters.[53] Poetry that is not the personification of Nature, of the soul, did not exist for her. She wholly accepted the romantic poet Vasily Zhukovsky's statement that "Romanticism *is* the spirit" and considered it her duty to elevate the spirit, which

---

*Literally: quintessence. [M. Ts.]

she felt was crushed, despised, and undefended in the world about her. The contemporary world was to her a kingdom of middle-class ignorance, of the commonplace and the every-day, in which lies and imitations prevailed. Tsvetayeva called it "the world of the body" as opposed to "the world of the spirit." She vehemently rejected love, or what was accepted as love in "the world of the body." Perhaps overemphasizing the gulf between soul and body, she referred again and again to the antagonism between the soul and love. She wrote of her "dislove of love." In her letters to Rilke we find such phrases as "love hates the poet," and "I do not love love, I hold it in contempt." In her letter to Pasternak of July 10, 1926, she spoke of "the ancient, insatiable hate of Psyche for Eve—Eve, of whom there is nothing in me. Of Psyche—everything." And in the same letter: "I do not understand the flesh as such and deny that it has any rights whatsoever." Tsvetayeva often sang the praises of Psyche in verse, and called herself Soul. "Soul, that is my name," she said in a letter to Rilke of February 8, 1926. The words she wrote in May 1938, when Nazi Germany was preparing to invade Czechoslovakia, are typical: "I see Czechoslovakia as a free spirit over which the body has no power."[54]

The world of genuine love—in which there was a union of souls, not of bodies—was the sublime, radiant, beautiful world Tsvetayeva created in her poetry, and in this sense her dialogue with Rilke was a dialogue between lovers. She re-called the words spoken by the poet Voloshin when they first met, in 1911: "When you love a person, you want him to leave you so that you can dream of him."[55]

In her poetry as in her life, Tsvetayeva created situations isolating those who loved, including herself, so that they could not meet physically. She did not deny the accepted at-tributes and manifestations of carnal love—she used them in her poetry—but she always sought to strip them of their cor-poreal carapace, freeing them from the bonds of base matter

Introduction

and gross sensuality. She wrote to Rilke on August 2, 1926: "Why do I tell you all this? From fear, perhaps—you might take me for generally passionate (passion)—bondage." She went on to explain: "I sound quite different from passion." Tsvetayeva extols "the handclasp without hands," "the kiss without lips." The following is from a poem she wrote in 1922:

> In the world where the streams run back,
> On the banks of—a stream,
> Into a dream hand take
> Another hand's dream.[56]

And on August 22 she wrote to Rilke: "I do not live in my lips, and he who kisses me misses *me*."

One of the leitmotifs of her letters to him is "freedom from desire." In these letters, as in all of Tsvetayeva's epistolary prose, we find the touching of imaginary hands, the touching of words, the "meeting of souls."

For Tsvetayeva such a meeting was not a play of fancy; it was indisputable, a given. The touch of a word was for her as real an act as the touch of a hand. In that letter of August 22 she also asserted: "Love lives on words and dies of deeds." And "The word, which for me is already the thing, is all I want."

Thus "I love you" for her encompassed all the raptures and vicissitudes of love. She created a new reality, the reality of the spirit. And the more passionate and sensual her language in the ordinary sense, the more ideal it was in the poetic sense.

Hers, then, was a romantic and complex love aspiring toward the unattainable, the unachievable, the impossible, and based on the antithesis of the real and the ideal. Such a dualism assumes that the unachievable *here* is possible *there*. As Tsvetayeva wrote to Anatoly Steiger, "Don't forget that the apparent impossibility of something is the first sign of its naturalness—in a different world, obviously."[57]

38

This same duality is evident in Tsvetayeva's attitude toward Rilke's death: "This is the first time the best *for me* and the best *on this earth* have coincided. Isn't it only natural that he should have gone? How do *you* regard life? For you his death is not in the natural order of things. For me his life is not in the natural order of things, is in a different order, is itself a different order," she wrote to Pasternak on February 9, 1927, candidly contrasting her romantic perception of life with his acceptance of "the joy of existence." Tsvetayeva felt that the farther one got from reality, the nearer one came to the ideal; the farther away from each other people were in reality, the closer they were in spirit, as she expressed in her August 22, 1926, letter to Rilke: "The farther from me—the further *into* me."

Characteristically, Tsvetayeva utterly ignored this world and elevated the other world to the absolute. She wrote to Pasternak on January 1, 1927: "How well I know the other one! From dreams, from the ambient air of dreams, from the density, the essentiality of dreams. And how little I know of this one, how much I dislike it, and how hurt I have been by it! But the other one—just imagine!—light, radiance, things illuminated quite *differently*, with your light and mine!" In her creative work Tsvetayeva tried to rectify this imbalance: "With my fancies I push my way through to the pith of things."[58] In the context of her poetry, "fancies" meant "the ideal."

Tsvetayeva's concept of dreams derived from the same romantic approach. She regarded dreams as a means of escape from real life. It is significant that Calderón's play *Life Is a Dream* was held in great esteem by German romantics and Russian symbolists. Dreams seemed more real as well as more exalted than waking life—manifestations of a different, incorporeal world, in which souls lived and communed. For that reason Tsvetayeva thought communication in dreams more ideal and satisfying than communication in waking life.

"My favorite means of communication is otherworldly—to dream: to see in one's dreams," she wrote to Pasternak on November 19, 1922. In a letter to Steiger on August 8, 1936, she wrote, "This, and this only, is how I want it to be between us: in dreams while awake, in dreams while asleep, entering into a dream with you and living in it."[59] She touched on this theme in her letter to Rilke of June 14, 1926, and developed it in the culminating letter of August 2. "When somebody dreams of us together—that is when we shall meet," she assured him. And in her letter of January 1, 1927, written after his death, she implored: "Beloved, come to me often in my dreams—no, not that. Live in my dreams."

In her notebook Tsvetayeva daily wrote down the poems and prose she was composing and fragments that later became letters. Sometimes she did not bother to copy out her notes, as in her letter to Pasternak on February 14, 1925: "This is a chance something, Boris, out of my poetry notebook; the rest has blurred and evaporated. My life consists of an unending conversation with you. I am writing to you on a leaf from that same notebook, my very own notebook, as on a leaf from my soul." These letters are an integral part of her creative work and difficult to characterize. In no way can they be considered traditional epistolary prose. Communion with those akin to her in spirit evoked a creative mood approaching the ecstatic. Tsvetayeva rushed headlong into each new friendship, giving herself to it wholly. In letters to someone she worshiped she made no effort to restrain her passion, her impulsiveness, even obsessiveness. Indeed, her attitude toward letters themselves was highly romantic. "A letter is like an otherworldly communication, less perfect than a dream but subject to the same rules," she wrote to Pasternak on November 19, 1922. "Neither the one nor the other can be produced on command: you neither write a letter nor dream a dream when *you* want to but when *it* wants to: the letter—to be written; the dream—to be dreamed."

In her correspondence with Pasternak, Steiger, Alexander Bachrach, and a few others, Tsvetayeva was very much conscious of herself as an artist, and she did create works of art. She could not have poeticized more completely—or, in a sense, more destructively—her relationships with these people whom, as a rule, she had never seen, or seen but a few chance times. Yet she treated every letter as an artistic undertaking, made of it a work of literature, an outpouring of her soul. Such were all her letters to Rilke—a peculiar, untraditional literary genre that might be called epistolary lyric poetry.

Again and again Tsvetayeva insisted that she was concerned with life, not literature. The false and the contrived were repugnant to her. She was contemptuous of literature that did not reflect life and nature, regarding it as aestheticism, ironically referring to such literature as belles lettres, as in her letter to Rilke of May 12, 1926. She demanded of poetry, as a whole and in its every line, "the truth of this moment," to quote her letter to Rilke of August 22. All her work is connected with facts, events, or emotional experiences in her life. She avoided inventing characters, preferring at times to draw upon myth and legend. Much of Tsvetayeva's prose is addressed to people she knew personally (Bryusov, Bely, Voloshin, the poet and novelist Konstantin Balmont, the poet and playwright Mikhail Kuzmin, Sofia Holliday, and others), but her reminiscences bear little resemblance to traditional memoirs. Using as a point of departure certain individual characteristics that she remembered, Tsvetayeva constructed an artistic image, unfailingly remodeling and re-creating her character. Convinced that "the imagination rules the world" —a quotation from Napoleon used as an epigraph to a chapter in *Evening Album*—she assumed the greatest license in dealing with reality. "She created whatever she wished, paying little attention to actuality,"[60] wrote her sister, Anastasia, reproaching Marina for lack of restraint, for wantonly distorted portraits of their mutual friends. "The memory is compliant, and for me it is identical with the imagination," Tsvetayeva wrote to Vladimir Sosinsky,[61] and this was ultimately her point of view.

Many of Tsvetayeva's letters have this same creative cast. An unexpected encounter or a letter written for some definite purpose often served merely as an occasion to raise the theme to a different level, to a higher, poetic one. Tsvetayeva often forgot about the real person she was writing to, carried away by an image that the moment's inspiration dictated.

The worldly, commonplace attributes of her correspondent interested her only to the extent that they lent detail to the image. This led to the breathtaking flights and tragic falls of Tsvetayeva's writing, as can be seen vividly in her letters to Rilke. Immersed in the creation of an atmosphere of spiritual communion, she failed to notice the actual man, who at that time was mortally ill. His repeated attempts to draw her attention to this offended her: she thought he was trying to resist her impulsive outbursts simply to preserve his tranquillity. No doubt Rilke was so exhausted by her lack of understanding that he stopped answering her letters; she lost touch with him several months before he died.

To judge by his letters, Rilke at first placed great trust in Tsvetayeva and fully sympathized with her. Pasternak's first letter acted as a tuning fork, immediately setting the key of kinship among the three of them, determining the character, style, and tone of their dialogue. Their correspondence was the conversation of people who understood one another with the utterance of but a single word, as if they had been initiated into one and the same mystery and felt no need to explain it to one another. The uninitiated reader must labor over the reading of their letters and poems. The best example of their esoteric style is the wonderful "Elegy" Rilke wrote to Tsvetayeva as part of this correspondence. But their correspondence as a whole creates the impression at times that they were conspirators, accomplices, mutually aware of something no one else knew about. Each saw in the other a poet close in spirit and equal in strength. It was a colloquy and contest of equals—a luxury Tsvetayeva had dreamed of all her life. "The only equals in strength I ever met were Rilke and Pasternak," she declared in 1938.[62]

Rilke (or, rather, the image of Rilke that Tsvetayeva created in her letters to him) was the only person with whom she felt she could speak without fear of being misunderstood. And yet in the course of three months—from early May to mid-August—Rilke's attitude toward her changed. Tsvetayeva's letter of August 2 marked a turning point in their relationship. Rilke was intimidated by her impetuosity, her categorical demands, her unwillingness to take circumstances into account. Her avowed desire to be "his only Russia," her crowding out of Pasternak, her urgent insistence on meeting Rilke at any cost—all of this he found unjustifiably harsh and hyperbolic. In his last letter, that of August 19, he reproached her for being too hard on him and Pasternak. "I object to any exclusions," he writes, referring to her desire to exclude Pasternak from their relationship. According to a letter Tsvetayeva wrote to Rilke's last secretary, Yevgenia Chernosvitova, Rilke made no reply to her long letter of August 22: "He did not answer my last letter (from the Vendée). I sent it to Ragaz; do you know whether he ever got it?" Nor did he reply to a postcard she sent him from Bellevue, near Paris, even though he did write letters during those final months of his life.

The tragedy of Rilke's death significantly changed the relationship between Tsvetayeva and Pasternak and in many ways shaped the course of their lives. In diverse circumstances and contexts, both were to return repeatedly to the experiences described in the letters.

1

THE CORRESPONDENCE between Rilke, Tsvetayeva, and Pasternak was set in motion by a letter of congratulation Leonid Pasternak wrote to his old acquaintance Rainer Maria Rilke on the occasion of the latter's fiftieth birthday. This letter, begun in a stilted and slightly flawed German and continued in Russian, was the first communication between the two men after twenty years.

LEONID PASTERNAK TO RILKE

BERLIN
DECEMBER 8, 1925

[In German]
Most revered Rainer Maria Rilke, dear sir!

It is really not a dream that I, whose name—Leonid Osipovich Pasternak—you will probably recall, may allow myself the pleasure of embracing my dear former correspondent —now of European renown—and [greeting and] congratulating him most warmly on his 50th birthday!
[In Russian]

Do you remember charming old Moscow, now but a legend, a fairy tale? ... Do you remember Tolstoy, his house, his estate at Yasnaya Polyana? ... Do you also remember that beautiful warm evening in Rome, at a villa next to the

Borghese, and our discussion of, among other things, *The Lay of Igor's Host*? ... And do you remember our chance meeting in the aisle of a Swiss railroad car with a foaming mountain stream rushing below us? That was the last time we saw each other.

Since then "much water has flowed under," and unprecedented historical events have caught us up like a whirlwind —caught all of us up, but my people in particular.

At the time of our revolution, cut off from Europe and the world of culture, in the nightmarish conditions of our Russian life, we—that is, my family and I—bitterly mourned your death, rumors of which had reached our ears.

According to the Russian saying, you are therefore destined to live a long, long life, dear jubilarian. So you can imagine how happy I am to be able to send you, from a place not far away (although I don't know exactly where you are, your address), my heartfelt congratulations and to wish "many happy returns of the day" to our beloved poet!

If only you knew how my children cherish your every line—especially my elder son, Boris, who is a young poet already acclaimed in Russia. He is your most ardent admirer, one who thoroughly appreciates you, who, I may even say, calls himself your pupil; he was one of the first to spread your fame in our country, where you were as yet unknown.

We were overjoyed when, on reaching Europe, we discovered that you were alive and well, thank God, and at the height of your creative powers. Where are you living now, and how is your wife? In 1921, when travel abroad was legalized, my wife and daughters and I moved to Berlin, where my daughters are now finishing their university education and I am working mostly at portrait painting.* My two sons remained in Moscow. If you are ever in Berlin, do let me know. I long to paint your portrait before I die.

---

*My portrait of Professor Einstein was exhibited last year at the Secession. [L. P.]

Once again, many happy returns, and may the Lord multiply your fame and honor. Sincere greetings to your charming wife, and convey my congratulations to her, too. I wish you the best of everything.

Affectionately,

LEONID PASTERNAK

Not knowing your address, I am sending this to Insel Verlag with the request that they forward it to you.

———

Leonid Pasternak's letter reached Rilke at the Val-Mont sanatorium, where he was a frequent patient at that time. Rilke's first letter gave intimations of his tragic fate: the leukemia that was already exhausting him had forced him to resort to medical aid, but Rilke, who all his life had avoided doctors, innocently imagined that the cause of his discomfort was the solitary, ascetic life he was leading. (He wrote of this in his letter to Tsvetayeva of May 17, 1926.)

———

RILKE TO LEONID PASTERNAK

VAL-MONT PAR GLION SUR TERRITET (VAUD)
SUISSE
MARCH 14, 1926

[In Russian]

My dear Leonid Ossipovich* Pasternak!

No, I can't write to you in Russian, but I read your letter . . . [In German] and even if I could not read Russian any more (I still do quite well but, alas, don't get down to it very

———

*Rilke's admittedly shaky Russian is reflected in his misspelling of "Osipovich" and, in the first sentence of the letter, the improper choice of aspect for the verb "read."

often . . .)—but even if I couldn't do it any more, the joy and great surprise of reading you, my dear and cherished friend, would have returned to me for a moment all I once knew: *this* good letter I should have understood under any circumstances and in any language. And now I want to lose no time but express how much *your* language and everything to do with the old Russia (the unforgettable, intimate, and homely *skazka**) and everything you remind me of in your letter have remained close, dear, and holy to me, implanted forever in my life's foundations. Yes, we have all had to undergo a great deal of change, your country more than any: but even if we do not live to see it at its resurrection, the profound, the real, the other surviving Russia has only fallen back on her secret root system, as she did before, under the Tatar yoke; who could doubt that she is still there and is gathering her forces in that dark place, invisible to her own children, leisurely with her own sacred slowness, on to a possibly still-remote future?! Your own exile, the exile of so many of those most faithful to her, nourishes this, as it were, subterranean preservation; for as the real Russia has hidden herself underground, inside the earth, thus all of you have, after all, left only in order to remain true to her in her present concealment; how strongly, with what emotion did I feel this, dear Leonid Ossipovich Pasternak, last year in Paris: there I met again old Russian friends and found new ones, and the youthful fame of your son Boris touched me from more than one side. Moreover, the last thing I tried to read over there in terms of date were poems by him, very *beautiful* ones (in a little anthology by Ilya Ehrenburg,[†] which unfortunately I eventually gave away to the Russian dancer Mila Sirul; I say "unfortunately" because since that time I have often wished I could look at it again). It touches me now to know not only that he, Boris, already the

---

*Fairy tale.

[†]Ilya Ehrenburg (1891–1967): Russian writer and journalist.

noted poet of a new generation, has not ceased being aware of me and keeping abreast of my work, but also that for your whole family my existence has remained a matter of the heart, something you share—that you, dear friend, have seen to it that your remembrance, your sympathy for me should thrive and grow in those dear to you, thus infinitely enhancing a possession I cherished. That you live and work in relative normality, surrounded by some of your family, is a good and heartening thing to know! And much as I am prejudiced against sitting for portraits, if physical proximity permits it and we see each other again, I shall be proud to occupy a modest place in the gallery of your models. But it is much more likely that you will come across Clara Rilke, who lives permanently in Germany (in the vicinity of Bremen), or with our daughter, who is married and living on an estate in Saxony, and who, a little more than two years ago now, made me a grandfather through the arrival of a daughter!

You know that before the war Paris was coming to be more and more my permanent place of residence. When the calamity of the long war began in 1914, I happened to be visiting in Munich, and there I waited out those dreadfully long, almost lethal years; in 1919 I moved to Switzerland, where I now inhabit an old château from the thirteenth century, situated in the magnificent Canton du Valais (Wallis), just above Sierre, in a landscape that reminds one of Spain and Provence —in complete solitude, occupied with my work and the roses in my little garden. From time to time I go to Paris for a few months or to Italy, whenever the excessive solitude of my residence, to which I owe so much, threatens to become more than life-size and turn into a menace. I am not at home at the moment; since last December I have been in this sanatorium of Val-Mont, just above Territet, because of certain disturbances in my previously always fairly dependable health. This explains my late reply. (I hardly write any letters here.) It is my hope now that over these pages you will forget my delay and forgive it. Give my heartfelt greetings to all yours and be warmly and gratefully embraced.

Your

RILKE

Just now, in its winter issue, the very beautiful, important Paris periodical *Commerce*, edited by Paul Valéry, the great poet, has published very impressive poems by Boris Pasternak in a French version by Hélène Izvolskaya* (whom I also saw in Paris).

As mentioned previously, Leonid Pasternak, his wife, and his daughters moved to Germany in 1921 because of his wife's illness. The younger daughter, Lydia, stayed in Berlin with her parents, while the elder, Josephine, went to live with her husband, Fyodor, in Munich. The parents corresponded regularly with their sons in Moscow. The following postscript was attached to a long letter Leonid Pasternak wrote his sons on the day he received Rilke's March 14 reply.

LEONID PASTERNAK TO BORIS PASTERNAK

MARCH 17, 1926

I have good news for you: I just received a delightful and priceless letter (especially for you, Borya) from Rainer Maria Rilke. Before, we were in doubt as to his very existence, and suddenly, six months or so ago, we learned from the papers that the literary world was about to celebrate his fiftieth birthday, articles about him were printed, etc., etc. In my joy at learning that he was alive and well I resolved to add my

----

*Poet and translator, a friend of Marina Tsvetayeva's in the early 1930s.

congratulations to the others, hoping to revive old memories; in a word, I wrote him a few words from the heart, some of them in Russian. In speaking of the past I told him, among other things, that my children, especially my elder son, "who is a young poet already acclaimed in Russia," were his sincere and ardent admirers. Not knowing his address, I sent it to him through Insel Verlag. It took some time to reach him (he was in Switzerland), but I got a long, interesting, and joyful reply—joyful because he spoke ecstatically of you, Borya (he began his letter "in Russian," but he has forgotten some of it); not long ago he read some of your poems, translated by Valéry [sic] in a Paris journal. Next time I will send you excerpts from his letter, copied out by Lydia—I'm afraid to send the original for fear it will get lost. I am forwarding it to Josephine—she will be delighted.

PAPA

For Boris Pasternak this letter was a bolt out of the blue. In a period of mental depression and acute creative dissatisfaction, worn down as he was by Moscow's hard living conditions, Pasternak received the news that Rilke was alive and knew of his, Pasternak's, existence as the voice of fate. That voice seemed to be telling him that even though prewar Europe had collapsed, intellectual life was being preserved in its highest manifestations, that in a divided world there was still a European commonality of interests capable of creating poetry as a natural thing, a part of life itself. And this stunning news came to him simply, domestically, in a letter written in his father's familiar hand. He yearned to see and read Rilke's own words directly, not in his father's paraphrase. His impatience was only increased by the promise of excerpts after a prolonged family perusal.

It was at this moment of heightened sensitivity that he

came by chance upon Tsvetayeva's "Poem of the End," one of her finest and most powerful works. Already an admirer of her lyrics—Pasternak began his correspondence with Tsvetayeva with an ecstatic letter inspired by her *Versts*—he was now enraptured by this long poem. Because her work proved to him that there was something in the world commensurate with his own aspirations, Pasternak became convinced that it was possible to labor fruitfully, and he came to believe in himself. Much later he expressed these feelings in a letter to Tsvetayeva's daughter, Ariadna Efron: "For a number of years I was kept on an exalted plane by everything your mother wrote, by the ringing, ecstatic resonance of her inspiration, thrusting her ever forward without a backward glance. For you two I wrote *The Year 1905*, for her alone—*Lieutenant Schmidt*.[1]

Toward the end of March, Pasternak sent Tsvetayeva a spate of letters. He accepted the happy coincidence of events as a gift from fate, whose voice he had heard in his father's letter.

PASTERNAK TO TSVETAYEVA

MARCH 25, 1926

At last I am with you. Since all is clear to me and I believe in fate, there is no need for me to speak. I could leave everything to fate, who serves me with an undeserved loyalty that makes me dizzy with joy. Yet this is joined to so much feeling for you—if not all of my feeling—that I can scarcely cope with it.

[Tsvetayeva's "Poem of the End" evoked in Pasternak a sense of the deepest spiritual affinity and prompted him to address her with the intimate form of the second-person pronoun—*ty*—for the first time.]

You are filled with such beauty, you are a sister to me, you are my life, sent directly from heaven, and at the time of my soul's greatest ordeal. You are mine and have always been mine; all of my life is—you.

[The following are reconstructions based on passages quoted in Ariadna Efron's memoirs.]

Four evenings in a row I have thrust into my coat pocket a fragment of a haze-moist, smoke-dim Prague night, now with a bridge in the distance, now with you there, before my very eyes; I lurch into someone seen standing in line or fished out of my memory, and in a trembling voice recite to him that endless sequence of poignant lyrics of Michelangelesque breadth and Tolstoyan quietude which is called "Poem of the End." I came upon the poem by chance, a typed copy, without punctuation.

What else is there to say but to describe the table on which it lay?

You made me think again of our God, of my own self, of my childhood, of that part of me which always inclined me to look upon a novel as a textbook (of you know what), and upon a lyrical poem as the *etymology* of feelings (in case you missed the point about the textbook).

Truly, truly. Precisely that, precisely that thread which is spun by reality; precisely that which a person always *does* and never *sees*. As when a genius, that half-crazed creature, moves his lips. Just as you do in the first part of your poem. With what excitement one reads it! As if playing a part in a tragedy. Every sigh, the slightest nuance, is explicit in the verse.

"Excessively, excessively, that is,"
"But when the train had drawn up, the hander-in,"
"With business secrets and talcum for ballroom floors,"
"That means one needn't, it means there's no need,"
"Love is of flesh and blood,"
"We're pawns, you see, and someone plays with us,"
"Separating, coming apart?"

(By these phrases, you realize, I express whole pages at a time, so that:

> "All I am is a beast with someone's charge in the belly,"
> "Aforesaid by the chess game.")

Probably I have left something out, the poem lies at my right hand, I could pick it up and verify it but I don't wish to, it is better this way, from memory, more alive, with the exclamations I keep uttering wherever I go: "A gift from heaven!" "Beloved!" "Astonishing!" "Marina!" or anything else you can pull out of my depths just by rolling up your sleeves and reaching for it.

This is how it affects people. After reading it aloud to them (and *how* I read it!) there is silence, surrender, an atmosphere in which they begin to feel "the assault of the tempest." How is it achieved? Sometimes by the mere lifting of an eyebrow. I sit bent, bowed, aged. I sit reading as if you were watching me, and I love you and want you to love me. Then, when my listeners are reborn through your greatness, your wisdom, your unqualified profundity, all I have to do is murmur, without changing my pose, merely lifting an eyebrow, "Well? What do you say? Isn't she colossal?" to cause my soul (open to everyone when I chatter, but, despite occasional slips, preserved in secrecy by its own nature) to plunge into the vast spaces you open up.

What a great, what a devilishly great, artist you are, Marina!

But not another word about the poem or I will be constrained to drop you, my work, my family, and, turning my back on everybody, sit down and write about art, about genius, about the revelations of objectivity (a subject that has not yet been worthily treated), and about the joyful gift of feeling a oneness with the world, because you, like any true artist, have fixed your sights upon the bull's-eyes of these lofty targets.

I have but one small criticism to make, of an expression you use. I fear we are not always at one in our choice of words, that even though we both withdrew from the world at an early age you and I have not fought off prevailing clichés in the same way. You perhaps left the words "artist" and "objectivity" to the circles you ran away from. If this is so, you naturally hear in them only Sivtsev-Vrazhek* overtones, enveloped in cigarette smoke and stained with wine; you parted company with them forever by dropping them in some familiar vestibule.

I picked them up. I will say nothing about artistry—if that theme does not constitute my entire theology, at least it makes a volume too big and heavy to lift. As for objectivity, this is what I would like to say. It is a term I apply to that magical, elusive, and rare feeling you know in the highest degree. There, I have put it in a nutshell. As you read this, see if it doesn't fit you, consider your poems, meet me halfway.

When Pushkin said (you can quote this more exactly; forgive my ignorance and approximation) "Can you believe it? My Tatiana is getting married!" he was probably giving fresh and novel expression to a feeling unacknowledged in those days.

Throughout his life Pasternak concentrated his attention on principles he had worked out in his youth, and which he prized above all else. As the son of a professional painter, Pasternak felt no repugnance for such terms of the trade as "artistry" and "objectivity"; yet he and Tsvetayeva felt a kinship because they both abhorred literary criticism and the theorizing of dilettantes. The smoke-filled air of would-be literary discussions

---

*A small street in the Arbat district of Moscow, in an area where the aristocracy and the intelligentsia lived. Tsvetayeva lived on this street for some time before her marriage in 1912, and Pasternak rented a room there in the winter of 1915–16.

common to Moscow intellectual circles was equally repellent to them both.

Elaborating a principle that perhaps can be traced back to the Marburg school of philosophy and its leader, Hermann Cohen, Pasternak asserted that the artist's subjective creativity can, to the extent that the artist is capable of embodying his experience in a work of art, continue its existence objectively, thus becoming part of the human heritage, and of creation. In passing from the subjective to the objective, works created by man become greater and more significant than their makers. Art creates characters who live their lives independently of the author, who merely watches from the sidelines. It is in this light that Pushkin's words about his heroine Tatiana are to be understood.

Pasternak experienced this sense of the objectivity of a work of art—the feeling that the force that produced the work is above and beyond the artist who is responsible for the work—when he wrote *My Sister, Life*. From that time on he considered the definitive criterion for appraising a work of true art to be its objectivity. He wrote Tsvetayeva: "In order to express the feeling of which I am speaking, Pushkin ought to have spoken not of Tatiana alone but of the entire poem: 'Fancy, I read *Onegin* as once I read Byron. I do not know who wrote it. As a poet, he is greater than I am.' Subjectively, it is what the poet has just written. Objectively, it is what he is now reading, or correcting in the galley proofs; something written by a being greater than himself."

Pasternak found substantiation for his idea in Tsvetayeva's "Poem of the End," in which she forever identified herself with what she saw and described, experiences offered her simultaneously in different places—in a den of thieves in Prague, or on a bridge from which unmarried mothers threw themselves and their unwanted babies into the river. Later Pasternak returned to the idea that his relationship with Tsvetayeva was predestined, that it would have existed regardless of their feelings, desires, or mutual admiration. He recalled that even in their letters of 1923–24 they had seen their alliance as preordained, a fulfillment of destiny.

Tsvetayeva formulated it thus: "I am perfectly serene now. No feverishness. My days pass blissfully. For the first time in my life I live with knowledge instead of enchantment. The world sees you for what you are without my help."[2]

When Pasternak remembered how often those he had considered geniuses and devoted friends turned out to be false, how bitterly disillusioned he had felt at the destruction of his idols, he marveled and rejoiced all the more that fate had made him the contemporary of a genuine poet, and a woman at that! And he noted a parallel in the great French poet Marceline Desbordes-Valmore, whom Tsvetayeva too admired.

"And suddenly here you are, not created by me, born to respond to my least stirring with every fiber of your being. That you are fiercely mine yet not created by me—this defines my feeling."

He continued in this vein in his next letter.

PASTERNAK TO TSVETAYEVA

MARCH 27, 1926

You are an objective phenomenon, above all you are talented, you are a *genius*. Please underscore this last word. In daily parlance it is a cheap word, a hairdresser's word. I am infuriated every time I meet it, as no doubt you are, too. One of these days it will be thrown at you—or perhaps not. Be that as it may, it is not a negative hypothetical rating but a positive and inescapable word that hovers above you like a roof in the air, beneath which you ply your alchemy year after year.

The main thing is what you are engaged in. The main thing is that you are building a world *crowned by the mystery of genius.* In your time, in your life, this crown, this dome, merges with the sky, the live blue sky above the city where you live, or which you see in your imagination as you ply your alchemy. At another time other people will walk beneath it and the world will see other epochs. The soil of the cities is roofed over by the mysterious genius of other centuries.

... You write of not being understood at a first reading, of the complete silence following upon it. My experience follows the same or almost the same rule. Only my raw things, written fifteen years ago (literally my very first efforts), were comprehended immediately (if only by two or three people). Soon I came to regard a two-year interval between the work and the understanding of it as but an instant, the two aspects an indivisible unit; once in a great while this was expanded to three or more years. ...

Certain pages of Pasternak's philosophical observations are interspersed with expressions of the almost unbearable anxiety that was growing within him and seeking an outlet. They give us fleeting glimpses of the true reason for his anxiety, as when, in an off moment, he said: "You will be bored by my next letters if you are not *with* me and do not know who is corresponding with *whom* and why. As for Rilke, a part of our lives, the man who has invited you and me to visit him in the Alps next summer—of him I will talk later, in another letter."

While awaiting a copy of the Rilke letter, Pasternak conceived and nurtured plans, though these were doomed to failure, as can be seen in the correspondence that follows.

He made no attempt to hide his frenzy of impatience in letters to his relatives in Germany. With an insistence not at all typical of him, he pressed his parents and sisters to send him Rilke's letter, the very news of which had changed his life.

The following is one of these letters, to his sister Josephine in Munich. The importance Pasternak attributed to the Rilke letter elevated his joy at learning of it far above ordinary family rejoicing at the praise his cousin Olga Freidenberg had received from the linguist Marr, the recognition accorded his brother Alexander by the eminent constructivist architect Mendelson, the honor accorded his father of having his portrait painted by Lovis Corinth, the foremost German impressionist, or the pleasure of family gatherings around the tea table and musical evenings with the amateur musician Yakov Maximovich Romm.

BORIS PASTERNAK TO JOSEPHINE PASTERNAK

MARCH 28, 1926

Dear Zhonya,

Bandits, that's what you are, and cannibals! Are you in your right minds? Merely to mention in an offhand way that Father has received a letter from Rilke and have Father send it first to you for domestic consumption, to be subsequently passed on to me for domestic consumption—and not all of it but only a part, the part that concerns me alone—thrust, as it were, into my napkin ring like one of those family triumphs such as "Olya has been praised by Marr" or "Alexander by Mendelson," or even "Papa has been painted by Corinth." To offer me such a napkin (I haven't even seen it yet, but I have fearful fancies of what a Hamlet-like breastplate Papa pushed forward about his son's being "an acclaimed Russian poet"— just imagine how that must sound in German!), to promise it to me and expect me to wait with a happy smile on my face (instead I burst into tears and haven't been able to sleep for

three nights, because this is not "Corinth" and not "praise")
and go to the toilet and do my daily stint (I was told to go on
working, mind!) and to play with my son, and love Mama and
Papa, etc., etc., and—"it will be sent in the next letter." How
very kind. Come, let's all sit down and wait for Yakov Maximovich to pay us a call. . . . I don't know what would have
become of me if there had not been added to the reason for
my agitation, which you gave me a sly glimpse of and then
lovingly snatched away, a more overt and direct reason be-
longing to the same species but issuing from a different source.
Quite by chance I came across a typewritten copy of one of
Marina Tsvetayeva's latest works, "Poem of the End." My agitation was fortunately not subdued by anyone or anything,
and it found an outlet in that poem. I have Tsvetayeva's address, and I wrote telling her precisely who she was and what
she was doing. Ah, what a supreme artist she is, and how I
love her, more than anything else in the world, as I do Rilke. I
am not telling you this by way of exchanging confidences,
but for the following reason: you must read her: I don't doubt
that you have friends in Paris, or at least Fedya* does. Ask
them to send you everything of hers that is available, and
read it. Probably in Paris they are saying the same things I
hear in Moscow. Interspersed with stormy, imperfect passages of mediocre value one constantly comes upon bits of
great and perfect art testifying to talent that often rises to the
level of genius. The only others who have excited me to this
extent are Scriabin, Rilke, Mayakovsky, and Cohen. Unfortunately I know none of her latest writings. A visitor from
abroad brought me her Russian folk tale called "The Swain,"
dedicated to me. Splendid romanticism, but not to be compared with the finest passages in "Poem of the End." A little
of my influence is felt here. But heavens! Into what hands that
little has fallen! Be sure to get it—not for me but for yourself;

---

*Fyodor Pasternak, Josephine Pasternak's husband.

even if you were to send it, there is little likelihood of my ever receiving it. At such moments one feels: Ah, what a great, if honorable, tragedy we are acting out—paying for it with our souls. Not one writer could produce such a work here.

Yours,

BORYA

Do send me the Rilke letter as soon as possible. And don't be angry with me.

My best to Fedya. All my "interest in history," my absorption in actuality, in fact all to which I have been disposed lately, has been shattered to pieces by Rilke's letter and Marina's poem. It's as if my shirt were split down the front by the expansion of my heart. I'm punchdrunk. Nothing but splinters all about me: there *are* kindred souls in this world— and how extraordinary they are!

JOSEPHINE PASTERNAK TO BORIS PASTERNAK

APRIL 7, 1926

Dearest Borya,

You must hate the sight of our letters because of what has happened to you, but nobody is to blame. I could have wept when I read your postcards and letters. A mere misunderstanding has caused all this pain, has created something unforgivable, *was nicht wieder gut zu machen ist,* * simply because it cannot be undone: no, it has been done, hurting you frightfully, unbearably, shatteringly. I suppose there is no sense in answering, but I cannot leave your heart-rending appeal without response. I only wish to give you a calm chronological account of what happened, for if we are in any way to blame for your suffering, our guilt is enormous.

On the evening of March 18 I received the letter from Mama

---

*Which cannot be set right.

and Papa with which Rilke's letter was enclosed. I read it. No, I cannot say that it seemed to have come from a different world; it presented too great a contrast to what I would have expected: the simple schoolboy handwriting, the leisurely style, as contrasted with poetry that for me is the finest, the most exalted in the world. But there is no sense in telling you all this, especially now, and little chance of conveying the awe I felt.

Let me say only that I wanted to make two copies of the letter immediately, one for you and one for myself. But Fedya said—and I agreed with him—that there were weighty reasons for not sending you the entire letter; it would be more prudent to send you only those passages in which he speaks directly of you. And so, since Mama and Papa had specified that we were to return Rilke's letter as soon as we had read it, so that they could send it on to you, I did not wish to hold it back even for the time it would take to make a copy for myself. I sent it off instantly, certain that they would copy out what could be forwarded and dispatch it at once.

A new week began and I wrote you another letter (on the 25th), the one in which I spoke of Zhenya.* I did not even mention Rilke, confident that you would receive—or rather, had already received—the excerpts *before* you got my letter about Zhenya. They had promised to do it in Berlin. To write that I was in ecstasy, or deeply moved, or weeping from conflicting feelings, one of which was my love for you, that I wept as I read that letter, etc.—I did not wish to write all that; it would be a watercolor compared with the oil painting of his living words before you.

On the other hand, I feared that the family had not yet written you and that I, by referring to something you had not read or seen, would unduly upset you, that . . . to make a long

---

*Yevgenia ("Zhenya") Pasternak (née Luriye; 1899–1965): Boris Pasternak's wife at the time. In the spring of 1926 Josephine Pasternak was instrumental in getting Zhenya admitted to a sanatorium near Munich for treatment of a lung condition.

story short, by being overcautious I did *not* do what Papa *did* do, evidently without giving thought to the consequences and thereby causing you such pain. In the letter I wrote you about Zhenya I *deliberately did not mention* Rilke.

Then all of a sudden I received your first postcard. I was horrified. I mailed it to the family, begging that you be sent a copy of the passages referring to you immediately or that the letter be returned to me so that I could do so. I received a reply saying that Lydia had already taken care of it. I was reassured. But then came your letter and second postcard, as disturbing as the first. I did not forward them to Berlin for fear of upsetting Papa—I saw no point in it, the harm had already been done. By that time you had, of course, received Lydia's copy and their letter. This letter of mine is of no importance now, but I couldn't help writing it.

In a few days I will write again. God be with you.

Love,

ZHONYA

It was not until April 3 that Pasternak received the long-awaited copy from his sister Lydia. Deleted from it was the whole passage beginning "Yes, we have all had to undergo a great deal of change, your country more than any" and ending "how strongly, with what emotion did I feel this, dear Leonid Ossipovich Pasternak, last year in Paris."

The next week Boris Pasternak sent Rilke an impulsive, unrestrained, inspired letter.

Thirty years later, this is what Pasternak said of the event:

He played an enormous role in my life, but the idea of writing to him was too daring even to consider until, twenty years after he had begun influencing me (unbeknownst to him), I suddenly found out that he had read my poetry in Hélène Iswolsky's French translation. I would never have imagined that the mail could serve as a bridge to that inaccessible world, so different from the world around me, to which I was bound only by admiration. Suddenly it turned out that this bridge had been thrown across by circumstances in which I had not participated in any way. Only then did I realize I could write to him. But diplomatic relations with Switzerland had been severed. I was, however, corresponding with Tsvetayeva, my close friend, who was living in Paris at the time and admired Rilke no less than I did. Incidentally I wanted to make her the gift of acquainting her with Rilke. I asked him not to waste valuable time on writing to me, but to indicate that my letter had been received by sending his *Sonnets to Orpheus* and *Duino Elegies* to Tsvetayeva in France.[3]

BORIS PASTERNAK TO RAINER MARIA RILKE

Moscow
April 12, 1926

Great, most beloved poet!

I don't know how this letter might end and what would distinguish it from life if I were to give full voice to my feelings of love, admiration, and gratitude, by now of two decades' standing.

I am indebted to you for the fundamental cast of my character, the nature of my intellectual being. They are your creations. I have words for you of the kind one has for distant events that come to be regarded as mainsprings of happenings that have seemed to emanate from there. The passionate joy I feel at being able to make confession to you as a poet is as uncommon with me as what I would feel when confronting Aeschylus or Pushkin, if such a thing were conceivable. The sense of fateful tension, of the presence of the incredible, of impossibility surmounted, which penetrates me as I write to you cannot be reached by verbal expression. The magical coincidence that I should come to your notice was a staggering event to me. The news that reached me about this was like an electric short circuit of the soul. I was alone in a room; none of my family were here when I read the lines about this in L[eonid] O[sipovich]'s letter. I rushed to the window. It was snowing, people were walking outside. I could take nothing in, I was crying. Then came my son with his nanny, and later my wife. I was silent. For hours afterwards I was unable to talk.

Hitherto I've owed you a limitless debt of gratitude for the broad, lasting, and unplumbed boons of your poetry. Now I thank you for the sudden and intense boon that has intervened in my fate and is manifest in this strange coincidence. To elucidate this further would mean making undue claims on your attention, a thing I am unwilling to dare unless you grant it to me. This would also entail having the ability to comprehend and relate a series of tragic events in history—which is probably beyond my power.

There is one lesson, though, which our life experience here alone teaches everyone who is willing to learn: a great thing is most full of contradictions when it takes an *active* form; in its reality, it is also *small* within its magnitude, and sluggish within its activity. Such is our revolution, which is a contradiction in its very appearance: a fragment of gliding time in the form of an immobile, fearful tourist attraction. Of such a nature are our personal fates, too, *immobile* temporal *subjects* of the somber and exalted historical portent, tragic even in its smallest, even ludicrous detail. But what am I talking about! As far as poetry and the poet are concerned, that is to say, the special refraction of the general light of European intimacy, of our contemporaries' countless confluent privacies of fate—as regards poetry, things are as they were. As it does in eternity, thus *here* and now, too, all depends on the kindness of chance, which, experienced deeply and at the right time, is precisely what yields the missing refraction. Then all becomes simple, stupid, unhistoric or time-fathoming, free and fateful.* Then one becomes a poet all over again, after having missed that exhausting happiness for eight years. This is what has happened to me these last few days. Before, through those long eight years, I was deeply unhappy and as good as dead, although I never forgot even in my deepest vexation the tragic grandeur of the revolution. I was quite unable to write; I lived by inertia. All had already been written in the years 1917 to 1918.

And now I am as if reborn. Two accidents brought this about. I have already spoken about the first. It struck me dumb with gratitude: however much I may write about this, it is nothing compared with the feeling itself. Permit me to speak also about the other accident, the more so since I experienced these facts as related to each other, and since it involves a poet; a poet who loves you no less and no differently from myself and (however narrowly or broadly one may wish to conceive this) may be considered, just like myself, as a part of your own poetic history, outreach, and effect. On the same day as the news about you, I received by those roundabout means of ours a poem, truly and genuinely conceived in a way that none of us here in the USSR now write. That was the second inner upheaval of the day. The poet is Marina Tsvetayeva, a born poet, a great talent of the caliber of Desbordes-Valmore. She lives as an emigrant in Paris. I dare to wish—oh, please, please, forgive me this audacity and what must seem an imposition—I would wish, I would dare wish, that for her part she might experience something akin to the joy that welled in me thanks to you. I am imagining what one of your books, perhaps the *Duino Elegies*, which title I know only by hearsay, would mean to her, with an inscription by you. Do,

---

*Pasternak uses here the German word *fatal* (meaning "painfully, or comically, embarrassing"), but he doubtless has in mind the French *fatal*, meaning "fateful."

please, pardon me! For in the refracted light of this deep and broad fortuity, in the blindness of this joyful state, may I fancy that this refraction is truth, that my request can be fulfilled and be of some use? To whom, for what? That I could not say. Perhaps to the poet, who is contained in the work and who goes through the courses of time by different names.

Her name is Marina Ivanovna Tsvetayeva, and she lives in Paris, 19th arrondissement, 8, rue Rouvet.

Allow me to regard your fulfillment of my request concerning Tsvetayeva as an answer from you, as a sign that I may write to you in the future. Of a direct answer I do not want to dream. As it is, I have taken a great deal of your time with this lengthy letter, which I am sure teems with mistakes and absurdities. When I began it I thought that it would be a proper *"hommage."* The revelation which you are for me and will forever remain suddenly arose before me as it had numberless times before. I forgot that feelings of this sort, which are spread over years, lifetimes, and various places and situations, never submit to suddenly being gathered into one letter(!); thank God that I did forget it, or I wouldn't have written even these powerless lines. As if there weren't whole sheets of writing lying here which I shall never dare to send your way because of their prolixity and immodesty. Aren't there also two sheaves of poems* lying about which I meant, by the first impulse of the moment, to send to you as tangible lumps of sealed earth† for the letter, and which I am leaving where they are lest you might at some time or other take it into your head to read this sealed earth. But all this becomes superfluous as I say what is the first and the last of it. I love you, as poetry wants to and should be loved, as culture in its progress celebrates, admires,

---

My Sister, Life and *Themes and Variations*, written by Pasternak in 1917–18 and published in 1922 and 1923 in Moscow and Berlin.

†*Terra sigillata*, a medicinal earth, used as a remedy against suppurating wounds and snake bites. Pasternak's metaphoric use of the term here is not clear, unless he thinks of sealed earth as an antidote to festering poetry.

and experiences its own peaks. I love you and can be proud of the fact that I do not lower you by this love; neither I nor she, my greatest and probably only friend, whom I have already named. If you were to make me, too, happy with your autograph, I would ask you to use that same address, Tsvetayeva's. One can't be sure about mailings from Switzerland.

Your

BORIS PASTERNAK

———

Pasternak asked Rilke to write him through Tsvetayeva not only to bring Marina into direct contact with the finest European poetry, to strengthen her position as an émigrée, and help her to become independent, but also for a purely practical reason: there were neither diplomatic nor postal relations between the USSR and Switzerland, and communicating with Rilke through his parents or his sisters was both too intimate and too slow, as had been proved once already. Now he had further grounds for finding this method unacceptable: Pasternak had sent his first letter to Rilke via his parents in Berlin, asking that the letter be forwarded at once; Rilke did not receive it until twenty days later.

———

LEONID PASTERNAK TO BORIS PASTERNAK

BERLIN
APRIL 22, 1926

... I will forward your letter to Rilke, to his present address. For the moment I have sent it with Stella* to Josephine.

———

*Stella Samullovna Adelson (Frishman) 1901–88: a close friend of the Pasternak sisters, at the time visiting them.

We all liked it and wanted to give Zhonya a chance to read it. I will probably get it back tomorrow and send it to him immediately.

I cannot help drawing your attention to a certain *faux pas* you made in your letter to him which even an outsider would find offensive. I deliberately said nothing, waiting to see if Mama or Lydia would notice it. Of course it made the same impression on them. I know you had nothing offensive in mind when you wrote, "In your letter to L. O. . . ." I do not have the letter here, so I don't remember the sentence it appeared in; the point is that there is an implied "somebody-or-other" in that abbreviated form (it looks even worse in German); if you do not feel it I cannot explain it, but it would have been simpler to say "to my father." It reminds me of some newspaper reporters who came to interview me once and began, "Begging your pardon, do you happen to be L. O.?" . . . I said nothing at first and am reminding you now in this offhand way because I am convinced of your good intentions (you certainly did not mean to slight me); so I am not offended, and *Schwamm drüber.**

But I am not quite sure that in asking Rilke to send his autographed book to Marina Tsvetayeva, a writer personally unknown to him, you were not carried away by your sincere and wholly disinterested enthusiasm, which I can only admire. Perhaps there was nothing indelicate about it (I well understand that he may, and probably does, know and admire her poetry). But we fellows, we "oldsters," are always finicky in our relationships—perhaps more so than is good for us. Can it be that among poets the exchange of books with total strangers is accepted practice? At any rate, your display of generosity to a friend and disinterestedness for yourself cannot help pleasing him as it did me, and I am sure he will appreciate it and comply with your request.

---

*Let's forget it.

Forgive me for poking my nose into your *Angelegen-heiten*,* but it would be sad if I did nothing but praise you, disingenuously passing over these two objections; "let the boy write whatever he likes, it's none of my business." How many times have I sworn to "let the boy write whatever he likes" (unforgivable parental indifference) and to *keep my nose out* of your affairs—and even now my conscience troubles me for bringing up these points....

... Here is Rilke's address (Lydia gave it to you in her letter, I believe): Val-Mont par Glion, s/Territet (Vaud), Suisse. He is in this sanatorium temporarily; he did not give me his permanent address, which is in a 13th-century castle in the Canton du Valais (Wallis).

LEONID PASTERNAK TO
RAINER MARIA RILKE

BERLIN
APRIL 30, 1926
BAYREUTHERSTRASSE 17

[*In Russian*]
My dear and distinguished poet,

Surely you can imagine what delight, what exceptional happiness your letter brought me and my family. We were touched to the depths of our soul by it. Its unexpectedness made the impression all the greater, for I assure you I had not counted on receiving a reply. Suddenly, out of a clear sky—your letter! Hurrah! Thank God our poet is alive! Alive and *that same* unparalleled Rilke! The joy of your letter came first to us who were on the Bayreutherstrasse (my wife, my younger daughter, and I); this same joy was then forwarded to Munich, where my elder daughter lives; finally this joy kin-

---

* Affairs.

dled a blaze of excitement in Moscow,* the consequences of which you will find in the enclosed letter from my son Boris.

This series of forwardings explains my delay in answering, for which I beg your forgiveness.

Thank you, my dear friend, for giving all of us such great pleasure, for your touching attention and kind feelings. Is it possible that you are already a grandfather? ... *Sed fugit, fugit interea*, that implacable *tempus*. How I should like to catch a glimpse of you, a recluse in such poetic surroundings; would I recognize you after so many, and such difficult, years? Certainly I would! But it is hard to recognize you in the two portraits I happened to see not long ago.... They helped me to understand and sympathize with your reluctance to "pose for your picture." A copy of one of the portraits was published quite recently in the magazine *Querschnitt*; I don't remember the artist's name but he seems to have caught a slight resemblance. In the second one by the rather well-known (and talented, I believe) Paula Modersohn, I could discover nothing that reminded me of you in any way. Could you have changed so? It must be a misunderstanding or a mistake in identity—the wrong name, perhaps.... But enough of this.

How delighted I was to read the description of your solitary life among the beauties of nature. I rejoice that fate has made it possible for you to enjoy the greatest blessing an artist can know on this earth, *die gesegnete ungestörte Einsamkeit*,† pursuing your beloved art among your beloved roses, which demand nothing of you while constantly giving of their own charm and beauty. I would like to believe that in such benevolent circumstances you have been able to mend your health. God willing, we may meet in Paris, where I have

---

*I did not send your letter to Moscow, only excerpts from it, fearing that the censor might not deliver it to my son and might perhaps destroy it. [L. P.]

†Blessed, undisturbed solitude.

been planning to go for the last three years. If we are to meet there, it will be at the beginning of June.

I regret that I cannot write fluently in German and so have tortured you with my Russian. A thousand pardons. My son Boris has asked me to forward his letter to you because he does not know your address.

My fondest regards, dear friend, endless gratitude, and best wishes from me and my family.

Yours,

LEONID PASTERNAK

2

IN EARLY April, a growing uneasiness made Pasternak decide to join Tsvetayeva in France without delay in the hope of going with her to see Rilke: "What would you and I do if we were together? . . . We would go and see Rilke." Later, in her letter of May 22, 1926, Tsvetayeva quoted these words.

At the same time that Pasternak replied to Rilke's letter, he wrote to Tsvetayeva telling her of his desire to join her. He referred to Rilke in an offhand way: "If you hear from him, let me know. If he writes anything for me, take a look—it may require transcribing. I don't believe we have any postal communication with Switzerland."

On April 3 Pasternak mailed Tsvetayeva a questionnaire to fill out, asking her to answer the questions "in any way and at any length." The questionnaire was sent out by the Section on Revolutionary Literature, part of the Department for the Study of Revolutionary Art at the Academy of Art, and its purpose was to gather data for *A Bibliographical Encyclopedia of Twentieth-Century Writers*. It requested the following information:

1. Last name (pseudonym), first name, patronymic
2. Address
3. Place and exact date of birth
4. Social origin (peasant, worker, employee, clergy, aristocrat)
5. Brief biographical information: a) environment in which you were raised; b) childhood influences;

    c) present source of income; d) travels; e) evolution
    of your creative writing
6. General and special education
7. Basic profession
8. Literary, scholarly, social activities
9. First publication
10. First review
11. Literary influences
12. Favorite authors
13. Periodicals and collections in which you have been
    published
14. Membership in literary organizations
15. Chronological list of works
16. Bibliography of works

Tsvetayeva's answers, sent to Pasternak via someone going to Russia, were as follows (the lengthy and unverified chronological list of her works has been omitted):

TSVETAYEVA, MARINA IVANOVNA
Born September 26, 1892, in Moscow.
Of noble birth.

Father—son of a priest from the Vladimir *guberniya*, a philologist working in European languages (among the fruits of his research, *The Oscan Inscriptions*); doctor *honoris causa* of Bologna University, Professor of the History of Art, first at Kiev University, then at Moscow University; the founder, the heart and soul, the one and only collector of all the exhibits in Russia's first museum of fine arts, the Rumyantsev Museum* in Moscow, of which he became director. An indefatigable

---

*Now the Pushkin Museum of Fine Arts.

worker. Died in Moscow in 1913, soon after the opening of the museum. He left all that he had (not much, because he was always helping others) to the public school in Talitsy (the village where he was born in the Vladimir *guberniya*). He left his entire vast library (laboriously compiled by his own efforts), every last volume, to the Rumyantsev Museum.

Mother—of aristocratic Polish blood, a pupil of Rubinstein, a woman of rare musical talent. Died early. My poetic talent comes from her. She, too, gave her library and her father's library to the museum. So from us, the Tsvetayevs, Moscow received three libraries. I would give my own, if I had not been forced to sell it during the years of the revolution. Early childhood. Moscow and Tarusa (a nest of Khlisty* on the Oka River). Sojourns abroad from the age of 10 to 13 (year of mother's death). Lived abroad sporadically until 17. Never lived in a Russian village.

Principal influences: mother (music, nature, poetry, Germany, passion for Judaism, one against all, Eroica). Father's influence no less but not so direct (dedication to work, contempt for careerism, simplicity, self-denial). Combined influence of mother and father—Spartanism. Two leitmotifs in a single home: Music and Museum. Atmosphere of the home neither bourgeois nor dilettantish; chivalrous. Life on a lofty plane.

Sequence of intellectual development: early childhood—music; 10 years old—revolution and the sea (Nervi, near Genoa, a nest of émigrés†); 11 years old—Catholicism;

---

*A sect of flagellants that arose in the seventeenth century.

†I.e., anticzarist émigrés.

12 years old—first sense of patriotism (the *Varyag*, Port Arthur,* the Russo-Japanese War); from 12 to the present day—love of Napoleon, supplanted briefly in 1905 by the Russian heroes Spiridonova[†] and Schmidt[‡]; 13, 14, 15 years old—the populist movement, the Zna-niye[§] collections, the Don River dialect, Zheleznov's political economy,[||] Tarasov's poetry[#]; 16 years old— a break with all "causes," love for Sarah Bernhardt (*L'Aiglon*), an outburst of Bonapartism; from 16 to 18— Napoleon (Victor Hugo, Béranger, Frédéric Masson, Thiers, memoirs, *Kult*), French and German poets.

First encounter with revolution—in 1902, 1903 (émi-grés); second in 1905, 1906 (Yalta, Social Revolution-aries); no third encounter.

Sequence of favorite books (each of them an epoch): *Undine* (early childhood), Hauff's *Lichtenstein* (ado-lescence). Rostand's *L'Aiglon* (early youth). Later, and to the present: Heine, Goethe, Hölderlin. Russian prose

---

*During the Russo-Japanese War the Russian cruiser *Varyag* (Viking) was sunk by its crew after a valorous but unsuccessful attempt to escape blockade in a Korean port and reach Port Arthur.

[†]Maria Spiridonova (1884–1941): Social Revolutionary who assassinated the head of the reactionary Black Hundreds organization.

[‡]Pyotr Schmidt (1867–1906): naval lieutenant who led a mutiny on his ship, the *Ochakov*, during the 1905 revolution in Russia; the rebellion was quelled and Schmidt was executed. He is the hero of Pasternak's *Lieutenant Schmidt*.

[§]Journals published by the Znaniye (Knowledge) publishing association (1898–1913), the most progressive Russian publishing house.

[||]Vladimir Zheleznov (1869–1933): Russian democratic economist who combined the ideas of classical English political economy with Marxist economic theory.

[#]Yevgeny Tarasov (1880–1943): Russian poet who became well known for his mili-tant verse during the revolution of 1905.

writers—speaking for my present self—Leskov and
Aksakov.* Of my contemporaries—Pasternak, Russian
poets—Derzhavin and Nekrasov.† Of contemporary
poets—Pasternak.

Favorite poems in childhood—Pushkin's "To the Sea"
and Lermontov's "Hot Springs." Twice beloved—"The
Forest King" and "Erlkönig."‡ Have loved to distraction
Pushkin's *Gypsies* from the age of 7 to the present day.
Never have liked his *Eugene Onegin*.

My favorite books in all the world, those one takes with
one to the stake: *The Nibelungs*, the *Iliad*, *The Lay of
Igor's Host*.

Favorite countries—ancient Greece and Germany.

Education: from the age of 6—the Zograf-Plaksina Music
School. Age 9—4th Women's *Gymnasium*; age 10—no
school; age 11—Catholic boarding school in Freiburg
(Black Forest); age 13—*Gymnasium* in Yalta; age 14—
Alfyorova's boarding school in Moscow; age 16—Bryu-
khanenko *Gymnasium*. Finished seven grades, left in
the eighth. At the age of 16 attended a summer course
in Old French literature at the Sorbonne.

Commentary on my first French composition (age 11)—
Trop d'imagination, trop peu de logique.§

---

*Nikolai Leskov (1831–95) and Sergei Aksakov (1791–1859).

†Gavrila Derzhavin (1743–1816) and Nikolai Nekrasov (1821–77).

‡Goethe's poem "Erlkönig" was translated into Russian by Vasily Zhukovsky (1783–1852) under the title "The Forest King."

§Too much imagination, not enough logic.

I have been writing poetry since age 6, publishing since 16. Have written poems in French and German. First book—*Evening Album*. I myself had it published while still a schoolgirl. First review—an encouraging one by Max Voloshin. I know no literary influences, only human influences.

Favorite writers (of my contemporaries): Rilke, Romain Rolland, Pasternak. Have been published in the following journals: *Severnyye zapiski* (1915); now, in Europe, mainly in *Volya Rossii*, *Svoimi putyami*, *Blagonamerenny* (these are of the literary left wing), occasionally in *Sovremennyye zapiski* (more rightist). Newspapers: *Dni*, sometimes in *Posledniye novosti* (more rightist). I have never printed in rabid rightist publications, because of their low cultural level.

Never have and never will belong to any school of poetry or politics. In Moscow I belonged (for purely material reasons) to the Poetry Section of the Writers' Union.

Things I hold most dear: music, nature, poetry, solitude.

Completely indifferent to public opinion, the theater, the plastic arts, spectacles. Feel possessive only toward my children and my notebooks.

Would inscribe on the finished product: *Ne daigne.** Life is a railroad station; soon I will set out—for where? I will not say.

MARINA TSVETAYEVA

---

*Never condescend.

PASTERNAK TO TSVETAYEVA

APRIL 20, 1926

Tomorrow I will be a different person, I will take the bull by the horns and get to work. But I will spend this night with you. At last they have withdrawn into two rooms. I have begun five letters to you today. Our little boy has the flu. Zhenya is with him. So are my brother and his wife. In and out, in and out. The stream of words you drank of as you pumped them out of me was constantly interrupted. We bounced away from each other. One after another my letters went into the wastebasket. How marvelously you work! But don't destroy me. I want to live with you for a long, long time.

Yesterday I read about your mother in the questionnaire you filled out. This is all so amazing! At the age of 12 my own mother played a Chopin concerto with, I believe, Rubinstein conducting. At least he was present at her concert in the Petersburg Conservatory. But that's not the point. When she finished playing he lifted her in his arms, kissed her, and, turning to the audience (it was a rehearsal attended by musicians), said: "*That* is how it ought to be played." Her name was Kaufman; she was a pupil of Leschetizky.* She is still alive. I believe in her talent. She is the very embodiment of modesty, not a trace of the prodigy, has given all of herself to her husband, children, us.

But it is about you I am writing. When I woke up this morning I thought about the questionnaire you filled out, about your childhood, and with my cheeks wet I sang it, ballad by ballad, nocturne by nocturne, all that you were brought up in—you and I. I wept. Mama never played in public again after we were born. I remember her as being always sad and loving.

---

*Theodor Leschetizky (1830–1915): composer and piano teacher whose pupils included Paderewski.

I had occasion to write to Voloshin and Akhmatova.* Soon
two sealed envelopes lay on my desk. I felt the urge to talk to
you—and immediately I was aware of the difference. It was as
if the wind had ruffled my hair. I could not write to you. I
wished to go outside to see what one poet's thinking of another poet had done to the air and the sky. I saw our shackles,
I saw you and me made for each other, and I saw the starva-
tion ration we must hold to for a year if you can survive on it
and promise me that I can, too. I am not joking, dearly
beloved; never before have I spoken so. Promise me that you
rely upon me, that you trust my intuition. Then I will tell you
why I have delayed, why I am not with you yet, and about
that summer night, and I. G., and L. M.,† and all the rest.

All of this I will explain later.

In contrast to your dream, I was with you in a happy,
translucent, endless dream. In contrast to my usual dreams,
this one was youthful and tranquil, and the transition to
waking was painless. It occurred a few days ago, the last day
I called happiness for you and me. I dreamed that it was
summer in the city, I was in a bright, immaculate hotel without bedbugs and away from everyday life, or perhaps it was
a mansion in which I was a servant. Downstairs there were
those same corridors. I was told that someone was asking
for me. Certain that it was you, I flew down a staircase that
was bathed in quivering light. And sure enough, there you
were in a kind of traveling cloak, enveloped in a mist of high
determination, appearing not suddenly but on wings, gliding
in much the same way that I had flown to you. What were
you? A fleeting vision of all that in the prism of momentary

---

*Anna Akhmatova (1889–1966): celebrated Russian poet. Pasternak had written her
and Voloshin at the request of the compilers of a literary anthology, to inform the
poets of payments due them for their contributions.

†The writer and journalist Ilya Grigoryevich Ehrenburg and his wife, Lyubov
Mikhailovna, who were living in Paris at the time.

emotion transforms a woman into something incommensurable with human dimensions, as if she were not a human but the sky filled with the beauty of all the clouds that have ever sailed across it. But that was but an element of your loveliness. Your beauty as revealed in photographs—beauty of your particular kind—by which I mean the manifestation of a great soul—was wafted to me in the air even before I found myself carried on the waves of that divine light and sound. It was a mood you yourself evoked. I cannot describe it, but this it was that gave joy and endlessness to my dream.

It was complete harmony, experienced for the first time in my life with an intensity equaling the experience of pain. I found myself in an atmosphere so full of passion for you that I was unaware of my own brashness and evanescence. It was more first than first love, as well as being the simplest thing on earth. I loved you as in life I had only *dreamed* of loving, long, long ago, loving to eternity. You were beauty in the absolute. In my dream, in the walls, the floor, the ceiling, with their semblance of reality, everywhere—you, Tsvetayeva, that is, in the anthropomorphic similitude of air and hours. You were the word revealing all that poets address themselves to throughout their lives without hope of getting an answer. You were a mighty poet, seen in the midst of a great outpouring of loving adoration, as close as the human can get to the elemental—not in the popular sense of the term ("natural," "cataclysmic") nor among people but in your own way and your own sphere.

Why is it that two years ago, when, in a similar mood, I tried to bring you back here and met with opposition from the Lanns,* I attributed no importance to the Lanns despite your opinion of them, and perhaps even today you would

---

*Yevgeny Lann (1896–1958), a writer and translator, and his wife, Alexandra Krivtsova (1898–1958), a translator from the English. Tsvetayeva and Yevgeny Lann had become friends in 1920.

deny that they occupy a place in your heart? Why is it that for me there exist only S. Ya.* and myself?

In respect to the lady with the dead fingers, you ask me: Perhaps you were in love with her? And this from one who sees me and says she knows me? Even if E. Yu.† were the exact opposite of what she is, *even then* it would require something exceptional, something returning time and people to life's fundamentals, to the source, to the beginning—in other words, it would require you—to shake me out of my rut and lead me on to a worthy path. I am not only married, I am also "I," and "I" is but a child in many respects. By that I mean that I am not exposed to frequencies that threaten to distort life. Once again: Do you understand me?

There have been occasions when Zhenya has suffered on insufficient grounds, that is, when I was enamored but not in love to the degree of taking the first step. There are *thousands* of women whom I would *have* to love if I let myself go. I am ready to run after any manifestation of femininity, and my mind swarms with such visions. Perhaps I was born with this trait so that my character would be formed by the development of a strong, almost unfailing system of brakes.

Well, anyway, E. Yu. was not among even those causes of Zhenya's suffering; her only virtue is her obvious dislike of me. I have only seen her two or three times, and always among people I did not find congenial. Whenever I put in an appearance she announced in a loud voice: Here am I, so-and-so and so-and-so, and he doesn't so much as look at me! Her tactlessness always embarrasses me, and I can only murmur that I am a cad or an unfeeling boor or whatever comes into a person's head in such circumstances. I had to call on her not because of her reproaches but because of your

---

*Sergei Yakovlevich Efron (1893–1941): Tsvetayeva's husband, often referred to in the letters as "S. Ya." and "Seryozha."

†Elza Yuryevna Triolet (1896–1970): French writer, born and raised in Moscow.

Yesenin,* because of that natural law by which the value of anything that increases my chances with you, however alien it may be to me, is multiplied out of all proportion. She read some of her prose to me and I praised it whenever possible. She is not without talent but I told her that the value of a writer and what he writes is determined by a third dimension—depth; it is this that raises the text in a vertical line off the page, and, most important, separates the book from the author. I told her her writing lacks this quality but it would probably come with experience. I can't understand why she seeks me out and tries to like me. I know of no reasons why she should want to be my friend. What I am trying to say is that, given all these things, I ought to be a zero for her, or at least she ought to feel indifferent, as do most of those who are touched by the same madness of trying to imitate me, etc. I came to dislike her actively after your letter, and surely I don't have to assure you it was not because of what she said about "Gapon"† (she heard it only once, and it was not to her I read it)—I have heard such opinions before—but because she came to me at night in your letter, your first letter, the one that made my life insufferable without you.

Allow me, Marina, to put an end to this self-torture, which can do nobody any good. Now I shall present you with a question without any comment from *my* side because I believe in your reasons, the reasons that you must have and that must remain unknown to me, but form a part of my life nevertheless. Answer me as you have never answered anyone before, as you would answer your own self. *Shall I join you now or*

---

*Sergei Yesenin (1895–1925): Russian poet who committed suicide. Tsvetayeva planned to write a poem or a play based on his life and had asked Pasternak to help collect biographical data.

†The second chapter of Pasternak's *1905* was originally entitled "Gapon," after the priest who led the "Bloody Sunday" demonstration of 1905.

within a year? There is *nothing foolish* about my indecision; I have good reasons for hesitating about the time, but I lack the strength to choose the second alternative (within a year). If you support me in the second choice, it follows that I will spend this year working with maximum concentration. I will make progress and advance not only toward you but also toward the opportunity to *help you* in your life and destiny (it would take volumes to explain this)—help you more than I have been able to do so far (please understand this in the broadest possible sense).

In this event I beg you to help me. Try to imagine *how* I read your letters and what they do to me. I will stop answering them, i.e., I will no longer allow myself to give free rein to my feelings; I will dream of you and you will never hear of it. One year—this is my time limit, and I will observe it. I am speaking *only* about work, about fortifying myself, about continuing efforts aimed at restoring to history a generation that seems to have dropped out of it, the generation to which *you and I belong.*

We are not speaking about anything else. I have an aim in life and that aim is you. But you are becoming less my aim than a part of my labor, of my misfortune, of my present uselessness, because the happiness of possibly seeing you this summer eclipses everything else and I no longer see the component parts of the whole, which may be visible to you. To enlarge upon this would only be to obscure it. I implore you, Marina, to do as I ask. Look about you and reflect upon *your* surroundings, those things that concern *you alone,* even if they include, among such things as conversations overheard among your French fishermen, *your* perception of what I am. Look about you, and in what you see and hear discover your answer; only let it not be guided by your desire to see me, for you must desire this, knowing how much I love you.

Send me your answer as soon as possible.

If you don't stop me I will come now, and *only to you*, but empty-handed and with not so much as an inkling as to where to go from there or why. Don't succumb to the romantic impulses that are so much a part of you. They are bad, not good. You are much more than just that, and I am like you. If, incidentally, fate is a factor in life (and this spring I became convinced that it is), then here in our Russian atmosphere (and perhaps in the whole world) we cannot depend on its being benign—or better, on its fortuities answering the poet's need. No, we must load the gun with our own hands. And that requires one year. Yet I am almost certain that I will join you at once, abandoning my work. I cannot begin it anyway until you make order of my chaos.

I am sending you my photo. I look like a monster. I am exactly what the picture shows—it's a good one. My eyes are slits because I am looking at the sun, which makes me appear worse than ever. Don't look at the eyes. Hold your hand over the eyes.

Don't listen to me. Answer freely. I beg you to.

———

Tsvetayeva had just returned from London, where she had traveled for two literary evenings arranged for her by the Russian critic Dmitry Svyatopolk-Mirsky. Her response to Pasternak's impetuous outburst was somewhat reserved, since she was just about to leave for the seashore village of St.-Gilles in the Vendée with her children, and a visit from Pasternak did not fit in with her plans. Unlike Pasternak, who by his own admission held everything—including her and Rilke —"in a single embrace," Tsvetayeva regarded any joining—in this case, of plans—as unthinkable.

———

PASTERNAK TO TSVETAYEVA

MAY 5, 1926

Your reply will come any day now. Perhaps it will require answering by telegram, in which case this protracted pause will be broken for you by the staccato bark of a wire. Long, long ago, so long that I have forgotten when, I received your chilling letter from Paris. On that day I found out that I would not see you in St.-Gilles. I knew it before the letter arrived. The coldness of the letter mitigated the harshness of the fact.

And yet, put me on ice as you will, the fact is unendurable. Forgive the excesses I allowed myself then. I should have shown restraint. I should have kept everything to myself as a vivifying secret until the day we met. Until then I could and should have hidden from you a love that can never die, for you are my only legitimate heaven and wife, so very, very legitimate that the force taking possession of the word makes me hear it in a madness that never dwelt in it before. Whenever I murmur your name, Marina, little shivers run up and down my spine from the cold and the pain of it.

I do not ask you whether you want this or not, I mean whether you approve or not, because, knowing how you aspire with all your being toward light and joy, I identify even my grief (the grief of having been rejected) with you—that is, with the poignant oneness that can never be shattered.

Without my saying a word, Zhenya understood everything, especially how deep and irreversible my feeling for you is. And in the searing wind of this discovery she has been growing spiritually day by day until I hardly recognize her. What terrible pain it is to see and understand and love her in her growth and suffering, without being able to make her realize that while all the world within me and around me is steeped in you, I embrace her no less tenderly than I do my son, even though I cannot say where and how my feelings are distributed and expended in time. If all goes well I will send her and the boy to my sister in Munich for the summer. And if my work allows it I will join them there in the autumn. If not, I am confronted by a dreadful, endless winter, and then— spring at last. No other time limits exist; I cannot allow, cannot imagine them.

What was the meaning of the last sentence in the form you filled out?—"Life is a railroad station; soon I will set out—for where? I will not say." (I don't have the form; I am citing from memory.)

The words did not disturb me; I took them as a declaration of immortality, I mean an emphasis on that, on the mystery and the faith, and not on the literal speed as Asya* did, filling me with dreadful alarm (because it was *your sister* who interpreted them in this way). Don't forget to answer this question. Bah!—how foolishly we chatter at times! This is not what I want to talk about. But tell me that my interpretation was the correct one, and if not (something inconceivable) I implore you to change your mind. The other day I received a letter from my sister in Munich. She assures me, she swears to me, that I will not die this year. For a passing moment her letter brought to mind two or three sleepless nights when I had been hounded by this fear. I must have mentioned it to her, although I cannot recall having done so. But for her letter, I would have forgotten all about it.

Oh, but what a spate of daily signs! People are joyous, they come running, they bring gifts, they swear allegiance. The signs are too many to list. Suddenly everybody loves me. They have remembered me and rush to me from every direction. How particularly wonderful you are when by the merest chance you become part of this whirlwind of felicity. All kinds of things have been said about me. Then, unexpectedly (let me add that the person who told me is unaware that you and I are acquainted), I am ecstatic to learn that *Versts* (yours)

---

*Anastasia Ivanovna Tsvetayeva (1894–1993): Marina Tsvetayeva's sister, a prose writer.

is among the hand-typed manuscripts making the rounds in Moscow.

Or in some letter I indirectly hear that the writer is sure some change must have taken place in me of late because he or she often dreams about me, etc., etc....

It's as if you had conjured me or assigned to me my own private Pythia. I have, insanely, begun to confuse two words: you and I.

MAY 8, 1926

I thank you, I trust you. How difficult to write! How much I scribbled and threw away this week. You pointed out the shoreline to me. Ah, how truly I am yours, Marina! Everywhere, everywhere.

Your reply is lying in front of me. Strange that it does not glow with phosphorescent light in the dark. I could not have anticipated anything so splendid. I kept circling around and around the problem. Twenty times I decided to set off on my journey, and twenty times I was stopped by a voice I hated as long as it was my own. Then you gave warning. And how beautifully! Are you aware that when you speak out you always surpass my finest imaginings, even though they are evoked by adoration?

A few days ago I expressed it this way to a certain person: I receive letters from a person I love to distraction. But this person is so immense, and the letters testify to this so vastly, that sometimes it almost causes me physical pain to hide them from others. Such pain is called happiness.

You do not know all. You sat me down to work. How can I thank you for making this separation easier through work, for taking the place of certain people and circumstances in my life these last three months.

I speak of you as of the source. How shall I explain it? People have come to treat me as if I were something pre-

cious—lovingly and solicitously, as if I were loaded with gold.
Since I am loaded with you, I love them for treating me so.
For their sensitivity, for surrendering themselves to what for
me is the breath of life.

I will write to you as soon as I finish *Schmidt*. Otherwise I
could not make myself concentrate on my work. It will be
three weeks or so. Then I will have a lot to tell you. Indeed
you are here with me and as palpably as any of the things surrounding me. But not a word of this today. When I write to
you I will be alone.

Yours was a rare and splendid reply. If what I said (at an impossible distance and in a divine, noble sense) about the legitimacy of our relationship seems to be at odds with your recent
words about marriage, cross it out so that you will never see
it again. As a matter of fact, I expressed the very soul and
essence of your own letter.

This summer, autumn, and winter there will be occasions
and periods when it will seem that we have defied spring,
have flown in the face of it. At such times I pray for you and
myself as well.

I am enclosing with this letter an unfinished one, begun
while I was waiting for your reply. Do not answer either that
letter or this one, in which I express to the sea sands of St.-
Gilles my humility and submission and anything else required to clear the air. Live and grow and be silent. Do not try
to catch up with me; I lag behind. For seven years I was a spiritual corpse. But I will catch up with *you*, you will see. I dare
not think about your awesome talent. I will understand it one
of these days; it will come to me instinctively. None can resist your clear, pure gift, which elevates a person by making
him *indebted* to it. *Freedom* is implicit in it, as in a beloved
calling, or in the realm in which *you* are to be found. The
summer of 1917 was a summer of freedom. I am speaking of
the poetry of time, and of my own poetry. In *Schmidt* there

is one part, very emotional, very much my own, that flashes forth, then sinks wearily into the following lines:

> O statehood's overpowering idol,
> Liberty's never-yielding door!
> Out of their cages aeons sidle,
> Beasts roam the Colosseum floor;
> An outstretched hand is ever reaching
> Into the ages' sodden gloom,
> By faith the fierce hyena teaching,
> And evermore a step is taken
> From blood games to the Church of Rome,
> And by that tread we too are shaken,
> We of the mines and catacombs.

The preceding verse has movement and is, perhaps, not bad. I quote these lines for the sake of the idea. Your influence is felt in the theme (Jews, conversion to Christianity, etc., from "Poem of the End"). But you took this as an eternal symbol, a tragic one; I took it to indicate constant transition, almost an ornamental canon of *history*: the arena becomes the first rows of the amphitheater; convicts become rulers; in a word, an examination of history leads one to think that idealism exists mostly so that it can be refuted.

Forgive me for the squeamish and petty request I am about to make, and do not wonder at my sudden display of practicality. Not all readers understand that when I write in "Potemkin,"* "They did not touch the meat but dined silently on bread and water...," the word "dined" is not a slip but is used intentionally. "To dine" is precisely the sailors' word,

---

*In the poem *1905*, "Potemkin" was the original title of the chapter ultimately called "Mutiny at Sea." As this letter makes clear, Pasternak considered including footnotes to explain naval slang; Tsvetayeva, however, dissuaded him.

or, rather, barracks usage, instead of "taking grub, chow, mess," "shoveling in," "filling up on," and other crude expressions. I took this from reliable sources. What I meant to ask you is: Ought I to provide footnotes for naval lingo, including "to dine"? If you approve, I could supply documented evidence: "It was impossible to dine on borscht so the crew had no hot meal and *dined on bread and water*." (From Case No. 3769, Year 1905, Police Department, Office 7, concerning the sailors' revolt on the battleship *Prince Potemkin of Tauris*. Testimony of seaman Kuzma Perelygin.) Naturally the original is in the old orthography.

In a document called "The Truth about the *Potemkin*," Afanasy Matyushenko, quartermaster first class from the engine-room section of the battleship *Prince Potemkin of Tauris*, wrote: "Why don't you *dine* on borscht, fellows?" "Dine on it yourself, we'll *dine on* bread and water." This excellent reminiscence (Matyushenko was hanged in 1907, betrayed by Azef) abounds in *dining on water*. I am surprised that some people find it strange. I believe the very soul of the language would have led me to use it myself even without documentary evidence. Perelygin's testimony would be enough for a footnote. The other footnotes would come under the words they refer to. *Shkantsy* means the middle section of the ship, the section most revered, almost sacred. *Knekht* is an iron post for fastening the hawser. *Skatit palubu* means to swab the deck after closing all the hatches. The *batareinaya paluba s bashnei* refers to the armored structure in the middle of a battleship with access to the engine and mine rooms as well as to the ship's arsenal. *Shchit* is a metal shield used as a gun target during maneuvers. *Kambuz* is the ship's kitchen. *Spardek* is the deck that forms a ceiling over the central part of the ship. *Yut* is the upper deck between the mainmast and the stern.

Perhaps all this is superfluous? Looks rather silly. What do you think?

How I loathe my letters! But since my real reply to yours is the continuation and finishing of "Luvers,"* and since any other letter I might write (instead of this nonsense culminating in these jumbled pages about footnotes) would amount to the same thing, I am sending it off to you—an outburst testifying to creeping mental paralysis.

I am serious about all this, Marina; a belief in fatality makes me fearless. Belief in the whole extended in time elicits contempt for the particular. There was a week when I totally withdrew from my family. Last winter I was often plagued by intimations of approaching age and illness. But it is amazing how suffering heals and rejuvenates. Suddenly I took a long look at my life and saw it for what it is. Forgive me this letter, the foolish poetry, the endless discourse on footnotes that are of course unnecessary. I will write well this summer, will examine everything from top to bottom. I will write you about you, about the ultimate, about what is most precious: about you unconditionally, "objectively." And about the meaning, as I see it, of my life's touching yours. When I speak I pile up verbal half-truths. That's because our relationship has become part of life.

I expect something from the English trip—perhaps some change in you or in my image of you. Perhaps it will become easier to live, easier for us to meet each other. Thank God you answered my question about the last sentence in the form you filled out. I cherish the fragments of your poetry that I find in your letters as trenchant models of virile and exalted lyricism. How splendid that we sing *these* praises to each other not in isolation but supported by many, many voices.

And still I feel that my not coming to you is a mistake, something lost. Life has become horribly difficult again. But this time it is at least life, and not something else.

---

*The Story "The Childhood of Luvers" (1922) was planned as the beginning of a novel that was never completed.

Common sense won out over the romanticism of Pasternak's first impulse to join Tsvetayeva. Pasternak realized that he could not possibly present himself to Rilke without having some worthy new work to justify his intrusion. On April 20 he had placed his fate in Tsvetayeva's hands, virtually asking her to serve as his better judgment and tell him not to come. He was pleased with her answer: she not only gave him freedom of choice but also reminded him of his duty, and this obviously postponed their meeting for a year.

Five years later, Tsvetayeva mentioned this letter when writing to Anna Tesková, a Czech friend with whom she corresponded for many years: "In the summer of 1926, after reading my 'Poem of the End,' B. was madly drawn to me, wanted to come and join me—I restrained him: I feared *total* disaster."[1]

For Pasternak, too, a drama "like a train wreck" was unthinkable: on March 25, 1926, he had written to Tsvetayeva about his wife, "I feel that my solicitude for her is dictated by the sense of duty you have inspired in me." To emphasize his agreement with Tsvetayeva's understanding of duty and marriage, Pasternak took back what he had said at an earlier time and in a different mood about the legitimacy of their relationship: "That you are fiercely mine and yet not created by me" is the definition of the feeling that allowed him "at an impossible distance and in a divine, noble sense" to call Tsvetayeva his "only legitimate heaven and wife."

Rainer Maria Rilke, Muzot, 1925

Marina Tsvetayeva
with her daughter,
Ariadna,
Paris, 1925

Ranier Maria Rilke,
Muzot, 1925

RAINER MARIA RILKE

DUINESER ELEGIEN

1 9 2 3

IM INSEL-VERLAG ZU LEIPZIG

Title page of Rilke's
Duino Elegies

RAINER MARIA RILKE
DIE SONETTE AN ORPHEUS

GESCHRIEBEN ALS EIN GRAB-MAL FÜR
WERA OUCKAMA KNOOP

Title page of Rilke's
Sonnets to Orpheus

Marina Tsvetayeva,
1924

Boris Pasternak,
Yevgenia Paternak, and
their son, Zhenya, 1924

Für

Марина Ивановна Цветаева /

Wir rühren uns, womit? Mit Flügel-
schlägen,
mit Fernen selber rühren wir uns an.
Ein Dichter einzig lebt, und dann und
wann
kommt, der ihn trägt, dem, der ihn trug,
entgegen.

Rainer Maria Rilke

/ Val-Mont, par Glion
(canton de Vaud)
Trina, im May 1926 /

Quatrain sent by Rilke
to Marina Tsvetayeva
with a copy of
his *Duino Elegies*,
May 3, 1926

Marina Tsvetayeva
with her husband,
Sergei Efron, 1926

Last page of Marina Tsvetayeva's letter to Boris Pasternak, May 26, 1926

RAINER MARIA RILKE

VERGERS

suivi des

QUATRAINS VALAISANS

avec un portrait de l'auteur par
BALADINE
gravé sur bois par
G. AUBERT

ÉDITIONS

de la **n**ouvelle **r**evue **f**rançaise

PARIS 3, rue de Grenelle **1926**

Title page of *Vergers*, Rilke's volume of French verse

12/IV 26. Mostad.

Großer, geliebtester Dichter!

Ich weiss nicht, wo dieser Brief endete und wodurch ich vom Leben unterschiede, gäbe ich den Gefühlen der Liebe, Bewunderung und Erkenntlichkeit die zwei Jahrzehnte zählen, volle Sprache.

Ich bin Ihnen mit dem Grundzüge des Charakters, mit der Art meines Geistesdaseins verpflichtet. Das sind Ihre Schöpfungen. Ich habe Worte für sie, die man für ferne Geschehnisse hat, die nachher als Quellen des Geschehens betrachtet werden, das von dort her zu sehen scheint. Die stürmische Freude Ihnen einmal Dichtergeständnisse machen zu dürfen ist nicht gewöhnlicher bei mir, als wie ich sie Aischylos oder Puschkin gegenüber fühlte.

First page of Pasternak's letter to Rilke, April 12, 1926

3

AT LAST, in early May, Rilke received the first letter from Boris Pasternak. It had traveled from Moscow to Berlin, to Munich, back to Berlin, and finally to Switzerland. With astonishing speed Rilke responded to Pasternak's request that he get in touch with Tsvetayeva.

RILKE TO TSVETAYEVA

VAL-MONT PAR GLION S/TERRITET
(VAUD) SUISSE.
MAY 3, 1926, A.M.

Dear Poet,

This very hour I received an infinitely moving letter from Boris Pasternak, a letter brimming with joy and a great flow of feeling. All the emotion and gratitude that his letter stirs in me is to go first of all to *you*, as I understand from his lines, and then through you to him! The two books (the latest I have published) that follow this letter *are for you, are your property*. Two further copies will follow as soon as I have any: these are to go to Boris Pasternak,* if the censorship allows it. I am so shaken by the fullness and power of his

---

*Name written in Cyrillic characters, as are "Leonid Osipovich" and "Marina Ivanovna Tsvetayeva" later in the letter.

message to me that I cannot say more today, but would you send the enclosed sheet to our friend in Moscow for me? As a greeting. Must I explain? You know that I am privileged to count Boris's father, Leonid O. P., among my close friends from Moscow days (over twenty-six years!). This winter (at the beginning of winter), after a long, long interval, a letter of his from Berlin found me, and I answered it with all the delight that this mutual rediscovery roused in me. But I didn't need the report from Leonid Osipovich to know that his son had become a poet of name and power: before that (last year in Paris) friends had put before me samples that I found gripping and heart-stirring. (I still read Russian, though it always takes some getting used to and practice; letters still easy anyway!) A stay in Paris last year, lasting almost *eight* months, brought me back into contact with Russian friends* I hadn't seen for twenty-five years. But why, I must wonder now, why was it not vouchsafed me to meet you, Marina Ivanovna Tsvetayeva?[†] After Boris Pasternak's letter I must believe that such a meeting would have resulted in the deepest innermost joy for both of us. Will we ever have a second chance to do this?!

RAINER MARIA RILKE

P.S. I am *just as* familiar with French as with German; I bring this to your notice in case you might be more conversant with that language, next to your own.

Enclosed with this letter was a note to Boris Pasternak. Tsvetayeva did not forward it immediately, but added a few phrases

---

*Including Yelena Voronina (Kazitsina), whom he had first met in Russia in 1899 (see p. 11 of the introduction).

[†]Tsvetayeva came to Paris in November 1925; Rilke had left the city in August of that year.

from Rilke's letter to her, those concerning the effect Pasternak's letter had produced on him. The idea of their meeting
and of the sacred joy it would bring them, mentioned by
Rilke at the end of his letter and seized upon by Tsvetayeva,
was to become the leitmotif of their relationship.

The copy of *Duino Elegies* (1923) that Rilke sent Tsvetayeva
at the same time as this letter bore the inscription:

> For Marina Ivanovna Tsvetayeva
> We touch each other. How? With wings that beat,
> With very distance touch each other's ken.
> *One* poet only lives, and now and then
> Who bore him, and who bears him now, will meet.
>
> Rainer Maria Rilke
> (Val-Mont Glion,
> Canton Vaud,
> Switzerland,
> May 1926)

He also sent his *Sonnets to Orpheus* (1923), inscribed

> To the poet Marina Ivanovna Tsvetayeva
> Rainer Maria Rilke
> May 3, 1926

TSVETAYEVA TO RILKE

St.-Gilles-sur-Vie
May 9, 1926

Rainer Maria Rilke!

May I hail you like this? You, poetry incarnate, must know,
after all, that your very name—is a poem. Rainer Maria, that

105

sounds churchly—and kindly—and chivalrous. Your name does not rhyme with our time—stems from earlier or later—has always been. Your name willed it so, and you chose the name. (Our names we choose ourselves, what comes after—follows).*

Your baptism was the prologue to the whole you, and the priest who baptized you truly knew not what he did.

You are not my dearest poet ("dearest"—a level), you are a phenomenon of nature, which cannot be mine and which one does not so much love as undergo, or (still too little) the fifth element incarnate: poetry itself or (still too little) that whence poetry comes to be and which is greater than it (you).

It isn't a question of Rilke the person (personhood: that which is forced upon us!), but of Rilke the spirit, who is still greater than the poet and who is what really bears the name of Rilke to me—the Rilke of the day after tomorrow.

You must look at yourself with, or out of, my eyes: your greatness through their bigness when I look at you: your greatness—across all that distance.

What is still left for a poet to do after you? A master (like Goethe, e.g.) one overcomes, but to overcome you—means (would mean) to overcome poetry itself. A poet is he who overcomes life (is to overcome it).

You are an impossible task for future poets. The poet who comes after you must be *you*, i.e., you must be born again.

You give to words their *first* sense, and to things their *first* words. E.g., when you say "magnificent" you say *"wreaking great things,"* as it was meant to mean originally (now "magnificent" is no more than a hollow exclamation mark of sorts).

---

*Tsvetayeva's syntax and punctuation (which consist chiefly of a not wholly artless anarchism, nautiluslike convolutions, parenthetic emendations, and showers of dots, dashes, and quotation marks) have been preserved in the translation as far as seemed advisable, and a little beyond.

I might have said all this to you more clearly in Russian, but I don't want to give you the trouble of reading your way into it, I would rather take the trouble of writing my way into it.

The first thing in your letter that hurled me up the tallest tower of joy (not lifted, not placed) was the word *May*,* the old nobility of which you restored with that *y* spelling. *Mai* with an *i*—that brings to mind the first of May, not the workers' holiday, which is going to be (may become) beautiful one day—no, the tame May of the bourgeoisie—of engaged and (not overly) enamored couples.

A few short biographical notes (only necessary ones): from the Russian Revolution (not revolutionary Russia; the revolution is a country with its own—and eternal—laws!) I went—by way of Berlin—to Prague, and your books went with me. In Prague I read for the first time the *Early Poems*. Thus did Prague become dear to me—on the first day—because of your having been a student there.

I remained in Prague from 1922 to 1925, three years; in November 1925, I went to Paris. Were you still there?

In case you were there:

Why didn't I come to you? Because you are the dearest thing to me in the whole world. Quite simply. And—because you don't know me. From injured pride, out of reverence for chance (fate, the same thing). From—cowardice, perhaps, that I'd have to endure your alien glance—on the threshold of your room. (What could your glance at me have been if not alien! It would have been a glance meant for anybody, after all, since you didn't know me!—and thus alien after all!)

One more thing: I will always be a Russian woman in your perception; you in mine—a purely human (divine) phenom-

---

*Spelled *Mai* in modern German.

enon. This is the difficulty about our too-individualistic nationality: all which in us is *I* is called "Russian" by the
Europeans.

(Same case as, with us, the Chinese, Japanese, Negroes—
very *far away* or very *savage*.)

Rainer Maria, nothing is lost; next year (1927) Boris is coming and we are going to visit you—wherever you may be. I
know Boris very little and love him as one only loves the
never-seen (already past or still to come: to come *after*), the
never-seen or never-been. He is not all that young—thirty-
three, I think*—but he is boyish. He doesn't resemble his
father by even the least little eyelash (the best a son can do:
I only believe in mother's boys; you, too, are a mother's boy,
a man taking after the female line—and therefore so *rich*
(duality)).

The premier poet of Russia, that's what he is. I know it
—and so do a few others; the rest are waiting for him to be
dead.

I am waiting for your books as for a thunderstorm that will
come whether I want it or not. Almost like a heart operation
(no metaphor! every poem (of yours) cuts into the heart and
carves it according to *its* knowledge—whether I want it to or
not). No wanting!

Do you know why I say *Du* to you and love you and—
and—and—because you are a *force*. The rarest thing.

You don't have to answer me; I know what time is and
what a poem is. I also know what a *letter* is. So there.

I was in Vaud, as a ten-year-old girl (1903), at Lausanne, and
still remember a lot from that time. In the boarding school
there was a grown-up Negro girl who was to learn French.
She didn't learn anything, and she ate violets. That is my
most vivid memory. Those blue lips—Negroes' lips are *not*

---

*He was actually thirty-six.

red—and the blue violets. The blue of Lake Geneva came only third.

What do I want from you, Rainer? Nothing. Everything. That you should allow me to spend every moment of my life looking up at you—as at a mountain that protects me (one of those guardian angels of stone!). Before I knew you, it was all right; now that I know you, permission is needed.

For my *soul* is well-bred.

I am going to write to you, though—whether you want it or not. About *your* Russian (the *Czars* cycle* and others). About a lot of things.

Those Russian characters of yours. *How touching it is!* I, who never cry, like a Red Indian (or Indian?), I was almost ready to—

I read your letter at the ocean; the ocean was reading along with me. We were both reading. I wonder if such a fellow reader troubles you. There won't be any others: I'm much too jealous (zealous—where you are concerned).

Here are my books—you don't have to read them—put them on your desk and take my word that they were not there before me (by this I mean in the world, not on the desk!).

MAY 10, 1926

Do you know how I got your books today (on the tenth)? The children were still asleep (seven in the morning), I suddenly got up and ran to the door. At the *same* moment—I had my hand on the door handle—the postman knocked—right into my hand.

I merely had to end my door-opening movement and from the same still-rapping hand receive the books.

---

*A cycle of poems in Rilke's *Book of Images*.

I haven't opened them yet, for if I did this letter wouldn't go off today—and it has to fly.

When my daughter (Ariadna) was quite small—two, perhaps three years old—she used to ask me often before going to bed, *"A ty budesh chitat Reineke?"* *

Reinecke—this is how Rainer Maria Rilke sounded to her quick, childish hearing. Children have no feeling for pauses.

I want to write to you about the Vendée, my heroic French homeland.† (In every country and century at least one—don't you think so?) I am here only because of the name. If one has neither money nor time, like myself, one chooses the most necessary thing: the indispensable.

Switzerland won't let any Russians in. But the mountains will have to move (or split!) so that Boris and I can come to you!

I believe in mountains.‡ (This line, in my altered version—which after all is not an altered one—for mountains and nights rhyme—you recognize it, don't you?)

MARINA TSVETAYEVA

Your letter to Boris is going off today—registered and commended to all the gods. Russia is to me still a kind of Beyond.

———

According to the postmark, the letter was sent on May 8. By dating it the 10th, the day Tsvetayeva assumed Rilke would receive it, she must have been trying to cancel out the time and space that separated them.

---

*Are you going to read Reinecke?

†In her youth, Tsvetayeva was enamored of royalist France.

‡An allusion to "I believe in nights," the concluding line of one of the poems in Rilke's *Book of Hours*.

The books she refers to in her letter were sent later. In *Poems to Alexander Blok* (1922), the inscription was:

> I don't care about the appearance of the book; that doesn't affect me at all! Be content with what's inside.
>
> For Rainer Maria Rilke
> —Marina Tsvetayeva
> (Have you noticed that my name is shorter than yours?)
> St.-Gilles-sur-Vie (Vendée)
> May 12, 1926
> I begin with the easiest books—with my youth.

In *Psyche: A Romance* (1923) she wrote:

> For Rainer Maria Rilke, my dearest on earth and after earth (*above* earth!)
> —Marina Tsvetayeva
> St.-Gilles-sur-Vie (Vendée)
> May 12, 1926

To make it easier for Rilke to understand her poetry, Tsvetayeva added marginal notes in German.

———

RILKE TO TSVETAYEVA

> VAL-MONT PAR GLION
> S/TERRITET (VAUD)
> SUISSE
> MAY 10, 1926

Marina Tsvetayeva,

Were you not here just now after all? Or *where was I?* It is still the tenth of May—and, strange thing, Marina,

Marina,* that was the date you wrote above the concluding
lines of your letter (cast forward into time, forward into the
timeless moment when I was to read you)! On the tenth you
thought you were receiving my books at the turning of a door
(as one turns pages in a book) . . . ; on the same tenth, today,
in the eternal today of the spirit, today, Marina, I received
you in my soul, in my whole consciousness, which trembles
before you, before your coming, as though your great fellow
reader, the ocean, had come breaking over me with you,
heart's flood. *What* to tell you? You have held your hands,
Marina, by turns extended and folded, in my heart as in the
basin of a flowing well: now, as long as you hold them there,
the displaced current goes over to you . . . let it be. *What* to
say: all my words (as though they had been in your letter, as if
facing a staged scene), all my words want to go out to you at
the same time; none of them lets another pass. When people
crowd one another as they leave the theater, isn't it because,
after having so much presence offered to them, they cannot
bear the curtain? Thus I find it hard to bear the closed-
up-again quality of your letter (once more, yet one more
time!). But look, even the curtain is comforting: next to your
beautiful name, next to this enchanting St.-Gilles = sur-vie
(survie!), somebody has written a large flattersome blue
"seven" (like this: 7!), the seven, my number of blessing. The
atlas was opened (for geography is not a science to me but a
relationship that is immediately put to use) and, *presto*, you
have been entered there, Marina,† on my internal map: between Moscow and Toledo somewhere I have made room for
the onthrust of your ocean. In reality, though, you see the
Île d'Yeu with the Pointe de Corbeau facing you. . . . And
Ariadne (how big might she be now, how high up does she
reach on you?) looks out with you, and . . . "children," you

---

*The second "Marina" is written in Cyrillic script.

†Name written in Cyrillic script.

say, "the children," in the plural? And yet in 1903, while I was already trying to come to terms with Rodin, you were still a little girl yourself, whom I'm shortly going to Lausanne to look for. (Oh, it will be easier to meet the Negro girl if one lures her with violets: this is how I saw her, painted by René Auberjonois*. . . how should I see *you*?)

You, poet, do you sense how you have overwhelmed me, you and your magnificent fellow reader; I'm writing like you and I descend like you the few steps down from the sentence into the mezzanine of parentheses, where the ceilings are so low and where it smells of roses past that never cease. Marina: *how* I have inhabited your letter. And what an astonishing thing when the die of your word, with the score already called, fell by a further step, showing the complementary number, the final (often still larger) one. A force of Nature, you dear one, that which stands behind the fifth element, inciting and gathering it? . . . And I for my part felt again as though through you Nature had assented to me, an entire garden of affirmation around a well. Around what else? Around a sundial. How you overgrow and overwaft me with your word-summer's tall phlox.

But, you say, it is not a matter of Rilke the person. I, too, am at odds with him, with his body, with which such pure communication had always been possible that I often did not know which produced poems more happily: it, I, the two of us? (Soles of the feet, blithe as often they were, blissful with walking across everything, across earth, blissful with primal knowing, pre-knowing, complicity of awareness beyond knowing itself!) And now dis-cord, doubly cored, soul clad one way, body mummed another, different. In this sanatorium ever since December, but not quite allowing the doctor in, into the only relationship between self and self that can stand no mediator (no go-between, who would make distances irrevocable; no

---

*Swiss painter (1872–1957) who lived in Paris from 1897 to 1914.

translator, who would break it apart into two languages).
(Patience, long snapped, tied up again . . .). My residence,
Muzot (which saved me after the snarled tangle and cave-in of
the war), four hours from here: my (if I may answer you literally) "my heroic French homeland." Look at it. Almost Spain,
Provence, Rhône Valley. *Austère et mélodieux*; knoll in wonderful harmony with the old turretry, which still belongs to it
just as much as it does to the one who inures the stones
to fate, who exercises them. . . .

RAINER MARIA

TSVETAYEVA TO RILKE

St.-Gilles-sur-Vie
May 12, 1926

The Beyond (not the religious one, more nearly the geographic
one) you know better than the Here, this side; you know
it topographically, with all its mountains and islands and
castles.

A topography of the soul—that's what you are. And with
your *Book* (oh, it was not a book after all, it was becoming a
book!) *of Poverty, Pilgrimage, and Death** you have done more
for God than all the philosophers and priests taken together.

Priests are nothing but intruders between me and God
(gods). You, you are the friend who *deepens* and enhances the
joy (is it joy?) of a great hour between Two (the eternal pair!),
without whom one ceases to feel the other, and whom, as one
is finally forced to do, *one loves exclusively.*

God. You alone have said something new to God. You are
the explicit John-Jesus relationship (unspoken by either). Yet
—difference—you are the Father's favorite, not the Son's, you

---

*Rilke's *Book of Hours* was divided into *The Book of the Monastic Life* (1899), *On
Pilgrimage* (1901), and *Of Poverty and Death* (1903).

are God the Father's (who didn't have one!) John. You chose (electing—choice!) the Father because He was *lonelier* and—impossible to love!

No David, no. David had all the shyness of his strength, you have all your strength's daring and risk.

The world was much too young. *Everything* had to come to pass—for you to come.

You dared *so* to love (to proclaim!) the unhuman (thoroughly divine) God the Father as John never dared to love the thoroughly human son! John loved the son with his arms (constantly hiding from his love at Jesus's breast), with his eyes, with his deeds. Word—heroics* of love, who always wants to be mute (in pure activity).

I wonder if you understand me, given my bad German? French I write more fluently; that's why I don't want to write to you in French. From me to you nothing should flow. Fly, yes! And failing that, better to halt and stumble.

Do you know how I fare with your poems? At the first blink of the eye. ("Flash of the eye" would be, and would sound, better; if I were German, I would have altered it: lightning, after all, is even quicker than a blink! And the flash of an eye is surely even swifter than ordinary lightning. Two velocities in one. Not so?) As I was saying, at the first blink of an eye (for I am a stranger), I know everything—then—night: nothing—then: God, how lucid!—luminous? And as I am trying to seize it (not allegorically,† almost with my hand), it is hazed: nothing but the printed lines. Lightning on lightning (lightning—night—lightning), that's how it takes me as I read you. It must be the same with you as you write yourself.

"Rilke is easy to grasp"—thus say, in the pride of the consecrated, the anthroposophists and other sectarian mystics

---

Heroica here may refer to Beethoven's Third Symphony (Eroica) or to needless "heroics," which misread the "needs" of love.

†Presumably she means "metaphorically."

(not that I have anything against them—better than socialism
—but still!...). "Easy to grasp." All chopped up, in pieces:
Rilke—the romantic; Rilke—the mystic; Rilke—the Grecian
of the myths; etc., etc.

Come, pit your strength against the *whole* Rilke instead.
Here all your clairvoyance is good for nothing. A miracle
needs no clairvoyance. It is *there*. Confirmed, seen by any
peasant with his own eyes. Miracle: inviolable: ungraspable.

For two nights I have been reading in your *Orpheus* (your
Orpheus is a country, therefore "in"). And just now I received
from Paris a purely literary Russian journal* (our only one
abroad) with the following lines in it:

"From this ('A Poet on Criticism'—notes, prose) we gather
that Mrs. Ts. is still disconsolate about the death of Orpheus,
and more ludicrous stuff of this sort...."

A critic† said about Blok, "The four years that separate us
from his death have reconciled us with it; more: almost con-
soled us about it."

I parried: "If four years are enough to console one over the
death of a poet like Blok, where does that leave Pushkin (d.
1836)? Where does it leave Orpheus (d. ?)? Every poet's death,
be it as natural as possible, is against Nature, is murder; hence
is unceasing, uninterrupted, eternally—within the moment
—enduring. Pushkin, Blok, or to name all of them, *Orpheus*,
can never have died, because he is right now (eternally!) dying. *V kazhdom lyubyashchem—zanovo, i v kazhdom lyubyashchem—vechno.*‡ Therefore—no consolation until we have
'died' ourselves." (More or less; it was better in Russian.)

This kind of thing of course doesn't belong in "literature"
(belles lettres); that's why they laughed at me. Had it been a

---

*The May 6 issue of *Vozrozhdeniye* contained a vicious attack by Peter Struve on
Tsvetayeva's "A Poet on Criticism."

†Georgi Adamovich.

‡In every lover—anew; in every lover—forever.

poem (a poet [a fool] who dares to write in prose)—were it a poem, they would have been silent or might even have sighed. (The old fable of Orpheus and the beasts, among which there were also—sheep?)

You understand that I am inviolable because I am not Mrs. Ts., etc., etc., as they of course think. I *am* sad, to be sure: the ever-true and ever-recurring story, which one would so gladly be rid of, of the poet and the mob!*

Your *Orpheus*. The first line:

A tree sprang up. O sheer transcendence!

There it is, you see, the grand manner (grand of kind). And *how well I know this*! The tree is higher than itself, the tree overclimbs itself—hence so tall. One of those whom God happily leaves unprovided for (they look after themselves!) and which grow straight into heaven, into the seventieth (we Russians have *seven*!). *Byt na sedmom nebe ot radosti.*† *Videt sedmoi son.*‡ The week—in Old Russian, *sedmitsa.*§ *Semero odnogo ne zhdut.*‖ "Sem Simeonov"# (a fairy tale). 7—a Russian number! Oh, there are lots more: *Sem bed odin otvet***; any number).

Song is existence†† (to be there; anyone not singing is not yet there, is still coming!).

"Heavy are the mountains, heavy are the seas…"†† as

---

*An allusion to a famous Pushkin poem.

†To be in seventh heaven with joy.

‡To have the seventh dream.

§Literally, a unit of seven.

‖Seven won't wait for one.

#"Seven Simons."

**Seven plagues, one remedy.

††Quotes from Rilke's *Sonnets to Orpheus* (1923).

though you were comforting a child, urging him to take heart . . . and—almost smiling about his unreason:

> . . . But the winds . . . but the spaces . . .*

This line is *pure intonation* (intention), therefore pure, pure angel speech. (Intonation: an intention which has become sound. Intention incarnate.)

> . . . We must not strain ourselves
> For other names. Once and for all
> It's Orpheus if it sings.*

If it dies, among poets; that's what I meant overleaf.

Is he from here?* And already one feels the coming (approaching) No. Oh, Rainer, I don't want to choose (choosing is rooting, polluting!), I cannot choose, I take the first random lines my ear still holds. Into my ears you write to me, by the ear you are read.

This pride out of earth* (the horse, grown out of this soil). Rainer! A book will follow *Craft*, there you will find a Saint George who is almost steed and a steed that is almost rider, I don't separate them and I name neither one. Your horseman! For a horseman is not the one who rides, horseman is the two together, a new figure, something that used not to be there, not knight and steed: rider-horse and horse-rider: horseman.

Your penciled notation (is this right? no, annotation, I suppose!)—those dear, airy three words: to a dog.† Dear one, this takes me right back to the middle of my childhood, age eleven; that is to say, into the Black Forest (into the very middle of

---

*Quotes from Rilke's *Sonnets to Orpheus* (1923).

†In the copy of *Sonnets to Orpheus* that Rilke sent Tsvetayeva, he wrote in the margin of Part I, Sonnet 16, "To a Dog."

it!). And the headmistress (Fräulein Brinck was her name, and she was gruesome) is saying, "This little Satan's brat, Marina, makes one forgive anything; all she has to do is say 'a dog'!"

("A dog"—yowling with ecstasy and emotion and wanting —a *Hund* with three *u-u-u*'s. They weren't pedigreed dogs, just street mongrels!)

Rainer, the purest happiness, a gift of happiness, pressing your forehead on the dog's forehead, eye to eye, and the dog, astonished, taken aback, and flattered (this doesn't happen every day!), growls. And then one holds his muzzle shut with both hands (since he might bite from sheer emotion) and kisses, just smothers him.

Where you are, do you have a dog? And where are you? Val-Mont (Valmont), that was the hero's name in that hard and cold and clever book, Laclos's *Liaisons dangereuses*, which—I can't think why, it's the most moral of books!—was on our index in Russia, along with the memoirs of Casanova (whom I love with a passion!). I have written to Prague to have them [send] me my two dramatic poems (I don't think you can call them dramas), "Adventure" (Henrietta, do you remember? his loveliest, which wasn't an adventure at all, the only one that was no adventure) and "Phoenix"—Casanova's end. Dux,* seventy-five years old, alone, poor, out of style, laughed at. His last love. Seventy-five years—thirteen years. You have to read that; it is easy to understand (the language, I mean). And—don't be amazed—it was my Germanic soul that wrote it, not my French one.

We touch each other. How? With wings that beat . . .

Rainer, Rainer, you told me that without knowing me, like a blind man (a seeing one!), at random. (The best shooters are the blind!)

---

*Dux, properly Duchov, is the "Château Dux," southwest of Teplice in Bohemia, where Casanova wrote his famous *Mémoires*.

Tomorrow is the Feast of the Ascension (*Vozneseniye*). How lovely! The sky in these words looks just like my ocean—with waves. And Christ—is riding.

Your letter has just arrived. Time for mine to go.

MARINA

TSVETAYEVA TO RILKE

ST.-GILLES-SUR-VIE
ASCENSION DAY 1926

... to him
You cannot boast of matters grandly sensed. ...*

Therefore, in a purely human and very modest way, Rilke the man. As I wrote this, I hesitated. I love the poet, not the person. (As you read this, you came to a stop.) This sounds like aestheticism, i.e., soulless, inanimate (aesthetes are those who have no soul, just five acute senses, often fewer). May I even choose? As soon as I love, I cannot and will not choose (that stale and narrow privilege!), you already are an absolute. And until I love (*know*), you, I may not choose because I have no relation to you (don't know your stock, after all!).

No, Rainer, I am not a collector, and Rilke the man, who is even greater than the poet (turn it whatever way you like, it comes to the same: greater still!)—because he carries the poet (knight and steed: horseman!)—I love inseparably from the poet.

By Rilke the man, I meant the one who lives, gets things published, whom one likes, who already belongs to so many, who must be tired by now of so much love. All I meant was the many, many human contacts! By Rilke the man I meant

---

*From the Ninth Duino Elegy.

the place where there is no room for me. Thus the entire set of poet and man—renunciation, abnegation, lest you might think that I am intruding into your life, on your time, into your day (working day and social day), which has been planned and allotted once and for all. A renunciation—lest it hurt afterward: the first name, the first date* that one collides with by which one is rejected (*Vorsicht—Verzicht!*).[†]

Dear one, I am very obedient. If you tell me: Do not write, it excites me, I need myself badly for myself—

I shall understand, and withstand, everything.

I am writing to you on the dune in the thin dune grass. My son (fifteen months old, George—in honor of our White Army. Now, Boris thinks he is a socialist! Do *you* believe that?)—well, then, my son, who is sitting astride me (almost on my head!), takes my pencil away (I happen to be writing in the notebook). He is so lovely that all the old women (*those costumes!* If you could be here!) have only one exclamation: "*Mais c'est un petit roi de Rome!*"[‡] A Bonapartist Vendée—peculiar? The king they have already forgotten, the word *emperor* is still resonant. Our landlords (fisherman and his wife, a fairy-tale couple totaling one hundred and fifty years of age!) still know a good deal of the last empire.

Children in the plural? Darling, I had to smile. *Children*—that word stretches (two or seven?). Two, darling, a twelve-year-old girl and a one-year-old boy. Two little giants from the children's Valhalla. Prize exhibits if ever you saw any. How tall is Ariadne?[§] Oh, almost taller than I (I'm not small) and twice as

---

*Or "datum."

[†]Caution—renunciation.

[‡]Why, he is a little King of Rome (Napoleon I's young son).

[§]Tsvetayeva uses the word "high" here. From this point on in the correspondence, she refers to her son as Mur or Mursik and to her daughter as Alya. Ariadna (Ariadne), the daughter, was actually fourteen years old at the time; similarly, Tsvetayeva takes two years off her age and that of her husband in the letter.

hefty (I weigh *nothing*). Here is my picture—passport picture —I am younger and brighter. A better one will follow, taken quite recently, in Paris. By the photographer Shumov, the one who photographed your great friend's works.* He has told me a lot about them. I was embarrassed to ask if he didn't have a picture of you. I would never have ordered it. (That I am asking you for your picture—straight out and quite without compunction!—please, that much you understand by now.)

... the fear and blue of childhood ...†

I still remember that. Who are you? Teuton? Austrian? (That used to be one and the same, didn't it? I am not very cultured—bits and pieces.) Your place of birth? How did you get to Prague? How to the Russian czars? There is a miracle here, after all: you—Russia—I.

All these questions!

Your earthly fate concerns me even more intimately than your other paths, for I know how difficult it is—all of it.

Have you been ill long? How do you live in Muzot? That magnificence. Large and somber and tall. Do you have a family? Children? (I don't think so.) Are you going to stay long in the sanatorium? Do you have friends there?

Boulevard de Grancy, 3 (and not far from Ouchy, I think), that's where you can find me. I have short hair (like now, I've never in my life worn it long), and I look like a boy, with a rosary around his neck.

Tonight I did some reading in your *Duino Elegies*. In the daytime I never get to reading or writing. The day's work goes on

---

*The works of Rodin, whose friendship Rilke valued enormously, and about whom Rilke wrote a book illustrated with photographs by Pyotr Shumov.

†From "Self-Portrait, 1906," in Rilke's *New Poems*.

deep into the night, for I have only my two hands. My husband—a volunteer soldier all his young life, barely thirty-one years old (I am turning thirty-one in September)—is very sickly, and a man, after all, cannot do woman's work, it looks ugly (for the wife, that is). At this moment he's still in Paris, but is coming here soon. He was in the *yunkerskoye uchilishche*,* they used to call him jokingly *astralny yunker*.† He is handsome: the handsomeness of suffering. My daughter looks like him, although more on the happy side, our son is more like me, but both are bright, bright-eyed, *moya raskraska*.‡

What to tell you about the book? The ultimate stair. My bed turned to a cloud.

Darling, I know *everything* already—from me to you—but it is still too early for a lot of things. Something in you must still get used to me.

MARINA

RILKE TO TSVETAYEVA

VAL-MONT PAR GLION
S/TERRITET (VAUD)
SUISSE
17 MAY 1926

"Marina! Spasibo za mir..."§

That your daughter should have been able to say this to you, Marina, and in the face of hard times! (Who in the days

---

*Service academy.

†The astral cadet.

‡My coloring.

§"Marina! Thank you for the world..." is the first line of a poem written by Tsvetayeva in 1918, included in the "Poems to My Daughter" chapter of *Psyche: A Romance* (1923), a book Tsvetayeva had sent Rilke.

of my childhood, what child—in Austria at least, in Bohemia —would have found the inner urge of assent to speak like this? . . . My daughter perhaps might have wanted to say this to me if the word and its mode of address had been more urgent in her; but almost the only time I really was with her was before any verbalness at all, from her birth to sometime after her first birthday: for as early as that, what had arisen, a little against my will, in terms of house, family, and settling down, was dissolving; the marriage, too, although never terminated legally, returned me to my natural singleness (after barely two years) and Paris began: this was 1902. Now my daughter has long since married and settled somewhere on an estate in Saxony, which I'm not familiar with; and my granddaughter, Christine, whom I also only guess at, from a lot of small snapshots, passed her second year in November and is growing well into her third. . . . But all of this is on a different plane from the one on which Muzot stands, which ever since 1921 (when the most wondrous circumstances, no, outright miracle itself, allowed me to find it and hold on to it) I have inhabited alone (not counting visits from friends from time to time—which are rare, though), as much alone as I've always lived, more so if anything: in an often uncanny intensification of what being alone means, in a solitude rushed to an ultimate and uttermost state (for formerly, being alone in Paris, and Rome, in Venice—where I have spent much time without being alone—in Spain, in Tunis, in Algiers, in Egypt . . . in that searching emphatic place, Provence . . . , there was still participation, being part of a web of relationships and tutelage). Muzot, on the other hand, more challenging than anything else, allowed nothing but achievement, the vertical leap out into open space, the whole earth's ascension to heaven within me. . . . Dear one, why do I have to tell you, since you have the *Elegies* in your hands, since you have the *Elegies* in *your* hand and over your heart, which beats against them in shared witness. . . .

These poems had been begun (1912) in no less grand a solitude, on the Adriatic, in the old (destroyed in the war) castle
of Duino (near Trieste); in Spain and later in Paris fragments
of lines turned up, and all of this would probably have con-
verged into achievement in 1914 in Paris if that great interruption of the world had not cut in, making me go rigid and
static. For years. Whatever I might have saved out of that
long winter of my being, I myself did not know when I was
finally (1919) able to take refuge in Switzerland, as on a soil
where something natural and guileless still had full authority; I did not find it out until 1921, at Muzot, in the first
lonely year I was in residence there, when the nature of
my temperament, which circumstances had repressed, drove,
within a few weeks, the unheard-of growth, first of *Orpheus*
(each part in three days!), then of the *Elegies* into its season of
completion, violently, almost destroying me with the passion
of its outbreak, and yet acting so gently and with such a sense
of pattern that not one (think of it), not a single pre-existing
line failed to be fitted into the place in which it was a natural
stair and a voice among the voices. How that healed together,
the earlier with its already aging fracture surface so intimately fitted onto the glowing one, taking on such new glow
from proximity and infinite kinship that never a visible seam
remained! Triumph and jubilation, Marina, without equal!
And *this* is what the overabundance of solitude, in all its
deadliness, was needed for. But, then, was it that I tried to
maintain the impossible conditions of intensified isolation
over and beyond what had been achieved, mastered? (This I
did, not from stubbornness or to wrest a bonus from grace,
but because letting in the "other," living by him and for him,
instantly [or just after the instant] entails conflicts and tasks I
had to fear at a time when I had accomplished *everything*
much too extremely merely to change to a new kind of
achievement.) Or is it (since the work itself, our great breathtaking labor, does not take revenge, after all; even when it

forces us outside and beyond ourselves, it leaves us, not fatigued or exhausted, but staggering under the reward), is it that, mechanically, I endured too long the same special conditions of seclusion, in a heroic valleyscape, under the almost sun-raging sky of a wine country—at any rate, for the first time in my life and in a treacherous fashion, my own aloneness turned against me with a physical sting, rendering this being-with-myself suspect and dangerous, and more and more threatening because of the physical disturbances that now drowned out what to me had been forever and ever the most primeval silence. Hence my presence here in Val-Mont, for the third time now (after two shorter stays in 1924 and 1925), hence my long sojourn in Paris (January to mid-August 1925), where in all conscience the opposite, the adversary, of the life offered by Muzot seemed to gain entry in all its guises and permutations; hence my reluctance to withdraw once more into my solid tower with all the danger that had invaded me and was rankly growing inside me.... What do the doctors think? A trauma of the nerve which they call *grand sympathique,* that large, beautiful tree of nerves which, if it does not bear our fruits, at any rate (possibly) brings forth the most dazzling blossom of our being....

...Disturbances of a more subjective than really factually or organically discernible kind (so far, at any rate); inroads upon that absence of bodily self-awareness from which harmony with our material stake (in ourselves) so involuntarily results; slight disorders of my body which render me all the more at a loss since I had been used to living with it in so perfect a concord, without a physician, that I was close to thinking of it as a child of my soul. This began at a certain turning point in my life (about 1899 and 1900, which coincided with my residence in Russia). Light and handy as it was and easy to take along into the most abstract spheres, how often voided, endowed with weight only by courtesy and still visible merely so as not to alarm the invisible! So intimately *mine;* friend, truly my bearer, the holder of my heart; capable of all my joys, disparaging none, making each my own in a more particular way; bestowing them upon me at the precise intersection of my senses. As *my* creature, ready for me and risen in service to my use; as pre-creature, outweighing me with all the security and magnificence of descent. A thing of genius, reared by centuries, glorious in the serene inno- cence of its not-I, touching in its eagerness to be faithful to the "I" in all its transitions and oscillations. Simple of mind and wise. How much I have to thank it, which, by dint of its nature, reinforced my delight in a fruit, in the wind, in walk- ing on grass. To thank it, whereby I am akin to the impene- trable into which I cannot force entry, and to the fluid element that runs off me. And it was still conversant with the stars by virtue of its heaviness. To sum up: distressing, this dissension with it, and too fresh a distress to be ready for compromise yet. And the doctor *cannot* understand what it is that distresses me so profoundly, so centrally, about these handicaps, which after all are tolerable, although they have set up their branch offices all over the body while they were about it. . . .

All this about *me,* dear Marina, pardon me! And pardon also the opposite, if all of a sudden I should turn uncom- municative—which ought not to keep you from writing to *me.* As often as the spirit moves you to "fly." Your German— no, it doesn't "stumble," it just takes heavier steps now and then, like the steps of one who is going down a stone stair- case with stairs of unequal height and cannot estimate as he comes down when his foot is going to come to rest, right now or suddenly farther down than he thought. What strength is in you, poet, to achieve your intent even in this language, and be accurate and yourself. *Your* gait ringing on the steps, your tone, *you.* Your lightness, your controlled, bestowed weight.

But do you know that I overrated myself? Because I read

Goncharov* in Russian as recently as ten years ago almost without a dictionary and still have relatively little difficulty reading letters in Russian, and from time to time see one in *that* light in which all languages are a *single* language (and this one, yours, Russian, is so close to being *all* of them anyway!), I was led to overestimate myself...: your books, even though you guide me through the more alien passages, are difficult for me—it has been too long since I have read consistently, save for scattered things like (in Paris) some of Boris's verses in an anthology. If only I could read you, Marina, as you read me! Nonetheless, the two little books accompany me from table to bed and in many ways outdo the ones easily read.

What keeps me from sending you my passport picture is not vanity but actually awareness of its lightning-flash fortuity. But I have put it next to your picture: get used to this first in pictures, will you?

RAINER

I shall have to go to Muzot for a day shortly, and there I'll pick up for you a few small, fairly valid pictures from two years ago. I completely avoid sitting for photographs or pictures: Shumov† has made no picture of me.

Send me that other one of yours soon!

---

*Ivan Goncharov (1812–91): Russian novelist.

†Written in Cyrillic script.

4

AFTER HIS decision to postpone his journey for a year, Pasternak's mood of elation gave way to dejection. That dejection was deepened by his not hearing a word from Tsvetayeva about Rilke and his reaction to Pasternak's letter. Pasternak's father had warned him that he had taken a risk in asking Rilke to answer his letters through Tsvetayeva; there was no telling how the older poet would feel about it.

A letter from Tsvetayeva received at the beginning of May made the strange request that he offer assistance to the poet Sofia Parnok, who had been Tsvetayeva's close friend in 1914–15. The poem from the cycle "My Friend" that she enclosed in this letter affected Pasternak like a live wire.

> There are some names which are like blossom scent,
> And glances dancing like a flaring lamp . . .
> And lips in shadow, dark and subtly bent,
> With corners that are deeply carved and damp.
>
> Women there are whose hair is like a casque.
> Their fans' perfume is ruinous and fine.
> They're thirty. So what good to you, I ask,
> Can be the Spartan maiden's soul of mine?[1]

Meanwhile, Pasternak's financial straits were becoming particularly acute, because he wanted to send his wife and son to Germany, where his wife's health could be improved. Working almost twenty-four hours a day on *Lieutenant*

Schmidt, he found it impossible to send Tsvetayeva the letters he wrote to her, and regularly destroyed them.

On May 18 Pasternak received the long-awaited reply from Rilke, in a registered letter sent by Tsvetayeva. "Getting this letter was one of the most momentous events of my life; I could not have dreamed of anything so staggering," he was to write thirty years later.[2]

RILKE TO PASTERNAK

VAL-MONT PAR GLION (VAUD)

My dear Boris Pasternak,

In the very hour in which your direct letter to me wrapped me about like the beating of wings, your wish was fulfilled: the *Elegies* and the *Sonnets to Orpheus* are already in the poet's hands! These same books, that is, other copies of them, are shortly going to go to you. How am I to thank you for having let me see and feel what you have so miraculously accumulated in yourself. It is to the glory of your fruitful heart that you are able to hold out to me so rich a yield of your inner self. May every bliss be over your being! I embrace you.

Your
RAINER MARIA RILKE

Tsvetayeva included with Rilke's reply a second sheet, on which she had copied out a passage in German from Rilke's letter to her: "I am so shaken by the fullness and power of his message to me that I cannot say more today, but would you send the enclosed sheet to our friend in Moscow for me? As a greeting."

Pasternak saved these two sheets of light-blue notepaper all his life. After his death, in the summer of 1960, they were found in an envelope marked "Most Precious," which he carried in a leather wallet in his jacket pocket.

PASTERNAK TO TSVETAYEVA

MAY 19, 1926

Three unmailed ones have preceded this one. That's an illness with me. I must overcome it. Yesterday I received your copy of his words. Ah, but your absence, the physically felt silence of your hands. I never knew that a beloved handwriting could, with silence, play such funereal music. I do not remember ever in my life having suffered the despair that engulfed me yesterday. Everything looked black to me. Aseyev* has a bad case of tonsillitis—a temperature of 104° for three days. I am afraid, afraid, and dare not admit what I am afraid of. This goes for everything. In such a spirit I cannot, will not, do not wish to write to you. I place the highest value on time, that living water associated with you, which only increases my thirst for it. I treasure the years, I treasure my life; I am afraid of panicking, afraid of squandering this unearthly treasure.

For the same reason I have not answered your letter about Parnok. I can do nothing for her, because she and I have never had anything in common; moreover, your letter arrived when we had just had another squabble: largely on her account I had left the editorial office of Uzel† the night before.

---

*Nikolai Aseyev (1889–1963): well-known Soviet poet, friend of Mayakovsky and Pasternak.

†The cooperative publishing house that brought out Pasternak's *Selected Poems* in 1926.

One would have to be a glutton for punishment, a veritable Saint Sebastian, to write about oneself as you did about yourself at the age of twenty. I am afraid even to glance at that Leyden jar of a letter charged with pain, jealousy, shrieks, and suffering, even though out of the corner of my eye I get a peep into the last century. I was innocently punished. I got the letter as I was leaving home for the *Izvestiya* office, where I hadn't been for four years. I was taking a poem, written in too great haste, about the general strike in England. I was sure they wouldn't accept it. I read your letter on the trolley car. A Leyden jar indeed, complete with anode and cathode and terrible force and deep dark mystery. Why should you have written it? Why, oh, why, my beloved little Spartan? Thus, upset by you and for you (although I had plenty of other things to upset me), I rushed into the editorial office. They didn't know what to make of me. The only sensible thing they said was that a poet in an editorial office is like a bull in a china shop. I talked too much there that day; perhaps my general sense of fear can be traced to then. Among other things, I said that having once begun to play at being beggars they had all become beggars—and monstrous beggars, the kind that would be exhibited in the zoo if nature . . . and so on and so forth.

Practical considerations force me to accept all that I have written about Schmidt in Part I, to have faith in the writing of Part II, and to hand in what is written. I will not stop working on it, though. I will bring it off. I had hoped to write a dedication to you when the work was finished, and to write it well. But it has to appear at the beginning. So yesterday, before handing it in, I wrote the best I could.

DEDICATION

A flash of arms and legs, and after it:
"At it, across the gloom of ages! Rouse

The horns more shrilly! Ho! Or else I quit
The chase and plunge into a dream of boughs."

The horn, though, breaks the lovely luscious pattern
Of years as real as foliage and as sound.
Calm reigns, and every tree trunk is a Saturn:
The growing turns again, the trail is round.

He'd float on verse to time's obscure relief.
In hollows and on lips such treasures dwell.
Instead, keep crying havoc, dell to dell,
And groans as genuine as the forest leaf.

Age, why have you no liking for the chase?
Reply in foliage, tree trunks, sleeping boughs,
In wind and grass reply to me and her.[3]

This, then, is the theme ("the fugitive spirit"): as expressed in the hero, the fatalism of history, man's passage through nature, and—my soul's dedication to you. The main thing, as you will see, is the acrostic of your name,* with which I began: to the left, the column with the letters of your name; to the right, the white margin and the fleeting traces of feeling. I wrote it in a strange mood, similar to what I felt— only worse, much worse—when writing the poem about England for the newspaper. But since this other one ends with the same tight, pulling-together, bucklelike words as the dedication, here it is:

Event on the Thames, which is stuffed with bran
Run by a drainpipe from pretension's van!

---

* Not reproduced here in translation; in Russian the first letters of each line, read top to bottom, spell *Marine Tsvetayevoi* (For Marina Tsvetayeva).

O future! Spirit thrusting at the throttle's arm!
Be stirred yourself, stir others not, be calm!

O roaring blast, O irresistible drag,
You crumple up a torn-off newsprint rag,
Inhale it, sweep it off and then release
Onto the street, left to our times' caprice.

Today is Sunday, and the cliché mill is dumb;
I've not a soul to swipe an anthem from.
Koltsov from questionnaires would make you a
    shoulder lock.
But Sundays there's no trading at Ogonyok.

And so, insurgent surf, I'm not to blame in any way
That were are face to face, alone, today.

Glimmer of asphalt, rattle of horseshoes, rush of
    clouds.
In the sweep of poles and horse is the age's sweep and
    course,
All rushes gaping like the whale, and somewhere
    gleams the goal,
And days join days to make the footway whole.

The patter of impatient hands runs up the frame.
Days laminate an age, cast lots who's to start the game—
This is your image, face of time, you're no live brook,
You are a shaft of hoops thrown up by hand.

Event on the Thames, you are a monogram in the crust
Of love-struck mountains, a gash from a glacier's thrust.
You, history, raise a mark, and as the days recur,
I'll meet the day on which I meet with her.

Although I am calmer today and remember why I am staying here for a year, and, accordingly, *for what purpose* I am staying, nevertheless I cannot touch on the subject of Rilke until I receive a letter from you.* His is the letter I longed for but in no way deserved. He answered immediately. When I begged you—remember?—for third-hand and effective support for my decision, I personally chose as a clue precisely this letter, or rather, the timing of its arrival. I had not counted on my letter's having, not two, but more than four destinations (it was delivered by hand to my relatives in Germany, from where it was sent to him, perhaps not directly); his answer went to the Rue Rouvet, then to the ocean, and only then from you to me. I had decided that if his reply were enclosed in the letter with your decision, I would listen *only* to my impatience and not to you or my "other" voice. And no doubt it is well that his letter and your decision parted company. But that you parted company a second time, that you were not with him when he came to me, sending only your handwriting—this shattered and frightened me. Quickly send me reassurances to calm me, Marina, my only hope. Pay no attention to the bad verse in my letters. Wait until you see *Schmidt* as a whole. If you find the dedication poor, hurry and stop its publication.

I have not yet fulfilled your request concerning Nad. Al.† You must forgive me. This, too, is a matter of self-preservation. I am afraid of having too much of you in my affairs and in my days. I will do what you asked, but later.

---

*Nor can I even think about him, let alone write to him. [B. P.]

†Nadezhda Alexandrovna Kogan, wife of the noted critic Pyotr Kogan (1872–1932) and a close friend of Tsvetayeva's in Russia. Tsvetayeva had given her some books for Pasternak, including Eckermann's *Conversations with Goethe*.

TSVETAYEVA TO PASTERNAK

MAY 22, 1926
SATURDAY

Boris!

My severance from life becomes more and more irrevocable. I keep moving, have moved again, taking with me all my
passion, all my treasure, not as a bloodless shade but with so
great a store of food that I could feed everyone in Hades. Ah,
wouldn't he give me a talking-to then, that Pluto.

The proof—my conscientiousness in performing my daily
duties, as roles are played: by memory. You don't know my
life in its personal aspect. And you never will know it from
my letters. I'm afraid to speak out, afraid to cast an evil spell,
afraid of intrusion, of ingratitude—I can't explain it. But evidently this blessed lack of freedom is so contrary to my nature that to preserve myself I keep moving into freedom
—complete freedom. (The ending of "The Swain."*)

Oh, yes—as for "The Swain," you were right (if you remember) and not Asya: "Owing to his unexampled goodness,
Borya read into the ending a proclamation of liberation and
rejoiced for you."

Boris, it's all the same to me where I go to escape. And

---

*In her essay "A Poet on Criticism," published in *Blagonamerenny* in 1926,
Tsvetayeva presented the idea behind her folk tale in verse, "The Swain": "When I
read [Alexander] Afanasyev's version of the folk legend 'The Vampire' I wondered
why Marusya, mortally afraid of the vampire, stubbornly refused to admit having
seen him, even though she knew that such an admission would save her. Why did she
say no instead of yes? Fear? But people don't merely bury their heads in the pillow
from fear, they also throw themselves out of the window. No, it wasn't fear. Or if it
was fear, there was something else besides. Fear and what? When I am told, 'Do this
and you will be free,' and I do not do it, it means I am not that anxious to be free, it
means being unfree is more important. What can make people prefer to be unfree?
What can make being unfree so precious? Love. Marusya loved the vampire and that
is why she did not admit to having seen him, and why, one after another, she lost her
mother, her brother, her own life. Fear and crime, fear and sacrifice."

that, perhaps, shows the depth of my immorality (lack of divinity). After all, I myself am Marusya: honest when necessary (tight-lipped when pressed), true to my word, defensive, evasive of happiness, only half alive (as far as others are concerned—less than half; but I know the truth), unaware of why I am like this, submissive to force brought to bear on me, and, even when choosing the path of the Cherubim, guided by a voice, by another's will, not my own.

I breathed a sigh of relief when the poem was done, happy for Marusya—for myself. What are they going to do in fire-blue?* Fly around in it forever? Nothing satanic. Cherubic? Well, that is what the simple folk wanted. (Read Afanasyev's fairy tale "The Vampire." It's all there.) And I must say they chose the right time for it.

Boris, I don't know what sacrilege is. All sins against grandeur of any kind (and there aren't many kinds) are one and the same. All others—a matter of degree. Love! Perhaps—degree of heat? Fire? Fire-red (with roses, the bedroom kind). Fire-blue. Fire-white (white for God). White in strength? In the purity of its burning? Purity. Which I invariably see as a black line. (Just a line.) That which burns without heat is God. And those vast trails of ashes—my ashes—floating in space—they are my "Swain."

Not for nothing did I give the poem to you. So far "Sidestreets" and "The Swain" are my favorites by me.

More about life. I hate things and the accumulation of them. Like a man who promises his wife that all will be put in order (and then she dies or something). She doesn't care about the *orderliness* of life based on reason; just the common mania for putting *things* in order. Suddenly, while speaking to a friend she hasn't seen for ten years, she interrupts with: "Oh, I've forgotten—are the towels hung up to

---

*This passage refers to the symbolism of "The Swain." At the end of the poem, the souls of Marusya and her lover ascend into fire-blue.

dry? The sun's shining. Must take advantage of it." And her eyes like glass eyes.

Like reciting a lesson, or the Lord's Prayer: you can't make a mistake because you don't understand a word you're saying. Not a syllable. (There are the most minute divisions of words. I believe it is with such words that "The Swain" is written.)

I could have written about myself what you wrote about yourself: love, love, love, on every hand. And it doesn't bring pleasure. I used to let anyone call me by my first name (without patronymic). Well, a name can become cheap. Now I don't forbid it. I just don't answer to it. (A name should be in the name of something.) Suddenly you have discovered America: me. That's not what I want. Be so kind as to discover America *for me*!

"What would you and I do if we were together?" (As if on a desert island. I'd know what to do on an island!) "We would go and see Rilke." I tell you Rilke is overburdened; he doesn't need anything or anyone. Strength, always attracting, distracts. Rilke is a recluse. In his old age the only person Goethe needed was Eckermann* (a recording ear and a strong will to support him through the second part of *Faust*). Rilke is beyond needing an Eckermann: he needs no link between God and the second part of *Faust*. He is older than Goethe and closer to the job at hand. He breathes upon me the bitter cold of the possessor, of whose possessions I am knowingly and by predestination a part. I have nothing to give him, all has been taken in advance. Yes, yes, despite the fervor of his letters, his unerring ear, and the purity of his listening—he does not need me, or you. He has grown out of having friends. For me this encounter is a great wound, a blow to my heart, yes, just that, the more so since he is right: in my best, high-

---

*Johann Peter Eckermann (1792–1844): Goethe's secretary, and author of *Conversations with Goethe*.

est, strongest, most self-sacrificing moments, I am as he is (not the coldness! the defensive divinity in him). And perhaps for *this* reason, seeking survival (the defensive divinity in me), for three years I walked beside him and, having no Goethe, was his Eckermann—even more—his Volkonsky!*
And this I never, in any circumstance, wanted to be.

> All life I meant to be like all the rest,
> The world, though, in its loveliness
> Refused to listen to my plea
> And wanted to be—like me.[4]

I give these lines without quotation marks. I remember hearing them read by Ehrenburg's wife in the spring of 1925. I like it better this way: you replaced "world" with "age" later, didn't you?

Ah yes: did Ehrenburg get back safely? And did he bring you my things? I am sending you another notebook for your verse.

Today is our first *pacific* ocean—not even a breeze. (Is it all right to send letters like this one?)

Not long ago I spent a beautiful day, all of it with you. I didn't let you go until late at night. Pay no attention to my "chilliness." There is always a sort of draft between you and me.

Send me *Schmidt*. His son visited me in Prague. The nickname "Ochakov" proved a calamity for the son. A charming boy, much like his father. I remember seeing him at the pier in Yalta in 1905.

Take care of yourself.

Love,
M.

---

*Sergei Volkonsky (1860–1937): Petersburg theatrical manager who wrote many volumes of memoirs. Tsvetayeva, a friend of his, copied the manuscript of one of his books, published an article about him, and dedicated a cycle of poems to him.

How well I understand your terror of words already mangled by use, already ambiguous. Your wary ear—how I love it, Boris!

———

Whereas it took no more than two days for letters to pass between Rilke and Tsvetayeva, so that the correspondents could read each other's letters before sending their responses, the conditions of the Tsvetayeva-Pasternak correspondence were entirely different. Letters from France to Moscow traveled five or six days, during which time the correspondents sent new letters developing themes touched upon in preceding ones without waiting for replies. For instance, Tsvetayeva's letter of May 22 was not in answer to Pasternak's of May 19, and in Pasternak's next letter, May 23, he was still under the impression that Tsvetayeva had sent him Rilke's letter without including any communication from herself—which meant, he felt, that she disapproved of his hopes for a lofty friendship among the three poets.

———

PASTERNAK TO TSVETAYEVA

MAY 23, 1926

I have a request to make of you: don't be disappointed in me too soon. This is not a senseless request, because, having tested myself by repeating the words "disappointed in me" over and over, I know that if I deserved them I myself would be capable of pronouncing them. Until such time, don't turn away from me, no matter what apparent cause there may be.

And another thing. I will not trouble you by bringing up incidents that have occurred in the past few months. Only let me believe that you and I breathe the same air and let me love this common air. Why do I ask this of you, and why do I try to persuade you? First—the reason: you yourself have filled me with alarm. It concerns Rilke. That is where the breeze is coming from. I have a vague feeling that you are gently pushing me away from him. And since I see the three of us as a unity, held in a single embrace, that means you are pushing me away from you, too, without openly acknowledging it.

I am ready to suffer this. What is ours remains ours. I called it happiness. Let it be misery. Never have I encouraged, or felt any desire to encourage, circumstances that could separate us. But the will of the poet transcends the demands of life. I personally have never been aware of exercising will power, only foresight, foretaste, and . . . accomplishment—or, rather, verification.

And suddenly, not long ago, with you, I had my *first* experience of will applied in the usual way, the way of strong-minded people.

In simplicity you revealed joy of a hitherto unknown degree. This degree has become my standard of measurement.*

I feel you are indignant, as if I had suddenly dropped into the *Plusquamperfekt*.† Nothing has changed.

It makes no difference—ours is the same aloneness, the same searchings and solutions, the same love for the labyrinths of literature and history, and the same role to be played out. Svyatopolk-Mirsky‡ wrote beautifully about you. His article was sent here by Zelinsky,§ who was ashamed and remorseful at the political calumny perpetrated by Kusikov,‖ a wretched nobody, not a bit better than the talentless creature whom I

---

*I have an unfinished story begun in 1916 on this subject (will power, transcendence, and simplicity raised to the nth degree). I have resolved to finish it this summer. [B. P.]

†Pluperfect tense.

‡In a review of "The Swain," published in the journal *Sovremennyye zapiski* in 1926.

§Kornely Zelinsky (1896–1976): Soviet critic.

‖Alexander Kusikov (Kusikyan) (1896–1963): Russian poet of the Imagist school.

got to know through the conflict in Berlin, where, taking over the *Nakanunye** editorial office, the two of them damaged Bely's reputation and, at someone's behest, attributed his work to a certain count in so shameless a manner that everyone expected to find all traces of Bely erased from the next issue of the magazine, and the signature under his picture changed to "Alexei Tolstoy."† There's Kusikov for you! But he's not really a bad fellow at heart. Forget what I've told you; it isn't worth remembering. He used to own a bookshop. When he opens a butcher shop, get revenge by buying your chops elsewhere.

The article is typed on fine embassy paper. Zelinsky not only regretted his involvement but found this article, singled it out, and gave it to a typist on the Rue de Grenelle. You thereby provided both of them with jobs. An excellent article, very profound and true—very true.

I admire Mirsky immensely. But I am not sure he is correct in his classification of me. I am not speaking of his judgment, merely of his classification. It resembles the tag you put on *The Noise of Time*‡: "still-lifeism." Do you agree? It seems to me I have begun—vaguely, by circuitous means, with difficulty, in muffled tones, and in realistic garb—yet have begun, I believe, to rescue and defend idealism, the very mention of which is now prohibited. The prohibition is not so important as the change that has taken place in everything: in readers, in physical geography (space and time), even in myself, involuntarily.

I recoil from the hateful term "first poet" and hasten to

---

*Newspaper published in Berlin from 1922 to 1924.

†Alexei Tolstoy (1863–1945): contributor to *Nakanunye* who became an eminent Soviet writer, best known for his trilogy, *Road to Calvary*.

‡Autobiographical book by Osip Mandelstam, published 1925; Tsvetayeva pronounced it "despicable."

defend you from it. You are a *great* poet. This is more enig-
matic, flexible, and greater than "first." A great poet is the
heart and substance of a generation. The first poet is but an
object of wonder for journals and journalists. There is no need
for me to defend myself against it. For me, Mayakovsky is
the "first," although he is also great like you, i.e., sheltered
and warmed at the breast of our generation, as Pushkin was
between Baratynsky and Yazykov.* "First," too, though. To
focus attention on that word in the article would be short-
sighted quibbling. Just a disagreement in definition. By "first"
Svyatopolk-Mirsky certainly means "genuinely great." I would
put it this way: Each generation is a unity—the poetic essence
is unique—unique in its struggle as concentrated in a given
person at a given time. Only our ability to be transmitters or
receivers of this uniqueness is constant. The waves transmitted or received are in perpetual motion. The essence of that
which is denominated is more awe-inspiring than the denom-
ination. A name given to things of the spirit is as the atom in
the study of matter: an approximate generalization.

I am referring to the article in *Sovremennyye zapiski*. I
don't have it here: as soon as I read it I sent it to Vylyam† in
Krasnoyarsk, hoping that Ehrenburg would soon bring another copy of it from Paris. That is why I am writing about it
so briefly—I must reread it.

I also want to explain why I am forewarning you. If I am
silent, don't take it as typical of me and don't let it raise foolish questions in your mind. Here is an example of how I
behave. Whenever something of mine is published in a magazine, the issue is sent to me. In the serious journals I always

---

*Yevgeny Baratynsky (1800–44) and Nikolai Yazykov (1803–46): poets contemporary
with Pushkin.

†Nikolai Nikolaevich Vylyam (Vilmont; 1902–86): scholar and translator of German
literature, once a friend of Pasternak's.

find something arresting, interesting, even commendable. At this difficult time, when I am trying to master realism through poetry, you will discover many things superior to mine; often the entire issue will have a kind of festive lightness setting it miles above my heavy day-laboring. I don't read these journals; I cannot read them, and not because of indifference. My heart is too troubled. If you were here I would probably devour them. If, for instance, you receive a bundle of new magazines with none of the pages cut except those on which my things are printed (so that I could make corrections), don't think it is because I am anxious for you to have the pleasure of reading my poor efforts and don't care a fig for the rest. That, of course, is not so.

I have a chance to send you a few magazines from which nothing has been deleted and which contain much that is good (in *Kovsh*, for example, everything is better than my contribution). I am taking advantage of this opportunity.

Spektorsky is definitely bad. But I don't regret that in *Spektorsky*, in *The Year 1905*, and in *Schmidt* (except for a few recent chapters), I allowed myself to be so dull and unrhythmical. I will set that to rights. But I had to allow it, because the nature of things made it inevitable, and also because it will enable me in the future to cut rhythm loose from traditional subject matter. Well, I can't talk about it in just a few words. You will misunderstand and think I am in favor of rhythm divorced from substance, rhythm as mere embellishment. Never. Quite the opposite. I am for rhythm that carries the word in the womb for nine months.

In looking through a lot of rubbish, I found, in a little collection from 1922, two pages I will stake my life on. I am offering them to you; read them slowly, don't let yourself be deceived by the form: these are not aphorisms but my own convictions, perhaps even fresh ideas. I wrote them in 1919. But since the ideas are an indivisible part of me, rather than something extrinsic that reaches out to the reader (sponge and fountain),* a certain aloofness may be perceived in the form, making the ideas hard to accept. Svyatopolk-Mirsky says that you and I are different. Read these. Are we different? Isn't this you?

I am sending my only copy. If you disagree with something to the point of wanting to argue about it, quote the passage fully or I will not know what you are talking about. As for the things in the magazines, should you find in the excerpt from *1905* (in *Zvezda*) two or three words deserving of admiration, that would be a great deal.

I am not writing to Rilke at present. I love him no less than you do. It saddens me that you don't understand this. How is it you didn't think of telling me how he inscribed the books he sent you, and how it all came about, and perhaps something from his letters? After all, you stood at the very heart of the explosion, and suddenly—there you are, off to one side. His blessing is what gives me the strength to carry on. If you receive anything for me, please mail it. I think it will reach me if it doesn't carry Swiss stamps.

I fear I will not be able to resist sending you the first part of *Schmidt*. After I had given it to the publishers, I found material immeasurably more valuable than the material I used. But I would have to be a wealthy landowner to rewrite it. Can't afford it. I am writing another chapter and inserting it like a wedge, as a result of which the stuff crumbles on both sides. I'll send it to you as soon as I finish the new chapter.

If you find this a weird letter, remember the request with which I began it.

Greetings to Alya, kiss the little boy, regards to Sergei Yakovlovich. Our two families may become friends some day. And that will not restrict our relationship but enlarge it. You will see. My hair began turning gray very fast this spring. Much love.

---

*See Boris Pasternak's definition of art, p. 147.

In commenting on the literary news relating to Tsvetayeva, Pasternak raised the questions (on which they had similar views) of the cheap rivalry between poets and of how critics distribute prizes. The difference between "first" and "great" poet, which Pasternak mentions in the context of Svyatopolk-Mirsky's article calling Tsvetayeva contemporary Russia's first poet, was an issue they had discussed earlier in respect to their own creative work. Tsvetayeva had written Pasternak on July 19, 1925, "You will never be First—first is a great mystery and a great fraud, Boris. First is a certain degree of last, or is that same last, only powdered, frilled, and rouged, and rendered innocuous. A first has a second. *A unique poet is never first* (Annensky, Bryusov)."

Tsvetayeva enlarged on this idea of a hierarchy in her article "Art in the Light of Conscience" (1932).

The pages Pasternak promised to send to Tsvetayeva were from an article he had written in 1919, which was published in the literary miscellany *Sovremennik*. This work, "A Few Principles," retained for him all its initial significance, upon which he was ready "to stake his life." It was directly connected with his collection of poems *My Sister, Life*.

The first version of the manuscript was entitled "The Quintessence." Believing that the principles he enunciated linked his creative work with Tsvetayeva's, he begged her to read it carefully.

Since the following letters refer, both directly and indirectly, to this article, some fragments from it are given here as elucidation.

1.
When I speak of mysticism, or of painting, or of the theater, I speak with the detachment and obligation with which a free-thinking amateur judges all things.

When the subject is literature, I think of books, and that robs me of the ability to judge. I must be shaken out of my physical absorption in books as out of a swoon; only then, and most reluctantly, overcoming a faint distaste, can I take part in literary conversations that touch not on books but on any other aspect—on readings of literary works, say, or poets, or schools, or new trends.

Never, under any circumstances, would I of my own free will cross the boundary separating the territory of vital concern from the territory of amateur lack of concern.

2.

Contemporary trends assume that art is like a fountain, when really it is like a sponge.

They have decided that art ought to gush, but it ought, rather, to suck up and absorb.

They assert that art can be divided into categories according to means of representation, when actually it is composed of organs of perception.

Art must always remain among the spectators and see things more clearly, more truthfully, more perceptively than the others, but in our day it has resorted to using face powder and dressing rooms and displaying itself on the stage. It is as if there were two forms of art and one of them, knowing that it holds the other in reserve, allows itself the luxury of perversion, which is tantamount to suicide. It makes a display of itself when it ought to get lost in the top gallery, in anonymity, and be unaware that it cannot help being discovered, that while shrinking in the corner it is afflicted with a glowing translucence, the phosphorescence that goes with certain diseases.

3.

A book is nothing but a cube of hot, smoking conscience.

It was assumed, in the not-so-distant past, that a book's episodes were invented. That is a misconception. What need has a book of inventions? One forgets that the only thing within our power is the ability to keep the voice of truth within us undistorted.

The inability to find and speak the truth is a failing that no talent for speaking the untruth can disguise.

5.

What is the miracle? The miracle is that once there lived a seventeen-year-old girl named Mary Stuart who, sitting at a window while outside the Puritans howled, wrote a poem in French ending with the lines:

> *Car mon pis et mon mieux*
> *Sont les plus déserts lieux.**

The miracle is, second, that on a day in his youth Algernon Charles Swinburne sat at a window, with October whirling and raging outside, and finished his *Chastelard*, in which the subdued plaint of Tsvetayeva's five stanzas sounded in the sinister throbbing of five tragic acts.[†]

The miracle is, third, that on a day five years ago a translator gazed out of the window and wondered which was the greater marvel: that the Yelabuga[‡] blizzard should know Scottish and be wailing, as on that earlier day, over the fate of the seventeen-year-old girl; or that the girl and the English bard who sang her lament were speaking to him in clear, soulful Russian about the tragedy they kept on reliving, the tragedy that would not let them go.

---

* For my worst and my best/Are more bleak than the rest. From the verses entitled "Farewell, Beloved France," written by Mary, Queen of Scots, on the death of her first husband, King Francis II of France.

[†] In 1916 Pasternak had translated the first part of *Chastelard*, which told the story of Mary, Queen of Scots.

[‡] The district in which Pasternak was living when he worked on the Swinburne translation.

What is the meaning of it? the translator asked himself. What is happening out there? Why is it so serene today (though the blizzard is still raging)? One would expect blood to be flowing. Instead a smile lights the faces beyond the window.

Therein lies the miracle. In the happy recognition of the oneness, the identicalness of the lives of those three and many, many others (eyewitnesses of three epochs; participants, readers). In the abiding truth of that October of an indefinite year that rages and roars beyond the window, on the hillside, in—art.

That is the miracle.

6.

... In setting the fancy free, poetry inevitably stumbles upon nature. The real world is the only source that, once having been successfully drawn upon by the imagination, never ceases to feed it. This goes on and on, constantly proving its validity. As a source it is reliable, profound, always alluring. There is never a letdown on the morning after. It renders the poet a far greater service than models and patterns....

———————

TSVETAYEVA TO PASTERNAK*

St.-Gilles,
May 23, 1926
Sunday I

Alya has gone to the fair. Mursik is asleep. The one who is not asleep is at the fair, the one who is not at the fair is asleep. I alone am not at the fair or asleep. (Loneliness deepened by

———————

*The beginning of this letter is a prose paraphrase of "From the Seaside," a poem Tsvetayeva was composing at the time.

being a loner. Everyone else must be asleep for me to feel that I am not asleep.)

Boris, this is not a real letter. The real ones are never committed to paper. Today, for instance, while pushing Mursik's carriage along an unfamiliar road—roads—turning here, turning there, seeing things for the first time, enjoying the bliss of being on hard ground at last (sand, sea), stroking some prickly flowering plants in passing as one strokes a strange dog, I talked to you all the time. Talked at you, Boris, loved it, breathed deeply, easily. At moments when you became too engrossed in your thoughts I took your head in both of my hands and turned it toward me: "Look, don't think this is beauty; the Vendée is *poor*, nothing striking, only bushes, sand, crosses. Donkey carts. Sickly vineyards." It was a gray day besides (the color of sleep), and no wind. But I felt Pentecost in this foreign air, I was touched by the children in donkey carts, the little girls looking very important in long dresses and hats (and *what* hats—they took me back to my own childhood—silly hats with square crowns and bows on the sides)—the girls looked like the grandmothers and the grandmothers looked like the girls.... But no more about that; it is about something else—and about that, too—about everyone—and about us, today, in Moscow or St.-Gilles, I'm not sure which, watching this festive, impoverished Vendée (as in childhood, pressing our heads together, temple to temple, in the rain, glancing out sideways at the passers-by).

I don't live in the past, Boris, I don't force on anyone either my six- or my sixteen-year-old self. Why do I feel drawn to *your* childhood, and why am I drawn to draw you into mine? (Childhood is a place where all remains *where* it was and *what* it was.) Now I am here with you in the Vendée in May 1926, playing endless games, switching from game to game, collecting seashells with you, cracking open green gooseberries the color of my eyes (not *my* comparison), running (for whenever Alya runs it is *me* running) to see whether the Vie is subsiding or rising (tide coming in or going out).

But there's one thing, Boris: I don't like the sea. Can't bear it. A vast expanse and nothing to walk on—that's one thing. In constant motion and I can only watch it—that's another. Why, Boris, it's the same thing all over again, i.e., it's my notorious, involuntary immobility. My inertness. My beastly tolerance, whether I want to be tolerant or not. And the sea at night?—cold, terrifying, invisible, unloving, filled with itself —like Rilke (itself or divinity, no matter). I pity the earth: it feels cold. The sea never *feels* cold, it *is* cold—it is all its horrible features. They are its essence. An enormous refrigerator (at night). An enormous boiler (in the daytime). And perfectly round. A monstrous *saucer*. *Flat*, Boris. An enormous flat-bottomed cradle tossing out a baby (a ship) every minute. It cannot be caressed (too wet). It cannot be worshiped (too terrible). As I would have hated Jehovah, for instance, as I hate any great power. The sea is a dictatorship, Boris. A mountain is a divinity. A mountain has many sides to it. A mountain stoops to the level of Mur (touched by him!) and rises to Goethe's brow; then, not to embarrass him, rises even higher. A mountain has streams, nests, games. A mountain is first and foremost *what I stand on*, Boris. My exact worth. A mountain is a great dash on the printed page, Boris, to be filled in with a deep sigh.

And yet, I'm not sorry I came. "One wearies of all things; never of you."[5] With this, for this, I came. That with which and for which I came is your poetry, i.e., the metamorphosis of material things. I was a fool to hope I could see *your* sea with *my* eyes—that which is beyond eyes, above eyes, within eyes. "Farewell, free-flowing waves..."[6] (when I was ten years old); "One wearies of all things..." (now that I'm thirty). This, then, is my sea.

I'm not blind, Boris. I see, hear, sense, breathe, *all* one is expected to do; but that is not enough for me. I haven't stated the main thing: only a sailor or a fisherman dares to love the sea. Only a sailor or a fisherman really knows it. Loving it on my part would be overstepping my rights (being a "poet," the most despicable of excuses, *doesn't hold here*. Here you've got to come up with hard cash).

Offended pride, Boris. On a mountain I'm as good as any mountaineer, but on the sea—I'm not even a passenger. A summer boarder who loves the ocean? . . . A pox on the breed!

I don't write to Rilke. It's too distressing. And fruitless. It upsets me, upsets my poetry. Is it a simple thing, do you think, to cope with a *Nibelungenhort*?!* Rilke has no need of it. It hurts me. I am no less than he (in the future), but I am younger than he. Many lives younger. The depth of a bow is a measure of height. He bows very deeply to me, deeper, perhaps, than . . . (no matter). What is it I was always conscious of? *His size.* I knew him earlier. Now I know him personally. I wrote to him: "I will not deprecate myself; that will not make you greater (or me lesser), it will only make you *more lonely*, for on the island *where all of us were born, all are like us.*"

> *Durch alle Welten, durch alle Gegenden, an allen*
> *Weg-Enden*
> *Das ewige Paar der sich-Nie-Begegnenden.*†

This couplet came of itself, as all of it does. Comes out as a kind of sigh, to which what has preceded it never clings.

My Germany requires the whole of Rilke. As usual, I begin with a rejection.

Oh, Boris, Boris, lick my wound. And tell me why. Show me that all is as it should be. No, don't lick it; cauterize

---

*The treasure of the Nibelungs.

†Across all the worlds, all the nations, along all the roads/Always the two doomed never to meet.

it. "It is not enough to apply honey to stings"—remember? Honey, indeed!

I do love you. The fair, the donkey carts, Rilke—everything, everything is within you, within your enormous river (not ocean, I won't say ocean). I so long for you, it is as if I had seen you only yesterday.

M.

MAY 25, 1926
TUESDAY II

You misunderstood me, Boris. I love your name so much that for me not to take advantage of the opportunity to write it in a letter to Rilke was genuine sacrifice, a real deprivation. Like not calling out of the window to someone who is going away (and for the next ten minutes *everything* goes away; the room left empty without you; filled only with longing).

I did it intentionally, Boris. So as not to weaken the joyful blow struck by Rilke's letter. Not to split the joy in two. Not to mix two fluids. Not to turn this event in your life into an opportunity in mine.* Not to do something beneath me. To have the strength to do this.

I would have been able to say to Orpheus: "Don't look back!" His turning was Eurydice's fault, a fault that echoed down all the corridors of Hades. Orpheus' turning was the result of either the blindness of Eurydice's love, or her impatience (hurry, hurry!), or—oh, Boris the very worst—remember 1923, March, the mountain, the lines:

> Orpheus need not descend to Eurydice
> Nor brothers violate their sisters' rest.

---

*Not to "exploit" the "opportunity" of writing a letter to Rilke and mentioning your name again. [M. Ts.]

153

Or could it have been a *command* to turn and thus to lose him? And to lose all that remained in her that was capable of loving—the last vestiges of her mind, her shade of a body, some shred of heart as yet untouched by the poison of immortality, remember?

> In deathlessness by an adder's sting
> A woman's passion ends![7]

All that still responded to her woman's name followed in his footsteps; she could not resist going even though by this time she may not have wished to go. In this light, transformed and exalted, I see the separation of Asya* and Bely—don't smile—and don't be alarmed.

Eurydice and Orpheus are echoed in Marusya and the swain—again don't smile. I have no time to think it through, but since it came to me instinctively, it must be right. Or perhaps simply a long-drawn-out "Don't be afraid" is my answer to Eurydice and Orpheus. Oh, now I see it: Orpheus came for her so that they should live; mine came for me so that we should not live. That is why she (I) rushed ahead. Had I been Eurydice I would have been . . . ashamed to go back.

As for Rilke. I have already written you about him (I don't write to him). Now I am suffering the tranquillity of the complete loss of the divine countenance—rejection. It came of itself. I realized it *suddenly*.

To put an end to the discussion of my absence in the letter (it was what I wished—*definitely*, actively, wished)—simple courtesy, Boris, is not entirely, or is entirely not, a simple thing. So there you are.

The leitmotif of your wonderful stag is *nature*. I always hear that word in italics, a sharp reprimand to those who do *not*. When a stag tears the foliage with his antlers, that is

---

*Anna Turgeneva (1892–1966): Andrei Bely's first wife.

natural (foliage and antlers go together). But when you use chain saws—oh, no. The woods are mine. The leaves are mine. (Did I read you correctly?) And the blazing green canopy spreading over all.

When I was six years old, Boris, I read a book (an old, translated book) called *The Green Princess*. Only it wasn't I, it was Mother who read it aloud. It was about two little boys who ran away from home. One fell behind, the other ran ahead. Both searched for the Green Princess. Neither found her. But the second one suddenly experienced a sense of bliss. A farmer comes into the story somewhere, too. That's all I remember. After Mother's voice had put a period at the end of the story and then had been silent for a little, she said, "Well, children, who was the Green Princess?" My brother (Andrei) quickly replied, "How should I know?" Asya hemmed and hawed and fidgeted. I got red in the face. Mother, knowing me and my blushing, said, "And what do *you* think?" "She was ... she was ... Nature." "Nature? Ah, you smart little monkey." (Was not my answer late by 100 years? Rousseau— 1800.) Mother kissed me and, in defiance of pedagogy, rewarded me with a book (unconsidered, in haste): "Here, dear, for listening so well." A horrible book: *Marions Tagebuch*. The worst thing was that Marion's diary, and Marion herself, and Aunt Hildebertha, and the "festival of the Three Kings" (*Dreikönigsfest*), were the very antithesis of natural. The antithesis of natural because the world of the book was divided into rich little girls and poor little boys, and the rich little girls showed their charity by giving the poor little boys their clothes (put them in skirts, do you suppose?). Alya also read the book and said that it told about a little boy who ran away to the woods (because the shoemaker beat him), but came back. In a word: How often does *nature* drag the unnatural in its wake? Was Mother, in giving me the book, trying to point out the costliness of having *one's own* nature? I don't know.

Boris, I've just come back from the sea, and one thing has become perfectly clear to me: constantly, *from the first moment of disliking the sea,** I have been trying to like it, hoping to have changed, or grown, or become different in some way. What if suddenly it should please me? As when a person falls in love. The same thing. And *every time*: No, it's not mine, I can't like it. The same violent revulsion (not compulsion, never that!) yet with an absolutely open mind, a sincere attempt to understand it through the word (the word is more of an object than any object: it is in itself an object that stands as a symbol; to name a thing is to give it substance rather than to give it a label)—and every time I am repulsed.

And every time—the unexpected bliss, which one forgets the minute one is out of it (out of the sea, or out of love)— gone without a trace, without recall. I jotted this down on the seashore so that I wouldn't forget to tell you. There are things that my feelings always make me reject: *the sea, love*. And can you believe it, Boris? As I was walking along the shore the waves were obviously bowing and scraping to me. The ocean, like a monarch or a diamond, curries favor from those who do not sing its praises. Not so the mountains. Mountains are grateful (divine).

Did you finally get my gift ("Poem of the Mountain")? If possible read "The Pied Piper" aloud, under your breath, with just the movement of your lips . . . especially "The Exodus." No, all of it, every bit. Like "The Swain," it is written for voice.

My letters are not written with any purpose, but you and I must *live* and *write*. I am redirecting my energies. I've almost finished that thing about you and me† (see?—I keep you with

---

*In my childhood I loved it as I loved love. [M. Ts.]

†"From the Seaside."

me!). The impression is that of something precious but frag-
mented. How marvelously the *word* reveals the *thing*! I keep
pondering certain lines. Oh, how I would love to describe
Eurydice: waiting, leaving, fading away in the distance.
Should it be done with the eyes or with the breath? I can't
say. If only you knew how vividly I *see* Hades! Evidently I
stand on a very low rung of the ladder of immortality!

Boris, I know why you don't go to get my things from N. A.*
Because of a feeling of dread, of self-protection, as one runs
away from a letter that takes everything out of one. Well, the
result will be that everything is lost, all my Goethe. Shouldn't
I (shouldn't you) ask Asya to go for them? I can't wait to get
Schmidt.

M. Ts.

Am I writing too often? I always want to talk to you.

MAY 26, 1926
WEDNESDAY III

Hello, Boris! Six in the morning, with everything blowing
and howling. I just ran to the well between rows of trees (two
opposite pleasures: an empty pail, a full pail) and I greeted
you with my whole body, and with the wind in my face. Back
at the house (now with a full one—the second in the parentheses), everyone was still asleep. I stopped and lifted my
head to see you. Thus I live with you, morning and evening,
getting up in you, lying down in you.

Ah, but you don't know that I wrote verses to you at the
height of writing "Mountain." ("Poem of the End" is another
thing. "Mountain" came earlier and shows a masculine face,
at first impassioned, of highest intensity from the very start,
whereas "Poem of the End" is a build-up of feminine grief,

---

*Nadezhda Kogan. See footnote on p. 135.

imminent tears, me when I lie down, not me when I get up. "Poem of the Mountain"—a mountain as seen from another mountain. "Poem of the End"—a mountain on top of me, me under a mountain.) The lines to you that inserted themselves are still a little raw, are the outcry to *you* within me, to *me* within me.

An excerpt:

> For bullets to trade—a Scythian,
> For the dance in Christ—a scourge,
> Sea! I venture forth on you like the sky.
> How at every verse
> As on a secret whistle note
> I halt in my track,
> I prick up my ears.
> At every line: stop!
> At every stop—a hoard.
> Eye! I fan out to you like light,
> Melt away. From grief
> In the way of guitars
> I feel my strings faltering.
> My things need altering . . .[8]

An excerpt. I am not sending the entire poem because of two gaps to be filled. When the spirit moves me the lines will be completed—these and others. You still happen to have three poems. I sent you my cycle "The Two" from Czechoslovakia in the summer of 1924: "Helen and Achilles—an unmatched pair"; "Thus we pass each other by"; and "I know that You alone equate with Me."[9]

Don't forget to answer. I will send the rest as soon as I hear from you.

Boris, Rilke has a grown daughter, married, somewhere in Saxony, and a two-year-old granddaughter, Christine. He was married when little more than a boy; two years in Czecho-slovakia and it came undone. Boris, the following is villainy (mine): he finds it difficult to read my poetry even though he read Goncharov's *Oblomov* without a dictionary ten years ago. . . . Goncharov—that's a mystery, isn't it? Made me wonder. Something emerging from the darkness of time (*Czars*)* is splendid, but *Oblomov*—infinitely worse. What a waste! For a moment I saw Rilke as a foreigner, i.e., myself as a Russian, him as a German. Humiliating. There is a world of hard values (and low values, hard in their lowness) that Rilke ought not to know anything about in any language. Goncharov (against whom I have no real objection inasmuch as he belongs to a quarter of a century of Russian literature) becomes too insignificant when mentioned by Rilke. One ought to be more compassionate. (Not a word to anybody about his daughter or his granddaughter or Goncharov. Double jealousy. Single is enough.)

What else can I tell you, Boris? My page has come to an end, the day has begun. I have just come back from the fair. The village is celebrating—the first sardines! In nets, not cans.

Can you believe it, Boris?—I'm beginning to feel drawn to the sea by a kind of morbid curiosity—so as to be convinced of my own instability.

I embrace your head—it seems to be so big because of what's in it—as if I were embracing a mountain—one of the Urals. "Semiprecious stones from the Urals." These sounds, too, bring back my childhood (Mother and Father went to the Urals to get marble for the museum). My governess said that at night the rats chewed her legs. Tarusa. The Khlisty. Five years old. Urals stones (from the wilds) and Count Harrach's crystal (from Kuznetsk)—there's my childhood for you.

---

*See footnote on p. 109.

Devil take it with its crystal and its millstones!

Where are you spending the summer? Has Aseyev recovered? Don't *you* get sick!

What else shall I say?

That's *all*!

M. Ts.

Have you noticed that I give you of myself *in pieces*?

5

THE CORRESPONDENCE between Tsvetayeva and Rilke was interrupted because she misinterpreted his tactful reference to his illness: she took as a sign of indifference and loss of interest Rilke's warning that, through no fault of his own, he might be unable to answer her letters.

After two weeks of suffering in silence, the ravages of which can be detected in her letters to Pasternak, Tsvetayeva wrote to Rilke again, returning to the point at which their relationship had begun, to her plan of visiting him with Pasternak.

————

TSVETAYEVA TO RILKE

St.-Gilles-sur-Vie
June 3, 1926

Much—everything, even—remains in the notebook. For you let me cite only the words from my letter to Boris Pasternak.

"When I used to ask you what we would do if we were together, you once answered, 'We would go to Rilke.' I tell you Rilke is overburdened; he doesn't need anything or anyone. He breathes upon me the bitter cold of the possessor, of whose possessions I am knowingly and by predestination a part. I have nothing to give him, all has been taken in advance. He does not need me, or you. Strength, always attracting, distracts. Something in him (what it's called is your guess) does not want to be diverted. Must not be.

"This encounter is a great wound, a blow to my heart (the heart not only beats, it also takes beatings—whenever it rises to a joyous higher beat!), the more so since he is right: in thinking that I (you) in our best hours are the same!"

One sentence in your letter: "... If all of a sudden I should turn uncommunicative—which ought not to keep you from writing to *me*. As often as ..."

The moment I read that—that sentence asks for rest. Rest took place. (You are a little rested, aren't you?)

Do you know what all this means: rest, unrest, request, fulfillment, etc. Listen, I suddenly seem to feel quite sure about this.

Before life one is *always* and *everything*; as one lives, one is *something* and *now* (is, has—the same!).

My love for you was parceled out in days and letters, hours and lines. Hence the unrest. (That's why you asked for rest!) Letter today, letter tomorrow. You are alive, I want to see you. A transplantation from the always to the now. Hence the pain, the counting of days, each hour's worthlessness, the hour now merely a step to the letter. To *be* within the other person or to *have* the other person (or want to have, want in general—all one!). When I realized this, I fell silent.

Now it is over. It doesn't take me long to be done with wanting. What did I want from you? Nothing. Rather—around you. Perhaps, simply—to you. Being without a letter was already turning into being without you. The further, the worse. Without a letter—without you; with a letter—without you; with you—without you. Into you! Not to be. —Die!

This is how I am. This is how love is—infinite time. Thankless and self-destructive. I do not love or honor love.

*V velikoi nizosti lyubvi**

---

*In the great lowliness of love.

goes one of my lines (*La grande bassesse de l'amour*, or—better still—*La bassesse suprême de l'amour*). So, Rainer, it's over. I don't want to go to you. I don't wish to want to.

Perhaps—some time—with Boris (who from afar, without a line from me, has "divined" everything! The poet's ear!)—but when—how . . . no meddling!

And—so you won't think me base—it wasn't because of the pain that I was silent, it was because of the ugliness of that pain!

Now it's over. Now I'm writing to you.

MARINA

RILKE TO TSVETAYEVA

CHÂTEAU DE MUZOT
S/SIERRE (VALAIS)
SUISSE
JUNE 8, 1926, EVENING

So my little word, as you erected it before you, has cast this great shadow, in which you, incomprehensibly to me, stayed away, Marina! Incomprehensibly, and now comprehended. That I wrote it, that sentence of mine, was not because I was overburdened, as you reported to Boris—no, free, Marina, free and easy, only so unpredictably called upon (which is what you mean, after all). Only so totally without prior knowledge. And, for some time past, probably on physical grounds, so apprehensive lest somebody, lest someone dear, might expect some action or attention from me and I might fail them, fall short of what is expected. I still manage the most difficult thing from a standing start—but suddenly I fear the necessity (even the inner, even the happy necessity) of a letter like the steepest of tasks before me: insurmountable.

I wonder if everything has to be the way your insight tells

163

you? Probably. This sense we have of experience pre-empted: should one bemoan it, exult in it? I wrote you today a whole poem between the vineyard hills, sitting on a warm (not yet warmed through for good, unfortunately) wall and riveting the lizards in their tracks by intoning it. You see I'm back. But first masons and other workmen must ply their trade in my old tower. Nowhere any peace, and cold and wet in this wine country, which used to be sure of its sun.

Now that we have arrived at "not wanting," we deserve some mitigation. Here are my little pictures. Will you "despite everything" send me that other one of yours some time? I don't want to stop looking forward to it.

RAINER

ELEGY FOR MARINA (TSVETAYEVA)

I

Oh, those losses to space, Marina, the plummeting stars!
We do not eke it out, wherever we rush to accrue
To which star! In the sum, all has been ever forereckoned.
Nor does he who falls diminish the sanctified number.
Every resigning plunge, hurled to the origin, heals.

Might it then all be a game, permuting of equals, a shifting,
Nowhere a name and scarce anywhere domiciled gain?
Waves, Marina, we ocean! Deeps, Marina, we sky!
Earth, Marina, we earth, we thousandfold spring, we larks
Whom an eruption of song flings past the borders of sight.
We start it as jubilation: already it wholly excels us.
All of a sudden our weight bends the song down to lament.
Yet: might lament not be a younger down-turned exulting?
Even the nethern gods would fain be exalted, Marina.
For so artless are gods, waiting like pupils for praise.

Praise, my cherished one, let us be lavish with praise.
Nothing is ours. A little our hand may circle the throat
Of unplucked flowers. On the Nile, at Kom-Ombo, I saw it:
Thus, Marina, sacrifice kings, themselves renouncing the
    vow-gift.
As the angels go marking the doors of those to be saved,
Thus we touch upon this and then that, apparently tender.
Oh, how far translated by now, how abstracted, Marina,
Are we even at heartmost pretext. Signal-givers, no more.
This most reticent thing—should one of the likes of us,
Able to bear it no longer, make up his mind and snatch—

Takes its revenge and kills. For, that it has death-dealing
    power,
That became clear to us all from its indrawn and delicate
    way,
And from that singular force that turns us from being alive
Into survivors. Not being: you know it, how often
A blind decree would bear us across that glacial forecourt
Of a rebirth . . . Bore . . . : us? Bore a body of eyes
Balking beneath uncountable lids. Bore in us the heart,
The flung-down heart of a whole generation. Bore the group
To a goal of migrant birds, the trope of our wafting
    mutation.

II

Those who love, Marina, they ought not, they must not
Know so much of perdition. Must be as new.
Old is at most their grave, only their grave remembers,
Darkened beneath the sobbing tree, remembers the eremost.
Only their grave caves in; themselves are supple as withes;
What would overly flex them, rounds them to opulent
    wreath.
How they disperse in the wind of May! From the center
    of Always,

165

Where you breathe and bode, the moment excludes them.
(Oh, how I grasp you, she-blossom grown on the same
Unwithering stock; how strongly I scatter myself to the
    night air
Soon to waft over you.) The gods learned early
To fabulate halves. But we, implied in the circling,
Filled ourselves out to be wholes like the disc of the moon.
Not in a waning phase, nor yet in the weeks of versation
Would there be ever one to help us to fullness again,
Save for our own lone walk over the sleepless land.[1]

                                        R.
                            (Written June 8, 1926)

———

A small envelope full of photographs was slipped into the letter. On five of them Rilke had written in French: "My study
(Muzot)"; "Garden (Muzot)"; "1. Muzot Castle (13th century,
restored in 18th century) sur Sierre (Valais)"; "2. Muzot
Castle in March 1926"; "3. Muzot Castle (entrance)."

6

SHORTLY AFTER the letter and elegy from Rilke, Tsvetayeva got two letters in a single envelope from Pasternak. He had just received the parcel she had sent him through Ehrenburg, which contained her "Poem of the Mountain" and "The Pied Piper," a large photograph of herself taken by Shumov, a sweater, a notebook (in which he was to copy Parts II and III of *Safe Conduct* four years later), and money received for the publication of his work abroad, which Tsvetayeva had arranged (probably a chapter from *The Year 1905* printed in the magazine *Versty* of which Tsvetayeva's husband, Sergei Efron, was an editor).

Two days later Pasternak decided to send her his manuscript of the first part of *Lieutenant Schmidt* and his early collection of poems *Above the Barriers*, published in 1917. He thought they might please her, reflecting, as he believed, her own ideas about what poetry should be. His own dissatisfaction with them, as expressed in his letter, caused him to rewrite the entire collection in 1929.

He was made more and more anxious by his ignorance of how the relationship he had initiated between Rilke and Tsvetayeva was developing. The hints she had dropped in her letters as to her discontent, resentment, and desire to discontinue the correspondence required urgent explanation, and until he received such explanation Pasternak was in no mood to write Rilke.

PASTERNAK TO TSVETAYEVA

JUNE 5, 1926

I thank you from the bottom of my heart for everything. Cross me out of your mind for two weeks, perhaps a month, but no longer. I'll tell you why. I am living through turbulent days, full of worries and domestic problems. And yet I must speak with you more seriously and at greater length than even in the last few months. The reason lies in your recent letters. By no means do what you suggest at present. I haven't even thanked Rilke for his blessing as yet, but I must put it off, just as I must put off my work on *Schmidt* and my reading of your poems (*serious* reading), and my discussion of them with you. Perhaps I am wrong about the time; I may get back to these things much sooner.

At present I have no corner of my own in which I can be alone with your large photograph, as I could with your small one when I was working in my brother and sister-in-law's room (they were away at work most of the day). I don't want to speak about the picture now: I would say so little compared with what I intend to say later. I spent a whole day with your "Poem of the Mountain" and "The Pied Piper." Then I was glad to turn them over to Asya, because, as I have just said, I don't belong to myself these days.

I only read them once. On the basis of this frustrating and unpardonable way of reading anything of yours, my impression was that in "The Pied Piper" (amazing for its design and composition) there are a number of magical and innovative passages particularly significant for their contribution to the poetic art. These passages are such that, on returning to them, I must work out how to *define* their elusive innovativeness, which is of a generic order and for which no name immediately comes to mind—I will have to search for it. So, for the present, consider that I have said nothing. More than at any other time I wish for your sake to be mature and *pre-*

cise. Asya liked "Poem of the Mountain" best (better even than "Poem of the End"). After a first reading my choice goes to "The Pied Piper," at any rate the part of it about which I have said nothing as yet.

Ehrenburg came to see me after he had been in Moscow, completely inaccessible, for a week. He hasn't given me everything yet. Of the offprints, only "Mountain" and "Pied Piper" in single copies. It is impossible to reach him at the apartment where he is staying.

Things are simpler with the sweater and the handsome leather notebook. I have put both of them aside, the sweater in anticipation of winter, the notebook in anticipation (hopeless) of exceptional inspiration. These items do not cause me the pain and bitterness provoked by the poems, which arrived at a time of my own barrenness. I dreamed of giving the money to Asya, but it came when I was suffering a financial crisis, so I had to postpone the dream.

At first glance this seems to be the situation: a certain man was stirred and exhilarated by gazing at a small photo, and he was given a large one; he was thrilled by certain passages of a poem, and he was given a second poem; gold was showered upon him, and with the drops still glistening in his hair he raised his eyes to the giver and all he could say was: I will repay you . . . some time in the future. However great the temptation to see me in this light, however great the resemblance to the truth, drive the image out of your mind, for it is not the truth. The best thing to do would be to comply with my request: forget me for a month. Now, please—don't explode. Although I am prepared to have you go to any extreme. My own hopes are so firm that I am ready to begin everything all over again.

I had the idea of sending you the half of *Schmidt* already written, *Above the Barriers*, and some other things, on condition that you write not a word about them until I begin talking to you like a human being again. But I don't want to make any excuses for *Schmidt* and so will not send it until it is finished. And that applies to everything else. Again I found examples of coincidence in the poems: our both referring to the sea as a saucer, many expressions, rhymes, etc.

I am anxious to settle my family affairs as soon as possible, remain alone, and get back to work. True, I am off to a bad start, but that can't be helped.

I can hardly face a summer in town—heat, dust, sleeplessness, exposure to the contagion of other people's beastliness: a kind of hell (formless suffering). If I accept any of the dozens of invitations extended to me, I am afraid I will be overwhelmed by the positive effects of my new impressions, enjoying a stimulation that will bear fruit not now, when needed, but only in a couple of years. I am afraid of freedom, of falling in love. That mustn't happen at present. I have no intention of setting aside the good things I hold in my hands. In a year I will have a better grip on them (an inappropriate metaphor). For the time being I am chained to this particular window sill and my workbench by having monstrous expenditures and a dwindling income.

This spring I was besieged by categorical demands. I struggled to free myself from humiliations imposed by Zhenya, you, my own self, and (what an odd order to list them in!) the world in general. I am depressed by what appears to be a return of the wholesale distribution of insults and injuries— this in reference to vague moral issues that are constantly being raised at a time when the *only* wholesome and certain place for them is in *work*.

No doubt you find this lamentable but inevitable. I do not.

JUNE 7, 1926

The congruence of our words and our manner of speaking is such that I am sending everything after all; I would not want it to appear that *Schmidt* and *Barriers* were written under the influence of "Pied Piper."

170

As for *Barriers*—don't despair. After about page 58 things begin to look up. The middle of the book is the worst. The beginning—the northern city, prosaic, dreary, a premonition of revolution (vague indications of revolt, labor exploding at every turn, inarticulate resentment in the factories, as in a pantomime)—the beginning, I believe, is tolerable. An unforgivable use of words. A free transference of syllable stress for the sake of rhyme—that doesn't matter; such arbitrariness is justified by local dialect or the Russian pronunciation of foreign words. A mixture of styles. The use of *fiakr* for "coach" and of the Ukrainian *zhmenya* for "fist" came about because Nadya Sinyakova, to whom the poem is dedicated, comes from Kharkov and uses such words. Oh, a great many weeds. Horrible technical impotence along with an inner intensity greater, perhaps, than in any of my later things.

Many people err in thinking this is my best work. *Some* of my blunders and heresies are like the errors in your philosophy of creativity (apparent in your last letters).

Forgive my boldness; I have given it thorough consideration and know what I am talking about.

There are more typographical errors than lines of poetry in *Barriers* because I was living in the Urals at the time (1916) and my friend Bobrov, the editor, did his best—the typical vice of one who is wholly devoted. He made the corrections and sent it to press.

A word or two about *Schmidt*. I was impatient to send it (physically *send* it, i.e., take it to the post office). There is an omission between 7 and 8. The omission is a letter to his sister (showing him as an entirely different person from the author of letters to "his beloved"). It is a most important addition. The book is almost finished, but I am sending you only the second part because not until here does the drama begin (a man becomes a hero for a cause he does not believe in, his spirit breaks, he perishes). I implore you not to write me a word about these things until I have written you in

171

detail about the "Pied Piper." Say nothing at all, not even whether you like them or not, there's a dear. I have already told you why I have included the other things.

Asya calls your husband "Seryozha," and I have made friends with the name. All who know him are enchanted and have only good to say of him. It seems to me I am fond of him because he causes me so much pain. No, I am simply fond of him as a man, I *respect* him.

*Komsomolskaya Pravda** called me up (unprecedented occurrence) and asked permission to print "Now I Am 14" (what a choice for Komsomols!). Once they have used it you could publish it in *Versty* if you wished, citing, of course, the *Komsomolskaya Pravda* issue in which it first appeared.

You hate me; I feel it.

———

In the interval between the two letters Pasternak received one from Tsvetayeva in which she enclosed copies of the first two letters Rilke sent her (May 3 and 10). After a period of devastating suspense, Pasternak at last had proof of the extent of Rilke's pleasure in their friendship. The force and sincerity of Rilke's second letter surpassed anything Pasternak had dreamed of.

———

PASTERNAK TO TSVETAYEVA

JUNE 10, 1926

I cannot overtake those two letters and bring them back. Tomorrow I will try to send another by airmail. There is

———

*A newspaper for Komsomols, members of the Young Communist League, who are between the ages of fourteen and twenty-eight.

nothing dreadful or wicked in them, but they speak of the dejection I felt until I read Rilke's second letter to you. Now I love everybody (you, him, and my own love) as immeasurably as I did that last time, on May 18, the day of your silent forwarding of his message. Do you know what has hung upon me so heavily of late? In what you said about him I caught glimpses of limitations assigned to things (your ideas about solitude and creativity) apparent to me no less than to you; but—and this applies to everything that is fundamental—as I come to know him and grow closer to him, I take these things more casually, more cursorily, invariably in some one aspect, and this makes them less weighty and more vital than your rigid, irrefutable rejection of them does. You presented them almost as lies. *I feared you did not love him enough.* It is hard for me to go over all this from the beginning, from the time when rapturous anticipation colored the spring: the anticipated visit to you, the letter to him, and all that was certain to follow, to reach out to us, to fly to us out of the future. I perfectly understood (and spoke of it in an undispatched letter) the good breeding and inner tact that dictated your reserve in sending me his message without including one from yourself. But I was distressed that this innate delicacy should have been given preference over the possibility of erring (if you had *not* kept silent you might have seemed to be made of an alloy rather than of pure gold).

That letter dimmed, if it did not obliterate, my sense of the everlasting. I failed to recognize in the beauty of your renunciation an aspect of my own everlastingness, anticipated through our relationship. Marina, you have no cause to be surprised or indignant: I will explain further if you will listen. I am not accusing you, I am trying to vindicate myself. Everything you wrote thereafter only deepened the misunderstanding. I see it all now.

I gave rein to my feelings on the assumption that you and I were translucent, i.e., that my letter to him passed through you and that my conjectures about our friendship with him were tantamount to facts. What you said about him, or, rather, the things you implied in response to my *confusion* and *anxiety*, served to deepen instead of allaying the confusion and anxiety. But I have already told you this. Your responses gave rise to two specters (all *my* fault). I imagined you yourself had limitations *I* could detect (fancy the scrupulosity of grief!). And I came to believe you did not love him as much as you could and should have; as much as I did (fancy this, too!). And all the while you kept pouring oil on the flames: Goncharov, *Marine*, and the rest.

Now these specters have been dispelled, though not by you. Even in your last letter ("laurels gobbled up") you go on hitting my sore spot: you harp on his supposed (imagined) boundaries and the limitations of your feeling for him, and on the specter of your own limitations, which, with all due respect for you (*Blagonamerenny*, Tsvetayeva*), were inevitable in this matter.

The specters were dispelled by his marvelous second letter to you. From his reply it is easy to deduce what your letters to him were like. It was this I yearned to know for so long, which I am astonished you did not realize. Instead of copying out his line about the force of *my* letter, you ought to have written if but a line (i.e., given me some indication) from his letter about *your* force, and, again from his letter, about the force he exerted over you. If you had done so our relations would not have become so terribly distorted. True, you told me at last how great was your feeling and how great his response, and, without seeing you, I would have been satisfied by that if in the same letter you had not grown testy for some reason, thus spoiling everything with this first attack of petty

---

*A reference to an article by Tsvetayeva entitled "On Gratitude," which appeared in the Paris periodical *Blagonamerenny*.

anger. Now all has been smoothed over, leveled out, and elevated to the high plane on which we set out; everything equal and on the whole auspicious. *There is no need to refer to it again.**

I sincerely believe that if you have already offended him in some way (and how should I not fear this, considering what you said in your letters) everything will have been put to rights long before you receive these observations of mine (I can imagine how loathsome you find them). I suffer greatly from not being able to write to him now, but the time is not ripe for it. I have told you my life is a muddle—dust and moths and getting money and sending the two Zhenyas† abroad. I have reread "The Pied Piper" and want to write you about it this very day. If they accept it for airmail you ought to get it in three or four days, right on the heels of this one. We must love each other according to your rule ("On Gratitude"). *I am not mistaken in you.* But I have such faith in your every word that when you began belittling him and cooling toward him I accepted what you said at its face value and was driven to despondency, in which state I would have remained but for his letter to you of May 10. It gave you back to me.

That happiness came to me yesterday. A little earlier, I had dreamed about you twice in succession. The first time was at night (I went to bed about four in the morning); the second time in the afternoon (I dozed off at twilight). Only the night dream remains in my memory, and that hazily. You had come here. I took you to see your younger sisters (who do not exist); they were living in various houses, each of which you

---

*By which I mean we mustn't "bring it up," "take it into consideration," "keep it in mind," etc. Just this once it *had* to be brought to mind—once and for all. [B. P.]

†Pasternak's wife and son.

recognized as a home of your childhood. They ran out to meet you, the same age as when you went away. In the shifting, pulsating sound of variations on a profoundly meaningful theme (I understood it; you were but a child, I was gray-haired in spirit) Moscow passed before us, rolling from hill to hill, up and down, a summer Moscow, hot, tumultuous, burning away with a still, white flame.

I embrace you tenderly. Forgive me everything.

———

Soon after receiving Pasternak's three letters, Tsvetayeva wrote Rilke a letter of apology that also thanked him for the photographs and the elegy. Her feeling for the elegy was unusual and deeply reverential. In it and through it she sought consolation for her life's grievances.

"The fear of someone else's gaze, of the evil eye, was typical of Marina with her inclination toward, and longing for, the *secret* possession of a treasure, be it a book, a landscape, a letter, or a human soul.... For Marina was highly possessive when it came to things immaterial; she could not bear shared ownership or shared experience," wrote her daughter, Ariadna Efron.[1] There is no evidence to confirm that Tsvetayeva showed Boris Pasternak the elegy—and in fact, a note in Pasternak's archives suggests he first saw it in 1959—but a year after Rilke's death she wrote the following to Boris's father, Leonid Pasternak:

> Some time—if we meet—I will read you his poem to me, the last of his *Duino Elegies*, written four months before he died. Boris is the only one besides myself who knows about it. But I will show it to you and I will also show you the letter in which, dear Leonid Osipovich, he wrote about you, writing your name in Russian characters.

When I die I will leave everything—poems, letters, pictures—to the Rilke Museum (a bad name)—to the Rilke-Haus—or even better, the Rilke-Heim, which will surely exist. I don't want them to be read before their time, and I certainly don't want them to be lost.

But in 1936 she decided to give the elegy to Anna Tesková, her beloved correspondent of many years:

Dear Anna Antonovna,

Here, instead of a letter, is Rilke's last elegy, which no one but Boris Pasternak has read. . . . I call it the "Marina Elegy"; it completes the cycle of his *Duino Elegies* and some day (after my death) will be included in them: it concludes them. Only one request: show it to *nobody* but yourself and your sister: nobody. It is my secret with Rilke, his with me. It is to this secret I always turn when I am injured by those unworthy to unloose the latchets of his shoes. My love to you. Many thanks for your letter.

M. Ts.

This is the *last* thing Rilke wrote: he died seven months later. And *nobody* knows.[2]

The exclusiveness and secretiveness to which Tsvetayeva laid claim and which she found so important did not really exist. Rilke wrote poetry to his last day, and, like the elegy, it was later published from the originals in his notebooks. The only difference between Tsvetayeva's version of the elegy and the published one was some minor punctuation changes made in the latter.

TSVETAYEVA TO RILKE

ST.-GILLES
JUNE 14, 1926

Listen, Rainer, from the beginning, so you'll know. I am wicked. Boris is good. And on account of my wickedness, I was silent—but for some phrases about your Russianness, my Germanness, etc. And suddenly the complaint: "Why do you exclude me? I love him as much as you do, after all."

What did I feel? Remorse? No. *Never*. Nothing. Without becoming feeling, it became deed. I copied out your first two letters for him and sent them off. What more could I do? Oh, I am wicked, Rainer, [want] no one to share the knowledge, even if it were God himself.

I am many, do you understand? Countless ones, perhaps (insatiable, astronomical figure!). None is to know of the others—that would get into the way. When I am with my son, then he (she?), no, *that* which writes to you and loves you must not be present. When I am with you—and so forth. Exclusiveness and seclusion. I don't even want to have a witness *in* myself, let alone *around* myself. That's why in life I am given to lies (i.e., given to silence and, if called upon to speak, mendacious), although in another life I am considered truthful, and am so. I cannot share.

And share I did (it was two or three days before your letter). No, Rainer, I am not prone to lying, I am too truthful. If I could scatter those simple permitted words over it all, like correspondence, friendship, all would be well! But I know that your name is not correspondence and not friendship. In people's lives I want to be that which does not hurt; that's why I lie—to all except myself.

Falsely situated all through my life. "For where I am bent, there I am a lie."[3] A *lie*, Rainer, not given to lying!

If I put my arms around a friend's neck, it is natural; if I tell of it, it's unnatural (to myself!). And when I make a poem about it, it's natural after all. So the deed and the poem are on my side. What is between accuses me. The between is mendacious, not I. When I report the truth (arms about neck), it's a lie. If I am silent about it, it's true.

An inner right to secrecy. That isn't anybody's business, not even that of the neck that was encircled by my arms. *My* business. And consider, after all, that I'm a woman, married, children, etc.

Renounce? Oh, it's never urgent enough to be worthwhile. I renounce too easily. On the contrary, when I make a gesture, I am pleased that I'm *still* making a gesture. My hands so seldom want to.

Letting it sink deep into me and after days or years—some time, unexpectedly—returning it as a play of fountains, depth having turned to height, been endured like pain, transfigured. But no telling: This one I wrote to, that one I kissed.

"Cheer up, do, it'll be over soon enough!"—Thus my soul speaks to my lips. And whether I embrace a tree or a person—for me it's the same. *It is one.*

That is one side of it. Now the other. Boris has made me a *present* of you. And, having barely *received* you, I want to *have* you for my own. Ugly enough. And painful enough—for him. That's why I sent those letters.

Those dear pictures of you. Do you know what you look like in the big one? Standing in wait and suddenly hailed. And the other, smaller one—that is a parting. One on the point of departure who casts a last glance—seemingly a cursory one (the horses are waiting)—over his garden, as one might over a page of writing before it is dispatched. Not tearing himself away—easing himself off. One who gently drops an entire landscape.[4] (Rainer, take me along!)

Clear eyes you have, clear as water—like Ariadna, and that

furrow between your eyebrows (vertical!) you have from me, I had that even as a child—always knitting my brows with thought and with anger.

(Rainer, you are dear to me and I want to go to you.)

Your elegy. Rainer, all my life I have been giving myself away in poems—to all. To poets, too. But always I gave too much, drowned out the possible response. The response took fright. I had anticipated the entire echo. That's why poets wrote no poems to me (bad ones—still none, less than none!) —and I always smiled: they leave it to him who is to come in a hundred years.

And, Rainer, your poem, Rilke's poem, the poet's, poetry's poem. And, Rainer—my muteness. Reverse situation. Right situation.

Oh, I love you, I can't call it anything else after all, the first word at random and yet the premier word and the best.

Rainer, last night I stepped out once more to take down laundry, for it was going to rain. And took all of the wind— no, all of the north in my arms. And his name was You (to-morrow it will be the south!). I didn't take it home with me, it stayed on the threshold. It didn't go into the house, but it took me along to the sea as soon as I went to sleep.

Signal-givers, no more.*

And about the lovers, of their being shut in and excluded ("From the center of Always . . .").*

And the long, still roving by the moon*

And yet there is no other meaning to it but:

---

*Quotes from the elegy. The final one is Marina's free paraphrase.

I love you.

MARINA

Dear one! I want to present you with one word, which perhaps you do not know.

> Woe is a true word, woe is a good word,
> Woe is a word full of grace.

Saint Kunigunda,
thirteenth century

The picture I don't have yet; as soon as I get it, I'll send it to you. Write to me from Muzot—have the masons gone? And is the sun there? We don't have an hour's worth of sun. I'd like to send you the whole sun; nail it to your piece of landscape.

Yes! Rainer! If I wrote something about you, it would be called "*Over* the Mountain."

The first dog that you stroke after this letter *is me*. Look out for the surprise* in his eyes.

———

Pasternak, unlike Tsvetayeva, was utterly innocent of any feeling of secrecy and possessiveness. In his joy he instantly sat down and copied Rilke's first letter to Marina and sent it to his father in Germany, thus vindicating himself of what his father had considered his tactlessness in forcing the acquaintance of Tsvetayeva upon Rilke:

It is painful and absurd that I have not yet answered Rilke. It is not because I do not love and admire him

———

*This noun could be "expression" or "surprise," depending on how much colloquial German Tsvetayeva commanded. The German is *"Pass auf, was er für Augen macht."*

enough—I love and admire him endlessly (I cannot say "too much," for it is impossible to love him too much, and "endlessly" is only enough). The cause lies in a misunderstanding that lasted a month. It was a certain inborn delicacy that led Marina, when forwarding his letter to me, to add no word of her own; she left us alone in the room, so to speak. And so I had no idea how things were going with them. At last, some two weeks ago, she copied out and sent me his first two letters to her. I have no right to quote the second (it is in answer to *her* letter, after he fulfilled my request to send her books). I cannot quote it, because it is so totally the letter of one poet to another; in it he addresses her as *Du* and presents her with a new and as yet unwritten part of *Malte Brigge*, unique in its emotional power. Only then did my spirits rise, knowing that my intuition and foresight had not betrayed me. We were bound by what ought to bind us. I am copying out for you what I can, justifying it because of the unchanging warmth of his affection for you, Papa, which he mentions again in his first letter to Marina. Well, then:

[Here Pasternak copied out Rilke's letter to Tsvetayeva of May 3 down to the words "I still read Russian, though it always takes some getting used to and practice," then paraphrasing the rest.]

At the end of his letter he says how sorry he is that he and Tsvetayeva did not meet and get to know each other in Paris. Evidently he had never heard of her. She wrote to him (in reply to this letter) and the correspondence of which I have already spoken began. Here is the letter to me, written in his own hand (that sheet of paper to which he refers in the above letter). [A copy of Rilke's letter to Pasternak is enclosed; see p. 130.]

I am tortured by the thought that today is exactly a month from the day on which I received it (and it had already made three journeys, since Marina was by that time at the seashore in the Vendée and it had been forwarded to her from Paris). I must have some time by myself to decide how to answer it. For God's sake, Papa, don't try to atone for my sins by writing to him in my behalf. And don't intrude in general. And don't be jealous. You have no idea what you mean to me, Papa, and how often I think of you; I write and talk to you whenever I can. But my voice can ring out pure and clear only when absolutely solitary.

Well, good-bye. I have to rush around getting money for the send-off. Welcome the best part of me (Zhenya and our son) with tenderness and an open heart, without strain.

Love,
Borya

View of St.-Gulles-sur-Vie, where Tsvetayeva lived for several months in 1926

View of Croix-de-Vie, on the French Coast near St-Gilles

Elegie
für Marina /

O die Verluste ins All, Marina, die stürzenden
                                            Sterne!
Wir vermehren es nicht, wohin wir uns werfen, zu welchem
Sterne hinzu! Im Ganzen ist immer schon alles gezählt.
So auch, wer fällt, vermindert die heilige Zahl nicht.
Jeder verzichtende Sturz stürzt in den Ursprung und heilt.

Wäre denn alles ein Spiel, Wechsel des Gleichen, Verschiebung,
nirgends ein Name und kaum irgendwo heimisch Gewinn?
Wellen, Marina, wir Meer! Tiefen, Marina, wir Himmel!
Erde, Marina, wir Erde, wir tausendmal Frühling, wir Lerchen,
die ein ausbrechendes Lied in die Unsichtbarkeit wirft!
Wir beginnens als Jubel: schon übertrifft es uns völlig.
Plötzlich, unser Gewicht biegt zur Klage den Sang, abwärts.
Aber auch so: Klage? Wäre sie nicht jüngerer Jubel nach
                                            / unten?
Auch die unteren Götter wollen gelobt sein, Marina.
So unschuldig sind Götter, sie warten auf Lob wie die Schüler.

Opening lines of the "Elegy for Marina" in Rilke's hand, June 8, 1926

Boris Pasternak, 1926

First page of an undated letter from Rilke to Boris Pasternak

First and last page of Rilke's letter to Marina Tsvetayeva, July 28, 1926

First and last page of Rilke's letter to Marina Tsvetayeva, August 19, 1926

Ranier Maria Rilke, Muzot, summer 1926

Wayside cross with Rilke's château of Muzot in the background

Rilke's study at Muzot

The church at Raron, Rilke's burial place

Rilke's grave at Raron

7

By MID-JUNE, Tsvetayeva and Pasternak had sent each other their most important work of this period: her "Pied Piper" and the first part of his *Lieutenant Schmidt*. The exchange led to literary analyses, but not to the appraisal of relationships and intentions that so often accompanied and inspired Pasternak's talk of literature; attempts at such an appraisal were left unfinished and were relegated to the desk drawer. Between the lines, however, we can sense mutual dissatisfaction. Although Pasternak detected restlessness, alarm, and irritation in Tsvetayeva's letters, he had no idea as to their nature or cause until Tsvetayeva explained, in her letter of June 21, what was happening in her life.

PASTERNAK TO TSVETAYEVA

JUNE 13, 1926

My friend,

I have read "The Pied Piper" again and have written half a letter on the subject of that astonishing poem. When you see it you will not be sorry. I cannot finish it at present. I will tell you everything later. In speaking about "Piper" I will make reference to a poem of my own—a recent one, no good ("Lofty Malady")—(I dislike it)—(I'm sending it); and another one, written long ago, something genuine, never published (I will copy and send it as soon as I have time to do so, and also to

finish this letter). Write nothing at all about what I am sending and have already sent (not even about *Barriers*) until you
receive "Another's Fate" (manuscript, 1916) and the letter
about "Piper." Then I will ask you to write about everything
as a whole, i.e., to give me your advice on what to do next,
and to say whether you think I can make up for the lost years.
Oh, yes; I am also sending the insert for 8—Schmidt's letter
to his sister. Look at all this stuff as evidence for a court trial.
I am sending it little by little so that it will be on hand when
we discuss everything. The letter about "Piper" will be not
only about this particular work but also about many other
things, some of them personal—in a word, everything sug-
gested by the poem itself. I have not reread "Poem of the
Mountain." That is why I have not mentioned it so far. I love
you with all my thoughts and embrace you tenderly. I have
no faith in the year that stands between us and our meeting.
My understanding of its significance will also go into the
"Piper" letter, if any explanations are needed.

PASTERNAK TO TSVETAYEVA

JUNE 14, 1926

I cannot finish the letter about "Piper" that I began a few
days ago. I will write another and tear that one up. I was
approaching it too broadly, from too many different angles,
too intimately, with too many remembrances and personal
regrets. In a word, my letter was too egotistical, and with a
plaintive egotism; it was a floundering of my entire being
touched off by your complex, many-faceted poem. "Piper"
seems to me less perfect but richer, more moving in its unevenness, more pregnant with surprises, than "Poem of the
End." It must be less perfect, because one has a lot more
to say about it. My delight in "Poem of the End" was complete. Its centripetal force drew even a jealous reader into the

text by communicating to him its own energy. "Poem of the End" is a unique, lyrically complete, highest-degree affirmation of life. Perhaps that is because it is of the lyric genre and written in the first person. At any rate, somewhere in this poem the ultimate in unity has been achieved, because even the creative basis of its power, its uniqueness (dramatic realism), is subjected to the lyrical fact of the first person: the hero = the author. The artistic value of "Poem of the End" and, even more, the lyrical genre to which it belongs, are conveyed through the psychological characteristics of the heroine. They belong to her. Insofar as the second part presents what one great person has to say about another great person, it surpasses the first; the one who is described enhances the greatness of the one who is describing.

What, in general, can serve as the basis of unity and completeness for a lyric that is not personal, not in the first person? So as to give a direct answer without undue pondering, I will trust to my intuition.

There are two focal points. Rarely are they equal. More often they are in conflict. To achieve the completeness of a work of art one must bring about a balance between the two centers (well-nigh impossible) or the total victory of one over the other, or, if the victory is only partial, the conviction that it is at least enduring. These focal points are, I believe: (1) The compositional idea underlying the whole (be it the acknowledged interpretation of a character from folk tale or legend, or a theme of lifelike credibility, or any other representational tendency). This is one focal point. (2) The second is the technical character of the forces used in the game and the chemical quality of the subject matter, which, manipulated by the first force (the compositional idea), produce a new world, a heavenly body amenable to spectroanalysis. The endlessness of the first creative impulse springs from the ideal immortality of the concept (the universe). The endlessness of the second, culminating in the impassioned, *real* immortality of energy, is in fact poetry—poetry in its inexhaustible flow. In "The Pied Piper," notwithstanding your inherent gift for composition, as displayed with such masterly skill and diversity in the Tales,* notwithstanding the tendency of all your cycles of verse to become long poems, and notwithstanding the superb composition of "The Pied Piper" itself (the concept of the entire poem concentrated in the image of the rats!! The social rebirth of the rats!!—an idea startlingly simple, a manifestation of genius, like the appearance of Minerva)—notwithstanding all this, the poetic originality of the fabric is so great that *probably* it rips apart the cohesive forces of compositional unity, for this is precisely the effect of the poem. What you have accomplished speaks with the tongue of *potential*, as happens so often with great poets in their youth, or with self-made men of genius—at the beginning. Yours is an astonishingly youthful thing, giving glimpses of extraordinary puissance. The impression of poetic raw material, or, more simply, of raw poetry, so completely outweighs all its other virtues that it would be better to declare this aspect the core of the work and call it madness through and through.

Perhaps that is how it was written, and further readings, keeping this in mind, may show me that indeed it does hang together. Svyatopolk-Mirsky was right in pointing out the necessity of reading the poem over and over again. I think it worth noting that in its very composition there are two factors leading you to strip poetry naked and to write it with pure alcohol. One of them is the use of taunting satire, condensing the image to the point of absurdity, and at the same time carrying the *excitement* of your technique to the highest pitch, to the point where, exploding in the midst of the tale, the *physical* aspect of speech assumes supremacy over the word, reducing it (the word) to second place, taking over

---

*Tsvetayeva's poems (folk-tale stylizations) "The Tsar Maiden" and "The Swain."

and moving within it as the body moves within clothing. This is a noble form of extravagance and one that poetry has made use of throughout the ages. It is good that you do not apply the method superficially, or only to the treatment of petty details, as the futurists did so often, but that in you it arises from a deep-seated mimicry and, like part of a musical composition, is governed by the structure of the whole ("Paradise City," for instance, and other sections). In addition it is rhythmic in the highest degree, with an almost corporeal rhythm.

The second factor leading to your denuding of poetry is the magic of music. This was a desperately hard task!—by which I mean it was severely complicated by the realism of your treatment. It is as if a fakir introduced his marvels with a disquisition on hypnotism, or a wizard by explaining his tricks —and then stunned and overawed his audience anyway. You understand, don't you, that if you had begun your poem with *Tri-li-li* or "Hindustán" it would have been a hundred times easier than to present first, in the same language and gestures, the appearance of reality (the rejection of miracles) and then—a miracle. In a word, no amount of praise can do justice to that aspect of your art, to *that* miraculousness. And yet, however much I speak about "The Pied Piper" as a complete world with its own peculiar properties, the rings typical of a thing *in potential* keep widening, like the rings of a pebble thrown into a pond. I speak of this work and find myself involved in a consideration of poetry as a whole; I speak of you and find myself confronted by my own personal regrets: the forces you manipulate in this poem are extraordinarily congenial to me—were especially so in the past. If I had not read "The Pied Piper" I would more easily reconcile myself to my present path of compromise (already become natural to me).

Your *unevenness* stems from a rhythmic substitution of one thought for another that leaps up in brackets (never going too far): *Figovaya! Ibo chto zhe list/Figovy (Mensch wo bist?);/Kak ne proobraz yeyo? (Bin nackt)./Nag, potomu robeyu.**

The demonic revolt of the rhythm (against itself), the mad crescendo of monotony, erases the individuality of words but confers upon the galloping intonation the character and external quality of words.

In the "Paradise City" part (up to the point of transition), this device is carried to the ultimate extreme: *Kto ne khladen i ne zharok,/Pryamo v Gameln poyez Zhai-gorod,*[†] and the entire theme, startling in its madness, plunges into the narrative like a horse into a river, which carries it swiftly forward until it is suddenly stopped by the horn of the night watchman. (Splendid!)

Again and again in the poem one comes upon this numbing, this anesthetizing of the word, which constantly serves either as mockery (almost like sticking out your tongue), or as the solidification of the leitmotif played by the flute. In this respect you are a Wagnerian in your use of the leitmotif as a deliberate and dominating device. For instance, the leitmotif charmingly runs over into the second chapter, where, besides being a reminder, it presents another kind of strong feeling (a wave of pride taking the place of sarcasm): *V moikh (cherez krai-gorod).*[‡] In this second chapter you make a splendid transition from the comparatively uneven rhythm of the discourse on dreams, regrettably and unintentionally overextended, to the part beginning *zamka ne vzlomav,*[§] which seems to express the indignation of the suppressed rhythm. This impression is not deceptive; as always with you, rhythm

---

*Figgess! Why the leaf, I mean?/Fig-ger (*Wo bist du hin?*);/Her prototype, then, I? (*Bin nackt*)./Naked, so I'm shy.

[†]Who's neither cold nor hot,/Off to Hameln-gorod.

[‡]In mine (round the bend-gorod).

[§]"Without breaking down the door" [into the Party].

in revolt begins to build itself into *lyrical judgments: Ne sushchnost veshchei—veshchestvennost suti. Ne sushchnost veshchei—sushchestvennost veshchi.*"* This is the poetic limit of inventiveness. In every sense. At least that is how it strikes me. Opposite poles can serve only as crowning points of a single homogeneous sphere. They are sufficient for its structure, i.e., they give all there is to give and exhaust all possibilities. What homogeneity connects Lermontov's finished lyrical sentiment with the execrable prosiness of some of his verse? (I have chosen Lermontov because, despite his occasional dilettantish affectation of a poetry of "things" quite foreign to his genius, despite his many really bad poems, despite his emotional ambivalence—on the one hand the genuine emotion of a poet; on the other, something assumed to be greater: a weak and inconsistent "sincerity"—he achieves, astonishingly, a dry, misanthropic *sentiment* that sets the tone of his lyrics, and if it does not establish his individuality as a poet, it at least offers a resounding, deathless, always infectious sense of depth.)

Well, then, the two extremes are connected by their common source: movement. Your heaping up of definition upon definition always drives to a rhythmic apogee, is always dependent upon it for form and substance, and is always natural precisely at the point where motion is accelerated to such a degree that it begins to think, to throw out definitions, formulas, Pythian mantissas, bits of well-formulated thoughts. In just the same way, excursions into the blind alleys of palpable words, i.e., into lip, throat, and neck-muscle sources of excitement or embellishment, result in the turning and twisting of the rhythm. But in this physics of poetry you are always far more successful in dealing with the "infinitely great" (definitions, sentiments, philosophical ideas) than with

---

*Not the beingness of things—the thingness of being. Not the beingness of things—the creatureliness of *a* thing.

the "infinitely small" (the root of a quality, the tonality of an image, its uniqueness, etc.). It was a pleasure to discover, on delving into the poem again, that the exposition also presented a leitmotif (*Zasova ne snyav, zamka ne zatronuv**). I have already remarked that in this poem you made a more careful selection of *detail* than you usually do.

> *Gusinykh peryev dlya notariusa,*[†]
> *Polka s mopsami v lavke glinyanoi.*[‡]

In the chapter "The Scourge" we again hear amazing music.

A few minutes ago Zhenya came in with the news that she has been granted a passport to go abroad. I must break off here: I've got to go raise some money. Naturally I'm excited and distracted. I had hoped to finish before she got back. Didn't succeed.

JUNE 18, 1926

Know what? I really think I'll send you this rubbish. Your ear will not deceive you. The flaccidity and inertia will inform you of the chaos in which, spasmodically, I have thrown together this appraisal. At the first opportunity (probably within the week) I will finish it and send the rest. The best chapters are undoubtedly "Exodus," "The Children's Paradise," and parts of "The Scourge." Knowing that I will certainly forget what I have written (because of *how* it was written), do not take offense if you find me repeating myself in the next installment.

There is something else I wanted to say. No doubt you

---

*Without lifting the latch, without touching the lock.

[†]Goose quills for the notary.

[‡]A shelf of pug dogs in a pottery shop.

will think this Sakulin-Kogan* sort of review is completely divorced from real life (yours, mine, anyone's). Well, then, how do you like this? For over a year we have been free of the rats that used to pester us (the result of neglect of the property). On the day I read your poem they invaded us again —came in from the yard, where repairs are being made. Interpret this however you like. Naturally I have no intention of living with them, even if they were lured here by the music of poetry. They shall be exterminated. But I find it curious.

I long to get down to work. The interruption has dragged on too long. As soon as I am back to work my mental state will become more lucid and orderly. At present I do not belong to myself.

If you are displeased with me despite the explanations and excuses your fancy supplies with alacrity whenever it wishes to—if you nevertheless are displeased with me, say so directly, without diluting your feelings in the general wash of your words.

Such a dilution is always harder to take than dissatisfaction in full strength, for it gives rise to suspicions and dejection.

I have also neglected to send you the addition to *Schmidt*. Or did I send it? The past few weeks are all mixed up in my mind. My writing desk could supply the answer if it, too, were not in complete disorder. In case I have not sent the addition, I am enclosing it now. I will begin writing Part II as soon as I see off the two Zhenyas. Oh, what a world of worries!

I have not even thanked Rilke yet. Will he forgive me?

I am sending it without reading it over. You will understand.

---

*Pavel Sakulin (1868–1930): Soviet literary critic who, with Pyotr Kogan (see footnote on p. 135), represented the sociological school of criticism.

TSVETAYEVA TO PASTERNAK

ST.-GILLES
JUNE 21, 1926

Dear Boris,

Just got *Schmidt, Barriers*, and magazines. Only writing to let you know they arrived. I haven't looked into them yet, because the morning is in full swing. In the same post I got a letter from Czechoslovakia demanding that I either come back at once or give up my Czech stipend ("give up" is not the right term; if I don't come back they will simply discontinue it).

I cannot go back now. I have rented and paid for this house until the middle of October. Besides, today is the first sunny day and the first real ocean, Boris. For *me* to go back is impossible, now or later: I have *lived out* Czechoslovakia, all of it has gone into my Poems "of the End" and "of the Mountain" (their hero got married on the 13th*). There is no more Czechoslovakia. I would return to a buried rough draft.

It follows (on my not going back) that I am homeless. I think this (the incomprehensible withdrawal of the stipend the Czechs had promised me until October at least) is an echo of the Parisian attack (on my "Poet on Criticism"),[†] or perhaps one of the Russians in Prague has been saying nasty things about me: that I am printed everywhere, that my husband is an editor, that he, Sergei, gets money for the issues (of *Versty*), etc. The fact is, No. 1 hasn't even come out yet, and No. 2 won't be out until October.

---

*Konstantyn Rodziewicz, who married Maria Bulgakova, daughter of the Russian philosopher Sergei Bulgakov; Marina claimed to have been instrumental in making the match.

[†]Marina's article stirred up heated protest in the Russian émigré press (from Mikhail Osorgin and Peter Struve, among others), particularly her quotations from Georgy Adamovich and disparaging remarks about A. A. Yablonovsky. She was especially upset about the review by Struve, which appeared in the newspaper *Vozrozhdeniye*.

I am writing to Czechoslovakia, asking them to try to get me a stipend *in my absence*, as they did for Balmont* and Teffi,† whom they support without ever having laid eyes on them (they saw *me* for three and a half years, always carrying a pail or a sack; didn't like the looks of me, I guess!).

I write them with full awareness that there is no point in doing so. Clearly it is the mischief of someone who envies me. (To envy *me*! After a moment's consideration: I may as well do it, but it's God, not the Czechs, I must ask to cross me off the list of dependents.)

Moreover (as to going back), there is nothing for Sergei to do in Czechoslovakia. No work, no hope. They won't even give him a job in a factory; they squeeze out Russians.

This, then, is the change in my life. Don't take it to heart; observe it from a distance, as I do. Why have I told you? To explain my delay with *Schmidt*. About three days will go into letter-writing—that is, the one and a half or two hours a day I can spend on writing letters or anything else.

Boris, where shall we meet? At present I have the feeling I don't live anywhere. In the Vendée for the time being—and then? I am suffering complete atrophy; I not only don't *live* here, I am never even present here.

There was an annihilating article by P. Struve (who never writes about literature), articles by Yablonovsky, Osorgin, and many others—all of the authors are offended (read "The Poet on Criticism" and you will understand)—this one envious, that one neglected—and me left homeless. Me? That's nothing. The children.

Mur has begun to walk, but, mind you, only on the beach, and in circles, like a heavenly body! He refuses to walk indoors

---

*Konstantin Balmont (1867–1942): Russian poet, one of the early symbolists.

†Teffi: pseudonym of Nadezhda Lokhvitskaya (1875–1952), author of humorous stories.

or in the garden—put him on his feet and he just stands there. At the beach he tears out of your hands and goes around and around (and falls down).

To get back to business. *Dni** reprinted an article by Mayakovsky about booksellers not being active enough. Here is a quote from it: "A bookseller ought to press the reader hard. Here comes a Komsomol girl with the firm intention of buying, say, Tsvetayeva. The bookseller should say to her as he blows the dust off the cover: 'Comrade, if you're interested in Gypsy lyrics, allow me to suggest Selvinsky.† The same themes, but how beautifully treated! By a man! But this is all passing stuff, which is why you ought to renew your interest in the Red Army. Here, try this book by Aseyev,'"[1] and more in the same vein.

Tell Mayakovsky I have some *new* covers he hasn't heard about.

Between you and me—this slur by Mayakovsky caused me more pain than the Czech stipend. Not for myself. For him.

"But this is all passing stuff," and

> Time is not an enormous grief:
> I live with your spirit. . . .[2]

I will write you soon. Boryushka; this letter doesn't count.

M.

[*In the margin*] I now have *Schmidt*; soon you will get a letter about you, and some of my poems. And an elegy (to me) by Rilke. I love you.

---

* A daily newspaper published in Berlin from 1922 to 1925, and then in Paris, where it became a weekly in 1928, under the editorship of Alexander Kerensky.

† Ilya Selvinsky (1899–1968): Soviet poet.

PASTERNAK TO TSVETAYEVA

JULY 1, 1926

Don't expect replies to your last three letters. The thought that you will find nothing in the hand held out to you causes me pain, ill-timed pain, by which I mean just one more devastating pain added to a general state of weariness and dejection. I don't wish to enlarge on this; it cannot be put into words. Now more than at any other time in my life I have to seek peace and moral equilibrium, pursuing my object selfishly, almost comically, like an old maid. I have remained alone in the city for many reasons (you hold the key to the main one), but with the sole purpose of working profitably, i.e., with greater and quicker monetary returns, so that next year I will have more money and leisure. I wish to mention in passing something you probably take the opposite view of, or which will be wholly incomprehensible to you. Perhaps it will reveal me to you in a new and unfavorable light, but I am not ashamed to acknowledge it. *I am afraid of a summer in the city* because it is nothing but an agglomeration of the most necessary necessities to keep a common drudge alive. Moreover, each of these necessities is distorted, twisted inside out, beginning with the sun and ending with whatever you like. Solitude assumes an aspect comparable to the solitude of the mad, or of the damned. Life, or, rather, its grossest aspect, is brutally and fanatically exaggerated, to the point of boring holes in the nervous system. Dust, sand, humidity, sweltering heat.

If I keep this up I will make you laugh; I will end up enumerating the temptations of Saint Anthony. But you mustn't laugh. Terrible truths are revealed by this senseless seething of the dammed-up blood. Forgive me for talking about it. Only in soul-shaking experiences are these truths discovered, but they, like groaning yokes, support a consequent nobility of spirit as thoroughly idiotic as it is divinely tragic.

205

This groan is the loudest note in the universe. I am inclined to believe that outer space is filled with *this* sound rather than with the music of the spheres. I hear it. I cannot reproduce it, nor can I imagine myself caught up in its rushing, multitudinous unity, but I do make my contribution to the elemental groan: I complain with every muscle of my heart, I give myself up so completely to complaint that if I were to drown I would go to the bottom, carrying a three-pood weight* of complaint in my upstretched hands; I complain that I could love neither my wife nor you, neither myself nor my life, if you were the only women in the world, if your sisters were not legion; I complain that I do not understand and sympathize with Adam in Genesis, that I do not know how his heart was constructed, how he felt and *why* he loved. Because the only reason I love, when I do love, is that, because I feel the cold of the right half of the universe on my right shoulder, and the cold of the left half on my left, my love circles around and around me in decent nakedness, like moths around city lamps in summer, cutting off sight of what lies before me and where I must go.

But I shouldn't be telling you this, dear friend. Perhaps it is a bitter thing that *I know* the mechanism of feeling because I have been hurt by it. Why should I reveal it to you? God only knows how you may take it. Besides, machines never smell good. How happy I am to be writing to you. In your company I become more pure, more tranquil. Basically you and I think alike. You misunderstood my jocular fear of "falling in love." This is a similar case. The same duality without which there could be no life, the same choking, heartbreaking grief caused by qualities eminently my own, deeply engraved, legitimately dwelling within me but tending to burst through my skin and then forever drumming upon me from outside.

But this is what the world is like. And I love the world.

---

*A pood equals about 36 pounds.

I long to devour it all, every bit of it. Sometimes this long-ing makes my heart beat so fast that the next day it hardly beats at all.

I long to devour the whole gigantic globe, which I have loved and wept over, and which surges all about me, travels, commits suicide, wages wars, floats in the clouds above me, breaks into nocturnal concerts of frog music in Moscow's suburbs, and is given me as my setting, to be cherished, en-vied, and desired. (Familiar? Don't you find it familiar?) Here again is the note of unity articulated by multiplicity for the *birth of sound* by fingers encompassing the octave. Once again—the paradox of depth.

God, how I love all that I have never been and never will be, and how sad that I am I. How all my neglected oppor-tunities or those that have flown past me through no fault of my own are as nothing compared with me! Dark, mysterious, joyful, glowing with adoration. One for whom the nights were made. Physically indestructible, deathless. I fear death only because it is *I* who will die, without having had the chance to be everyone else. But sometimes when I am writing to you or reading what you have written, I am free of this clattering, jostling threat. Now let me embrace you strongly, strongly, and kiss you with all the feeling that has accumulated during these reflections. All my thoughts have been tinged with ten-derness. Have you felt it?

I am speaking about the exclusiveness that does not make us exclude each other, about absolute values, about the *in-stantaneousness* of the living truth.

Thank God this is so. It will be easy for you and me—the common language of shared qualities. Do you know what I am writing about? About the Rilke letter, about Goethe, Hölderlin, Heine. About "the greatest on earth." But most of all about the instantaneousness of truth.

I have parted company with certain people on these grounds. For some time now I have been used to saying to myself that I can have a close, intimate, easy, and constant relationship with those who know that the instant (far more than hours and ages) is eternity's only rival. One has to succumb to the alien, the wholly uncongenial, to sit for hours with a person who feels at home in the hours. It is like mating fish and fowl. And how disastrous when this happens in love!

JULY 2, 1926

I am deliberately sending this off without reading it. The minute I wrote that last line I went to see Ehrenburg, who was getting ready to go to the railroad station. Maya* was there, as were Sorokin† and someone else I am not acquainted with. There was much drinking, and they kept unobtrusively filling my glass.

We were only a stone's throw from the station (he was leaving for Kiev from the Bryansk Station) and the apartment of his first wife (where he was staying) is at the Dorogomilov Bridge. He and I walked along the riverbank, which at this spot preserves the chaotic appearance of 1918–19. Twilight was settling in; people were bathing on both sides of the river. Here, if you remember, one is presented with a wide vista. The sun was screened by dust, or what appeared to be a dry, still, rigid haze—that gray exhaustion of the air characteristic of cities at sundown. Only in my faraway *Gymnasium* days had I experienced the feeling I did then—namely, an enormous expanse of sadness.

The scene emanated a kind of sorrow, as if it had just floated out of oblivion and was about to plunge back into it. I was about to say to Ehrenburg: "Tell Marina...," but I did

*Maria Pavlovna Kudasheva (1895–1985), later the wife of Romain Rolland.

†Tikhon Sorokin: historian and art critic, whose wife, Yekaterina, had previously been married to Ehrenburg.

not go on despite his insistent questioning, interspersed by sarcastic remarks, as if he were years older than I was.

I don't believe there is anything he can tell you. We have only seen each other a few times. Whom has he met? My family, perhaps, but only superficially. Me in the company of others. Me (in the first days of his being here) filled with hope, with the firm conviction that everything here that made him despair was but froth and spume, and that the substance remained whole and unimpaired. Then in the last days of his stay—me in an entirely different mood, which he might never have noticed had I myself not told him of the change. He is an admirable person—lucky, traveled, with a glittering life story, a man who thinks, lives, and writes with ease. In a word— trivial. I never shut up like a clam in his presence, but I don't remember ever having spoken my mind or opened my heart to him. I don't understand how he can like me, what he can like me for. He is not so simple that I find him commonplace, an everyday chunk of easygoingness like most of the people I talk to. Nor is he enough of an artist to turn me, during our conversations, into his toy of the hour, of the circumstances, or of the moment's mood. Since, despite his consistent good luck, I consider him a failure, I inwardly wish him well (never letting him know it), wish it determinedly and with immense flourish. I sincerely hope you will not agree with me, but will set me straight: "Why, he is not an artist at all!" I would *like* you to have a different opinion of him. If you find in him what I look for in vain, I will thereafter see him with your eyes. I feared his arrival after my letter about "Greed."* I had a feeling that he and I were sure to exchange harsh words. It never came to that. Everything went smoothly.

I have expounded a lot of nothingness about the beginning of "The Pied Piper." You must have found it unpleasant reading. According to the relative values of the parts, I ought

---

* A story by Ehrenburg (1925).

to write volumes about the second half, having expended so many words on the first. I will not, however, seek a balance. I will try to be brief. The best chapters are "The Exodus" and "The Children's Paradise." "The Scourge" is on their level (as to theme, but without the flute, and that is like a chess game without a queen). I like "In the Rathaus" less. As in the first half, one has to speak almost exclusively of the rhythm, of the musical characteristics of the components, of the themes. The privileges accorded rhythm in "Exodus" and "Children's Paradise" are practically limitless—a lyric poet's dream. Here we have the subjective rhythm of the writer, his passion, his ecstasy, his soaring flights of fancy—in other words, something that is rarely successful: art that makes itself the subject. To appreciate your own triumph you have but to recall the flat, vulgar descriptions of poets, artists, and eccentrics in most plays and stories. In "The Scourge" the rhythm paints the picture, and how well it does it! It is the natural rhythm of petty trading, so natural that it seems always to have been one of the potentials of music. Thanks only to the swift flash of it, are you able in a single instant to cover the entire market place and all its details in two or three rhythmic strokes. Wonderful in its force (in its wealth of possibilities) is the chanted motif (*a u nás, a u nás**), especially when it is repeated after the *stunningly* executed fugue of the rats. It seems that you drew individual rats and the entire swarm simultaneously and brought the whole picture together on a web of rhythm, using one of the threads as a whip to beat your way to the end, to that advancing, accumulating, accelerating finale! Here the rhythm resembles what it speaks of—a rare accomplishment. The rhythm itself seems to be made not of words but of rats, and not of word stresses but of gray spines.

I have spoken less of the best chapters: all my preceding observations were elicited by the magnetic perfection of these

---

*But with us, but with us . . .

central ones. And so, indirectly, much has already been said about them. "The Exodus"! (From now on I shall be laconic and follow no particular order.) I like the way the procession passes the Rathaus. "The Dream Monger." Very good for their unity of style are the lexical inventions of this chapter, lending a certain credibility to the fabulous kingdom to which the children are being led. These inventions tie together all the fantastic illusions. The imaginary destination has its own peculiar flora, climate, morals, and mysteries, and these explain the weird consistency of the vocabulary. Indeed, there is breathtaking lyricism in this fairy-tale chapter *Ti-ri-li*. The insistent repetition of this phrase is more powerful than the *realistic* characterization of the flute, for all its rhythmic modeling. Its realism is oddly expressed on page 44, where, after the double statement of this tune, *ne zhaleite** falls at the end of the line and suggests, between *zhaleite* and *alleike*, the rhyme *fleite*,[†] deliberately, even conspicuously omitted, but doubly present because of its apparent absence.

On the whole the Piper's rhythmic pattern (his leitmotif) is astounding. The first line of this most happy of musical phrases is perfect in intonation: *Hindustán!* The compression of the anapest $(UU—)$ into one word (an exclamation) gives it tremendous impact. The imagination, aroused and challenged by this anapest and unobstructed by a formal sentence, instantly forms the flutist's image, what you might almost call his *pose* (body bent forward in the saddle for the articulation of that same triple beat $UU—$ in the phrase *v pushinú*.[‡] The conceptual waves (waves of thought) at moments when the hypnotic awareness of the flute's theme dies away (for example, what could be finer than *miru chetvyorty chas i ni kotor god*[§])

---

*Don't be sorry.

[†] "Sorry," "lane," and "flute," respectively.

[‡] Into a flake.

[§] The world's four hours and no years old.

are astonishing. India here becomes overwhelmingly real. The massacre of shadings—well, you yourself spoke of your ruthless hand, and spoke correctly. In the new interweaving of leitmotifs of doubt and disillusion (from approximately the moment of the shift in rhythm: *tot kto v khobote vidit nos sōbstvĕnnў**), the flute theme develops striking *new* force.

Actually this is a funeral march, coming with magical unexpectedness from an unaccustomed direction—the back door; or perhaps it would be better to say it is let into the soul through the back door, whereas we are used to having a Beethoven, a Chopin, a Wagner, or any other funeral march let in by the door out of which the body is to be carried: the front door of a Te Deum. You display much wit and wisdom in "In the Rathaus." For the purpose he serves, your Ratsherr, borrowed from the Romanticists, is excellent. He is a character that might be among those surrounding and supporting Faust. The sarcasm of this chapter is deeply significant and in no way a caricature:

> *Plachte i bdite, chtob nam spalos,*
> *Mrite, chtob my plodilis!*†

The ego, the "I" theme, is just as good. You mold eternal attributes into symbols very adroitly. *Zhvachno-bumazhny.*‡ But when, at the end of the fifth chapter, the threat of a familiar voice is heard plowing a furrow into the exceedingly complex soil of your language (*Ne vidat kak svoyei dushi!*,§ imitating with irrevocable finality the folk saying *Ne vidat kak svoikh ushei!*‖), then you understand why, notwithstand-

---

*Who in an elephant's sees his own nose.

†Weep and be wakeful, that we may sleep,/Perish, that we may multiply!

‡Chewing the paper cud.

§Invisible like one's soul!

‖Invisible like one's ears!

ing its impressive merits, this chapter leaves us colder than Chapters 1 and 2. (As for the fourth and the last, they are beyond compare!) This is because after "The Exodus" our attention is so tightly glued to the Piper's fate, less in our eagerness to know the outcome than in our hope that he will be happy, that we cannot possibly concentrate on anything else, however interesting; as a result we pick out of the fifth chapter only that which serves the development of the theme, namely, the betrayal, the broken promise, which we instantly pounce upon, irritated by circumlocutions that delay the climax.

The genre pictures you paint in this chapter, perhaps more brilliantly than anywhere else, also annoy and exasperate. But perhaps that is what you wanted. A vexing chapter.

And again—pictures, pictures. Music and painting. How I do love you! How deeply and for how long have I done so! It was precisely this impulse, this love for you, formerly unidentified, that gnawed at me from within and darkened and saddened me from without, that weighed down my hands and shackled my feet. It is precisely because of the nature of *this* passion that I am languid and unsuccessful and just what I am. I am haunted by your femininity, and your ignorance of how and why we are to meet, and by my recent belief in approaching rapture, now delayed and hidden from sight by a year, as if wiped out. This is in line with my feeling. Nothing can be changed. I might be talking about "The Children's Paradise." A cruel and terrible chapter, coming straight from the heart, told with a smile, but—cruel and terrible. The part about school is marvelous. *Gul da ball. Gun da Gall.* * And filtered through that feverish, buoyant, early-morning rhythm:

> *Shkolnik? Vzdor. Balnik? Sdan.*
> *Livnya, livnya baraban.*

---

*Thrum and ball. Hun and Gaul.

> *Globus? Sbit. Ranets? Snyat.*
> *Shchebnya, shchebnya vodopad . . .**

Filtered through it, evidently, that "Hindustán" which showed
its force yesterday. The terrible anapest *UU—*, close to yesterday's rhythmic magnet, is now merely given a new sound.
The moment you recognize its melody, you want to rush forward to protect the children from its consequences (from a
knowledge of the end):

> *Detvorá*
> *Zolotýkh vecheróv moshkará!†*

All of the doomed children together enter the range of the
rhythm. A slight easing of the harshness is provided by making the flute sound for the rats like a real flute (unadulterated,
unrelieved, fatal realism), whereas for the children it is meta-
morphosed, calling to them like a trumpet (unconsciously, in
the sound of the rhythm: *tra-ra-ra*). Similarly, the funeral
march is lighter and purer. The harmony is broken up into
two elements: promise (which sounds almost like *truly* good
tidings: *Yest u menya . . .‡*) and the motif of the funeral service, *V tsarstve moyem . . .§* (which sounds like a biblical
canon): *Idezhe nest bolezn, ni pechal, ni vozdykhanye.‖* The
first motif grows in depth beyond the web of temptation; it
achieves firmness and true elevation, dramatically paid for by
the personal note that breaks through after the line *Dlya
malchikov radost dlya devochek tyazhest#*:

---

*Schoolboy? Rubbish. Gradebook? Done./Downpour, drumming downpour's thrum./
Globe? Shot down. Pack? Let fall./Gravelly gravel waterfall . . .

†Small fry homing/Golden evening midges swarming!

‡I have . . .

§In my kingdom . . .

‖Where there is not sickness, nor grief, nor sighing.

#For boys, rejoicing, for girls, sorrow.

Dno strasti zemnoi
I rai dlya odnoi.*

But enough of "The Pied Piper." I fear my meticulous analysis has made you hate it. *Summa summarum*: it presents the absolute and incontestable supremacy of rhythm. This flows naturally from the character of the subject matter. It reaches its highest manifestation in two dramatic chapters in which miracles are created; it extends over other chapters as well, the only difference being that in them rhythm is not in the first person; in all other respects it retains the same force and is the same source of ideas, images, transitions, and the interweaving of themes.

I received your letter about the Czech misfortune. I can't tell you how grieved I am. I beg you not to leave France. I feel you are nearer Russia there than in Czechoslovakia, although geography says otherwise. I can't explain it, but I think you feel the same. I have faith that it will all come right in the end, although I fully appreciate the difficulties that have suddenly engulfed you.

Oh, these eternal intrigues! I, too, have been the victim of them of late. It's a boring story, but a month ago my situation (materially and in terms of my prospects) was relatively good, and now things have changed for the worse; it looks as if this year will be like last. But in the name of all things holy, don't go back to Czechoslovakia. I was unaware of that quotation from Mayakovsky because I read nothing and know nothing about what is going on around me. Forget it! I will tell you about him. He's a very strange person. He may even think he was speaking warmly of you. He has been in the Crimea for some time now, or I would speak to him. Fond of him as I am, I have quarreled with him two or three times for similar reasons. Each time I found him completely ignorant of what I was talking about.

---

*The depth of earth's pain/And Eden for one.

Forgive me for this dull and verbose letter. At last I have cleared a path to "The Pied Piper." Now I can read it for pure enjoyment. After all, "The Pied Piper" is not a thing one can dismiss with "I liked it immensely." I was intrigued by the poem's originality and wanted to get to the bottom of it.

TSVETAYEVA TO PASTERNAK

JULY 1, 1926
THURSDAY

Dearest Boris,

The first day of the month and a new pen.

It's a pity you chose Schmidt instead of Kalyayev* (Sergei's words, not mine), and that you chose a hero of our times (timeless times) rather than a hero of ancient times, or, to put it more precisely (now quoting Stepun†): a victim of dreaming instead of a hero of our dreams. Who is Schmidt according to your historical poem? A Russian intellectual caught up in the revolution of 1905. He is not a sailor at all, so much an intellectual (see Chekhov's "At Sea") that all his years at sea had no effect on his intellectual slang. Your Schmidt is a student, not a sailor. An inspired student of the late nineties.

Boris, I don't like intellectuals and never consider myself one of them, they are all so *pince-nez*-y. I like aristocrats and the common people, the flower and the root, Blok of the blue skies and Blok of the wide spaces. Your Schmidt resembles the intellectual Blok. His jokes are just as awkward, just as unamusing.

There is less of yourself in this than in your other things.

---

*Ivan Kalyayev (1877–1905): member of the militant Social Revolutionaries who was executed for assassinating Grand Duke Sergei Alexandrovich.

†Fyodor Stepun (1884–1965): Russian philosopher, writer, and publicist.

Enormous as you are, this little man overshadows you.* I am
convinced that the letters are transcribed almost literally—so
unlike you are they. You give us a very human Schmidt, very
touching, with all his natural weaknesses, but how hopeless!

"The Elements"† is splendid. And quite naturally so. Here
the story is about great happenings and not about a little
man. "The Marseillaise"‡ is just as splendid. Everything is
splendid where he is absent. The poem rushes past Schmidt.
He is an obstruction. The letters are one continuous complaint. Why did you have to introduce them? If I had written
it I would have sent them to the very bottom of my memory,
drowned them, buried them. Why didn't you give "a hundred
blinding photographs"³ of Schmidt? Didn't you want us really
to see him—is that why? The dreariness of that face! Why
did you have to give us such a literal version? If you had presented him in action—a series of scenes—you would have
raised him above the reality imbedded in his words.

Schmidt is no hero, but you are. For using those letters!

(Now I see it clearly: my only objection is to the letters.
The rest is—you.)

Ah, yes—this is very important—how did the money business turn out? It remains a mystery. And why did you introduce the incident? It isn't very credible. A fine officer! And
the way he expresses his outrage! An officer is robbed of the
regiment's money, and his response?—"How beastly!" Only
documents can be so unreal!

Boris darling, I'm laughing now. I just reread *Schmidt* and
came to the lines in which you yourself marvel that you
should have used the incident and ask yourself what bearing

---

*That is, try as you will to be overshadowed, you don't succeed. You are the trees, the
flags, the pamphlets, the vows. Sch[midt] is the letters. [M. Ts.]

†Chapter 4 in the manuscript of *Lieutenant Schmidt*.

‡Chapter 5 in the manuscript of *Lieutenant Schmidt*.

it has upon the main theme. The next couplet provides the answer, but I am not convinced.

Boris, everything is perfectly clear to me now: what I want is for Schmidt to say nothing. Schmidt to say nothing and you to say all.

For a long time I did not understand your letter about "The Pied Piper"—for at least two days. I read it—everything was foggy. (You and I have different vocabularies.) When I stopped reading it, the thought cleared, emerged, stood solid. Your most apt criticism, it seems to me, was about the variety of the poetic fabric distracting the reader from the story. And you were right about the leitmotifs. Musicians have already spoken to me about my Wagnerism. Indeed, you were right in everything; I have no complaint to make. Even about how I hop, skip, and shout my way to the *idea*, which then possesses me for the next few lines. A jump with a running start. Isn't that what you said?

Boris, don't think I meant your entire *Schmidt* (the poem): I only meant the *theme*, your tragic faithfulness to the original. When I love, I see no weaknesses, only strength. Schmidt would not have been Schmidt in my version, or I would never have written about him, just as I cannot (as yet) write about Yesenin.* You give the live Schmidt—the Chekhov-Blok-intellectual Schmidt. (Ever since I was a child I have hated Chekhov for his jokes, mockery, smart sayings.)

Boris dear, have fewer letters in the second part or put more of yourself into them. And have him grow in stature just before he dies.

My fate is undecided. I wrote to all sorts of people in Czechoslovakia. *Blagonamerenny* has closed down. That leaves

---

*See footnote on p. 83.

no one who will publish me (I have quarreled with two newspapers and two magazines). When I have a free moment I will tell you about our meeting (I've lost what I already wrote about it). I am writing a long thing, very difficult.* Half my day is spent at the beach—walking, or, rather, sitting and taking care of Mur. I never work at night—I don't know how.

Perhaps I will go to the Tatra Mountains (in Czechoslovakia) in the autumn—to some godforsaken spot deep within them. Or to the Russian Carpathians. I don't want to go to Prague—love it too much, am ashamed of myself, that other self. Do write to me! But I suppose I will get a letter from you tomorrow, now that I have written you today. Have you seen your family off? Is it easier or harder to be alone?

Did Ehrenburg bring you my prose things, "The Poet on Criticism" and "Hero of Labor"? Don't write to me about them specially, only if something in them jolts you. I haven't read the magazines yet, only your poem.

I wish somebody would make me a present of free days. Then I would copy out Rilke's elegy for you, and some of my own things.

Write me about Moscow in summer. I love it best then, love it passionately.

It is interesting to compare what Tsvetayeva said in the preceding letter about *Lieutenant Schmidt* and what she wrote about it in her 1932 article "The Epic and Lyric in Contemporary Russia": "Nothing could be more touching than to find Pasternak trying to imitate, literally reproduce a person, reproduce with an honesty carried to the point of servility, as

---

*Tsvetayeva had completed the poem "Attempt at a Room," based on a dream of Pasternak's (see p. 80), on June 6, 1926. In July 1926 she finished "The Life and Work of the Back Stairs," later titled "Poem of the Stairs."

in certain passages of *Lieutenant Schmidt*. He is so inept at it (should he do this? should he do that?) that he copies everything as a schoolboy copies from his neighbor—even the mistakes. And what a withering contrast: the live Pasternak and his language, and the would-be objective language of his hero."

On June 30, Rilke sent Tsvetayeva a copy of his French poems *Vergers*, just published in Paris. On the flyleaf he had written the following:

> *Marina: voici galets et coquillages*
> *ramassés récemment à la française plage*
> *de mon étrange coeur... (J'aimerais que tu connusses*
> *toutes les étendues de son divers paysage*
> *dupuis sa côte bleue*
> *jusqu'à ses plaines russes.)**

> R.
> *(Fin de juin 1926)*
> *Muzot*

TSVETAYEVA TO RILKE

St.-Gilles-sur-Vie
July 6, 1926

Dear Rainer,

Goethe says somewhere that one cannot achieve anything of significance in a foreign language—and that has always rung false to me. (Goethe always sounds right in the aggregate,

---

*Marina: some seashells and flints/just picked at the French coast/of my strange heart... /(I wish that you knew/the whole of its view, which varies/from its shore of blue/to its Russian prairies.)

valid only in the summation, which is why I am now doing him an injustice.)

Writing poetry is in itself translating, from the mother tongue into another, whether French or German should make no difference. No language is the mother tongue. Writing poetry is rewriting it. That's why I am puzzled when people talk of French or Russian, etc., poets. A poet may write in French; he cannot be a French poet. That's ludicrous.

I am not a Russian poet and am always astonished to be taken for one and looked upon in this light. The reason one becomes a poet (if it were even possible to *become* one, if one *were* not one before all else!) is to avoid being French, Russian, etc., in order to be everything. Or: one is a poet because one is not French. Nationality—segregation and enclosure. Orpheus bursts nationality, or he extends it to such breadth and width that everyone (bygone and being) is included. Beautiful German—there! And beautiful Russian!

Yet every language has something that belongs to it alone, that *is* it. That is why you sound different in French and in German—that's why you wrote in French, after all! German is deeper than French, fuller, more drawn out, *darker*. French: clock without resonance; German—more resonance than clock (chime). German verse is reworked by the reader, once more, always, and infinitely, in the poet's wake; French is there. German *becomes*, French *is*. Ungrateful language for poets—that's of course why you wrote in it. Almost impossible language!

German—infinite promise (that *is* a gift, surely!); French—gift once and for all. Platen* writes French. You (*Vergers*) write German, i.e., your self, the poet. For German surely is closest to the mother tongue. Closer than Russian, I think. Closer still.

Rainer, I recognize you in every line, yet you sound briefer,

---

*Count August von Platen (1796–1835): German writer whose poetry was in the classical form, known for the metric "purity" of his verse. Tsvetayeva admired him but found many of his poems "cold."

each line an abridged Rilke, something like an abstract. Every word. Every syllable.

> *Grand-Maître des absences*—*[4]

you did that splendidly. *Grossmeister* would not sound like that! And *"partance"* (*entre ton trop d'arrivée et ton trop de partance*[†] . . .[5])—that has come from very far (that's why it goes so far!)—from Mary Stuart's

> *Combien j'ai douce souvenance*
> *De ce beau pays de France.* . . .[‡]

Do you know these lines of hers:

> *Car mon pis et mon mieux*
> *Sont les plus déserts lieux.*[§]

(Rainer, what would sound splendid in French is/would be the Lay of the Cornet![||]) I have copied "Verger"[#] for Boris.

> *Soyons plus vite*
> *Que le rapide départ***[6]

rhymes with my

---

*Grandmaster of absences.

[†]Between your excess of arrival/And your excess of departure.

[‡]First two lines of "Farewell, Beloved France," by Mary, Queen of Scots (see p. 140): "How full and sweet my memory runs/Back to the lovely land of France. . . ."

[§]For my worst and my best/Are more bleak than the rest." (First quoted on p. 140.)

[||]*The Lay of the Love and Death of Cornet Christoph Rilke*, Rilke's famous narrative-dramatic poem, published in 1899.

[#]"Garden," a cycle of seven poems in *Vergers*.

**Let us be swifter/Than the express is off.

Tot poyezd, na kotory vse
Opazdyvayut...[*][7]

(about the poet). And *"pourquoi tant appuyer"* with Mlle. de Lespinasse: *"Glissez mortels, n'appuyez pas!"*[†]

Do you know what new thing there is in this book? Your smile (*"Les Anges sont-ils devenus discrets!"*[8]—*"Mais l'excellente place—est un peu trop en face..."*).[‡][9]

Oh, Rainer, the first page of my letter might as well be completely omitted. Today you are:

> ...*Et pourtant quel fier moment*
> *Lorsqu'un instant le vent se déclare*
> *Pour tel pays: consent à la France*—[§][10]

If I were French and were writing about your book,

"Consent à la France"

would be the epigraph.

And now—from you to me:

> *Parfois elle paraît attendrie*
> *Qu'on l'écoute si bien,—*

---

[*] That train which everybody/Is late for...

[†] "Why lean so hard" and "Glide, mortals, do not lean!" Julie de Lespinasse (1732–76) was a French writer whose letters to her lover are famous as a tribute to an all-engrossing, unconquerable passion; these collected letters were one of Tsvetayeva's favorite books.

[‡] The Angels—have they become discreet!... But the excellent place is a bit too full-face.

[§] And yet, what a proud moment/When of a sudden the wind declares/For such a land: consents to France—

> *Alors elle montre sa vie*
> *Et ne dit plus rien.*[*][11] (You, nature!)

Still, you are a poet, too, Rainer, and from poets one expects *de l'inédit.*[†] Therefore a big letter, quick, for me alone, or I'm going to make myself out more stupid than I am and be "offended," "lacerated in my finest feelings," etc., whereupon you'll write to me after all (for the sake of peace and quiet! and because you are *good!*).

May I kiss you? It's no more than embracing, surely, and embracing without kissing is practically impossible, isn't it?

MARINA

[*Postscript on flap of envelope*]
Sender: Muzot s/Sierre (Valais) Suisse.

Muzot has composed your book of verse. So Muzot is sending it without making mention of you.[‡]

On August 10, 1953, in a letter to the poet Kaisyn Kuliyev, Pasternak wrote the following about Rilke's book of French poems:

> Rilke, Germany's greatest modern poet, now recognized as one of Europe's greatest poets, traveled much and loved Russia; he was well acquainted with Scandinavia and lived for a long time in Paris, where he was Rodin's secretary for a while and became a friend of French writers and artists. His last book of verse, written not

---

[*]At times she seems fondly aglow/To be heard so well,—/Then she lets her life show/And ceases to tell.

[†]Here, "unedited matter"; hence "spontaneous," "novel," even "unheard-of" things.

[‡]Rilke did not write his name on the envelopes of some of his letters.

long before he died, was in French. Probably he felt that he had exhausted his expressive possibilities in German (all abstractions and generalizations), and felt it was impossible to turn back to what he had begun with (even though it was basic to all his poetry), whereas if he resorted to French he could make a new beginning.

8

TSVETAYEVA'S answer to the letter in which Pasternak mentioned the temptations he was subjected to during his lonely stay in the city (July 1, 1926) reveals one of the basic differences in their outlooks. For Pasternak the Gospel precept of resisting temptation was a basic tenet of spiritual life. His complaining of the difficulty he found in resisting temptation unexpectedly aroused Tsvetayeva's indignation. Her letter also summarized her reflections on the possibility of joining her life to that of one she loved. These reflections (definitely related to Boris Pasternak) had cropped up in her earlier letters to him, and also to those to whom she had confided their relationship:

> February 11, 1923: Oh, but it will be hard, hard, hard for me, whose words are so irreproachable, so gallantly protective of my other virtues, to meet you in the flesh.

> March 9, 1923: If we should meet, you would not recognize me and would instantly feel easier. I find relief in words, as I shall some day find relief from the crookedness and aridity of this world in the righteousness and bountifulness of the other. Do you understand? In life I am incorrigibly wild; I will slip out of any hand.

> 1924: As for "living with you" ... I must confess my complete and everlasting inability to "live with an-

227

other," while living in him: to live in him while living
with him.[1]

February 29, 1925 [to O. E. Chernova]: B. P. and I could
never live together. I am certain of it. For that same reason, for those two reasons (Sergei and I) . . . : the tragic
impossibility of leaving Sergei, and the second, no less
tragic impossibility of building *life* out of *love*, eternity
out of separate days. I could not live with B. P. But I
want to have his son, so that *he would live in him
through me*. If this does not happen, my life, the purpose of it, will have been thwarted.[2]

May 26, 1925: Boris, you and I cannot live together. Not
because of you, and not because of me (we love, we pity,
we are linked), but because both you and I are *beyond*
life, have grown out of it. We can only meet.

TSVETAYEVA TO PASTERNAK

SATURDAY, JULY 10, 1926

I couldn't live with you, Boris, not because I don't understand
you, but because I do. To suffer for another's truth, which at
the same time is my own truth, indeed to suffer for truth at
all, would be a humiliation beyond endurance.

Up to now I have suffered only from untruth, I alone was
true; if the words (rarely) and the attitudes (more often) were
the same, the motivation behind them was always different.
Moreover, *what you hold to be yours* is not on your level—is
in fact not yours at all, less yours than not yours. In meeting
you I would meet myself, with all the barbs turned against
me. I couldn't live with you in Moscow in July, Boris, because
all your vexations would *erupt* on me.

I have thought a lot about this—even before you came on the scene—all my life. I have no use for fidelity imposed by an inward struggle (me, a springboard—how mortifying!). And I cannot understand fidelity as a constancy of passion. I have known only one kind of fidelity (perhaps it wasn't fidelity, I don't know, I'm not observant; then it must have been infidelity—a form of it): fidelity born of exaltation. A person so exulted in his exaltation that it swept away everything else; it was hard for him to love even me, so effectively did I deflect him away from love. Not exultation but exaltation. That was the fidelity I wanted.

What would you and I do in Moscow, Boris (or anywhere else)? Is it possible for a unit (any unit) to add up to a sum? It is different in quality. In atomic structure. A person's essence cannot be broken down into bits of daily living. Being heroic doesn't guarantee anyone an apartment. Apartments are needed by those who would make new heroes (of themselves).

I was wrong about understanding you. I understand you from a distance, but if I were to see the things that please you I would burst into contempt as a nightingale bursts into song. I would be infuriated by them. I would be cured of you in a second as I would have been cured of Goethe or Heine by one look at their *Käthchen-Gretchen*. I can accept the street as the multitude, but the street personified in a single person, the multitude presuming to offer itself in the singular with *two* arms and *two* legs (and you would be taken in by it?) —oh, no!

Try to understand me: I am speaking of the ancient, insatiable hate of Psyche for Eve—Eve, of whom there is nothing in me. Of Psyche—everything. And to trade Psyche for Eve? Conceive of the waterfall height of my contempt (one doesn't even trade one Psyche for another). To trade a soul for a body? I would lose *my own* as well as *hers*. You are now put in your place. I don't understand you, I withdraw.

Jealousy. I could never understand why Tanya, with a justifiably modest opinion of herself, is indignant with X for falling in love with other women. *Why?* She sees that others are more clever and beautiful than she is and she appreciates *the value* of the things she lacks. My case is complicated because what I have to offer is not my own; *ma cause,* the moment it ceases to be mine, turns out to be the *cause* of half the world: the *cause* of the *Soul.* Unfaithfulness to me is a *test case.*

Jealousy? I simply withdraw, as the soul invariably withdraws before the body (especially someone else's), because of disdain, of incalculable incommensurateness. Any suffering this may cause dissolves in indignation and endurance.

There has never been anyone so impertinent as to say to me, "I am exchanging you for a lady of instincts, one of the crowd, a nobody. I am exchanging you for my own blood." Or, even better, "I wanted a taste of the street." (Nobody has ever had the cheek to address me by the familiar pronoun.) I would stiffen at such frankness, would admire the exactness of the diagnosis, and perhaps would understand. There is no masculine street, only feminine—I am speaking of its composition. But it is the man who, in his lust, creates it. It exists in the countryside, too. Not a single woman would go after a ditchdigger (exceptions only prove the rule), but all men—all *poets*—go after street girls.

I have a different street, Boris, which flows along like a river, Boris, without people, with the endings of all ends, with a childhood, with everything but males. I never look at them, I simply don't see them. They don't like me, they scent me out. Their *sex* doesn't like me. You see my shortcomings, but some men have been enchanted by me, almost in love with me. Yet not one of them has put a bullet through his head for me—fancy that!

To shoot oneself for Psyche! Actually, she never existed (a special form of immortality). Men shoot themselves for the lady of the house, not for a mere guest in the house. No doubt in memoirs written by aged gentlemen who knew me in their youth I will stand at the top of the list. I will figure as their first love. But I don't count with today's men.

The leitmotif of the universe? I suppose so, I see it and believe in it, but I swear to you I have *never* heard it within me. It must be a male leitmotif.

What am I complaining about? About the impossibility of becoming flesh and blood. About the impossibility of drowning ("If I were to drown . . .").

This is all so cold and cerebral, Boris, but behind every syllable stands a real experience, still alive and, by virtue of its repetitiveness, enlightening. Perhaps if you knew the nature of each experience and with whom it had occurred, you would approve of my instinct (or the absence of it). "It is not strange that . . ."

Now for the conclusion.

I began with ". . . not because I don't understand you, but because I do." And I end with "I don't understand you, I withdraw." How can these be connected?

Different motors working on the same frequency—your multiplicity and mine. You cannot understand Adam, who loved only Eve. I cannot understand Eve, whom everybody loves. I cannot understand the flesh as such, and I deny that it has any rights, especially the right to speak out; I have never heard its voice. Eve is, no doubt, the lady of the house, but I am unacquainted with her. (I prefer blood; at least it *flows*.) "Abstemious blood . . ." Ah, if only my blood had something to abstain from! Do you know what *I* want—when I want? Darkness, light, transfiguration. The most remote headland of another's soul—and my own. Words that one will never hear or speak. The improbable. The miraculous. A *miracle*.

You will get, Boris (for in the end you will surely get me), a strange, sad, dreaming, singing little monster struggling to escape from your hand. That passage in "The Swain" with the flower—remember?* (How very much *me* "The Swain" is!)

Boris, Boris, how happy you and I would be together—in Moscow, and in Weimar, and in Prague, and in this world, and especially in the next, which is *already within us.* Your constant departures (that's how I see it) and—what gazes up from the floor with your eyes. Your being, on all the streets of the world, and in my house. I cannot bear being with other people and neither can you. We would get on famously.

Dear one, tear out the heart that is full of me. Don't torture yourself. Take life as it comes. Don't suffer because of your wife and son. I release you from guilt toward all. Take what you can while you still have the desire to take.

Remember that our blood is older than we are, especially yours, Semitic. Don't emasculate it. And take what you must from a lofty height, from the height of poetry—no, from the height of ethics!

Write to me about everything, or don't write, just as you wish. Above everything else—no, before and *after* everything else (to the first dawn!)—I am your friend.

M.

Versty has come out.† Your "Potemkin" is quatrains. Notes at the end. Our pictures on the same page.

---

*"*Khitry devitzyny pryatki! Glyadit: derevtze da v kadke. Lbom ob zemlu—chok! Da na vetku— Skok! — Tut k nei barin! Khvat! 'Govori kak zvat: Imya, zvane, rod!' Skhvatil—zamer—zhdet. Tut—nachalos! (Gdye vzyalos?) Plamenem vzmelos! Zmeyem vzvilos! Vyetcya iz ruk, Byetcya iz ruk, Rvyetcya iz ruk, Lyetcya iz ruk . . ."* (Girls' hide-and-seek's tricky fun!/Now she's a shrub in a tun,/Next—brow to the ground, flop!/Up a tree to a branch, hop!/Here comes Master, and wham!/"Tell me your name:/Given name, calling, dates!"/He's caught her—stands stock-still, waits. . . ./But she, here goes, what a lark,/Whirls up like a spark,/Uncoils like a snake,/Whips from his hands,/Slips from his hands,/Sneaks from his hands,/Leaks from his hands.)

†*Versty*, no. 1 (1926), contained Tsvetayeva's "Poem of the Mountain" and a chapter ("Potemkin"; later called "Mutiny at Sea") from Pasternak's *The Year 1905.*

Versty is splendid: a big, handsome volume, very austere. It's a book, not a journal. The critics will maul it and tear it apart for the coming year. I will send you the list of the contents in my next letter.

Svyatopolk-Mirsky is to arrive here in a few days. I will read your *Schmidt* to him. I have already read it four times and a long letter about it is brewing in me. I will let you know Mirsky's opinion. (At present the press is united in slashing him to pieces, mostly because of you and me.)

I will find out where I stand with Czechoslovakia in a day or two. One way or another we will meet. Perhaps from Czechoslovakia it will be easier for me to join you—somewhere. Perhaps all is for the best.

I'm off to the post office. Good-bye, beloved.

I understood your second letter about "The Pied Piper" instantly and in full. You read the poem as I wrote it: I read your letter as you wrote it and as I wrote the poem.

I must still write about you and me.* And Rilke's elegy. I haven't forgotten.

Have you received "A Poet on Criticism" and "Hero of Labor"? (They were given to Ehrenburg.)

PASTERNAK TO TSVETAYEVA

JULY 11, 1926

Dear Marina,

Of late I have *feared* that, without my wishing it, you would force yourself to write in praise of *Schmidt*. Precisely that: I feared it. I am not ashamed to admit my fear, but I dare not say what I feared, whether it was that the bedrock faith I

---

*"Attempt at a Room."

place in you would be shaken, or the spotlessness of your conscience smudged, or the integrity and nobility of my image of you spoiled. As always, you issued from this absurd misunderstanding true to yourself, unsullied. Creativity gives rise to crazy moods, in which A does not equal A and logic offers no aid or is drunk and obscene.

Regardless of the fear to which I have just confessed, I was disappointed in your letter.* That is not surprising, and the mood it induced was well deserved. To write something that turns out to be bad is an unexampled misfortune for the members of our brotherhood. But how are our feelings to be contained within reasonable bounds? And how are they to be defined? My entire *Year 1905* must be bad, for the same reasons.

It would be even worse to write a bad book. Worse still would be the recognition that you had long since fallen by the wayside and would never rise again. Finally, the crescendo of shame and bitterness demands that you make the briefest possible summing up, that you reduce the appraisal to a "round number," eliminating all fractions; and then the most painful thing of all (or so it is with me): seeing yourself as a parody of a man, a parody of a poet.

I quickly pass through all these sorrowful stages in my own mind, coming to rest on the last, for which your opinion is in no way to blame; indeed, it corresponds in every way with my own. There is good reason for my despondency. You ask whether I find it easier to be alone. I find it desperately hard.

I have certain painful peculiarities that are paralyzed only by weakness of will. They lie entirely in Freud's domain. I will speak of them briefly, just to point out their nature.

All the weak sides of sensibility, both Christian and, to

---

*Of July 1.

put it bluntly, carnal, are manifested in me and are easily exacerbated to the point of delirium, to the point of heart failure. The circumstances of my life *run counter* to the coils of my inner mechanism. I recognize this fact and am always conscious of it; in normal conditions I find it a cause for rejoicing. When I am alone I am left with nothing but these coils. If I succumbed to their action I would be ripped apart the minute I moved. But there is no one who, carrying within him such latent force, can be restrained by reason. I am no exception. Yet if I succumbed to it I would instantly and for all time have to part with all that is dear to me, all that has made up my life, all the people who have become my destiny. To make a long story short, let me say simply: after such an explosion I would find it impossible to look my son in the face.

This, then, is what restrains me, the dread of *this* night, which ever threatens to descend.

You see me as better and simpler than I really am. I have no end of feminine traits. I am acquainted with too many aspects of what is called the "penchant for suffering." For me this is not a single phrase defining a single shortcoming. For me it carries a whole world of meaning. A whole *real* world; i.e., I reduce reality (in matters of taste, experience, and painful response) to this "penchant for suffering," and it is not for nothing that the *heroine* of my novel—not the hero—embodies it.*

At present Nikolai Tikhonov† is staying with me. He spent seven years fighting at the front. He has violated my solitude, and I have frankly told him in what respects he is a hindrance and in what a help. He spoils my mood. I feel

---

*The never-completed novel (referred to earlier) that began with the story "The Childhood of Luvers."

†Soviet poet (1896–1979).

happier and less oppressed when reading his stories than when constantly in his presence.

There's a man for you! My qualities as compared with his must be called maidenly, not merely feminine.

> Ich habe Heimweh unbeschreiblich
> Von Tränen ist der Blick verhängt
> Ich fühle ferne mich und weiblich . . .*
>> Johannes R. Becher

Perhaps you don't know what I'm talking about? About the terrible influence wielded over me by appearances, chimeras, probabilities, moods, and fantasies. From earliest childhood to the present, through passing years and changing circumstances, I have surrendered to the lure of ideas I couldn't shake off, even though they were always morbid, always drained my heart's blood, always contradicted the actualities of life. The only thing that ever changed was the ideas themselves. I never have and never will see life as I suppose others see it—Nikolai Tikhonov, for instance.

I must tell you something about Zhenya. I miss her terribly. Basically I love her more than anything on earth. When she is absent I always see her in my mind's eye as she was before we got married, i.e., before I knew her family and she knew mine. But the time came when what had filled the air so richly that I did not have to search myself or ask myself what this something was, because it lived in her and moved beside me like a reflection in a glass—this something, I say, sank into the mire of a certain ability—my ability to love or *not* to love.

The spiritual essence of our union parted company with its transient, everyday play-forms. It was of vital importance that we recapture and reinstate this essence. I saw no success

---

*I miss my homeland more than I can say,/My gaze is draped about with tears,/ Female is how I feel, and far away. . . .

in our efforts. The dark shadow of our powerlessness fell across the years, spoiling the lives of both of us. That is why, in writing to you about her, I must often have made things look worse than they really were. You must meet her. If she comes to Paris, chance will throw you together; I am as sure of this as I am that I breathe.

I have a grave request to make of you. Allow me (without causing ill feeling) to remove the dedication to you from that mediocre work.* If you understand and consent you will take a great burden off my mind. I am tortured by the thought that I have connected your name (and that means your reputation) with so feeble an effort; that because of me you will be associated with it. Surely you can understand this. In this matter be as outspoken as you have always been.

Has any arrangement been made with the Czechs? My material affairs seem to be looking up. The State Publishing House is probably putting out new editions of both *Sister* and *Themes*.†

I am anxiously awaiting the poem that you say is to be about you and me. Or let me simply say I am awaiting some wonderful new poetry.

Yours,

B.

When you reply, don't forget to tell me about the dedication—I beg you not to. Tikhonov greatly admired "The Piper." Then I gave him "Poem of the End." He was enraptured. He said your voice was second only to Akhmatova's in today's serious poetry. If this doesn't please you (i.e., if you dislike the way he put it), remember that on the whole Tikhonov belongs to quite a different circle, and one not very close to you and me. But he is really a fine person.

---

*Lieutenant Schmidt. See Pasternak's letter of May 19.

†*My Sister, Life* and *Themes and Variations* were reissued in a single volume, *Dve knigi* (Two Books), in 1927.

Many years later, Pasternak explained his attitude toward Tsvetayeva's criticism of *Lieutenant Schmidt*, which he believed was dictated by her initial lack of understanding of his purpose: to reject in every way the poeticizing of Schmidt and to remove the romantic halo surrounding his image. This explanation was recorded in the tenth notebook of Alexei Kruchyonykh's *Meetings with Marina Tsvetayeva*.* Pasternak's phraseology is evident, and it appears that the passage either was a copy of a text written by Pasternak himself or was written at his dictation.

This acrostic [the "Dedication"] was printed in *Novy mir* as the dedication of *Lieutenant Schmidt* to Marina Tsvetayeva. Since it was never printed again, it is clear that the dedication was canceled. In 1905 and for some years thereafter, Schmidt was the hero of Marina Tsvetayeva's childhood and adolescence. That explains the dedication. The author, using contemporary source material, approached Schmidt realistically, unromantically, for his aim in writing both poems (*The Year 1905* and *Lieutenant Schmidt*) was to present a true picture of the times and its morals, if only from a historico-revolutionary point of view. Accordingly, however lofty and tragic the subject matter, if the research data showed limited outlook or bombast or was in any way ludicrous, all of this was included in the poem deliberately as an eloquent example of prevailing mores. To explain this in commentaries was out of the question. Yet without explanation certain ironies, such as those in Chapter 3 ("Letter About Squabbles"), and especially in "The Gentleman's Letter" (No. 6), which the author consid-

---

*See note 3 to the introduction.

ered a self-evident example of intellectual braggadocio, were unrecognized by most readers, even by such discriminating ones as Tsvetayeva and Mayakovsky.

The *idealizing* of heroes and heroic episodes was so widespread at the time that the ordinariness of the hero's psychology and circumstances, as deliberately portrayed in certain parts of the poem, was attributed to the author's lack of insight and empathy, resulting in failure. In her letters to Boris Pasternak, Marina Tsvetayeva again and again asked him to delete those parts of the poem. This difference in opinion as to the general tone of the poem affected the final version (which was less than half the length of the original) and placed in question the dedication, which now seemed indelicate. The matter is referred to in their correspondence from 1926 to 1928. In certain letters Tsvetayeva expresses her belief that the writing of *Schmidt* was a waste of time, since the poem would only be looked upon as an exercise in which one member of the intelligentsia extols another one, proving nothing. Yet even then Tsvetayeva seems to have understood at least half the task of vindication and rehabilitation that faces us today, a fact testifying to her sharp powers of perception at such an early point in the twentieth century. And from such a distant shore.

In a separate edition of Part I of *Lieutenant Schmidt* the author deleted the "Dedication," the "Letter About Squabbles," "The Gentleman's Letter," and certain stanzas from other parts of the poem. Later on he forgot what he had excised from Parts II and III. In 1926 the complete poem was published in *Novy mir*.

In July 1926, Tsvetayeva wrote Pasternak that their correspondence had come to a dead end. This letter has not survived, but its contents are clear from her reference to it in a letter to Rilke of August 14. In another letter, one written to Anna Tesková at the same time, she stated that she had definitely made up her mind to return to Czechoslovakia. This explains the consternation Pasternak expressed in his letter of July 30, and his insistence that she give him her new address.

Pasternak's view of will power, touched on in the preceding letter, had been a subject of discussion between them for some time. Tsvetayeva was inclined to play with different meanings of the word, as in her letter of February 1, 1925: "Our lives are similar; I, too, love those with whom I live, but that is a small part of it. You are my will, in Pushkin's sense: 'will' as a substitute for happiness."*

But at the present, dramatic moment, when she felt deeply hurt by Pasternak's identification of will with fidelity to his wife and son, Tsvetayeva responded by telling him she has decided to end their correspondence.

PASTERNAK TO TSVETAYEVA

JULY 30, 1926

If I attempt to answer you, our communications will continue in the practical, documental tone. Or perhaps you believe there can be a change? There cannot be; the main thing has been said once and for all. What we began with remains unalterable. We have been placed side by side—in what we do with our lives, in what we die with, in what we leave behind. That is our destiny, a decree of fate. It is beyond our will.

Speaking of will: it is my will not to write to you and to regard what you call the impossibility of writing to me

---

*"No happiness is there on earth, but peace there is, and power of will ..." (Pushkin, "It's time, my friend, it's time").

as a *promise* not to write. In saying this I am not considering either you or myself. Both of us are strong, and I'm
not sorry for either of us. God grant that others should be
so fortunate. I don't know how long this will last. Either it
will lead to some good or it will not. And don't ask me why.
The only genuine good is that based on active and absolute
truth.

Don't try to understand. I cannot write to you and you
must not write to me. But whenever you have a change of address, *be sure to let me know*. This you must do!

Allow me not to talk about myself and not to enumerate
the measures that I am taking voluntarily and with the best
intentions.

Until we really meet! Forgive all my blunders and the
wrongs I have done you. I will never give back to you your
pledge of friendship and your promise to come to me (under-
scored in pencil). I will end on this. I need not speak about
myself: *you know everything*.

Don't forget about changes of address—this I implore you.

Let me tell you about Aseyev before he tells you himself.
This winter I tried to read "Poem of the End" at the Briks'*
place. We were not on very good terms. I read this instead
of reading something of my own, as they had asked me to
do. I must have looked defiant. They took a cruel revenge.
Unable to bear their superciliousness, I stopped reading on
the second page. I became indignant, I began shouting, the
evening ended shamefully. Last week I gave Aseyev (who was
present that evening) "Poem of the End" and "Pied Piper." I
gave them to him for a month, so that he could read them at
leisure and form an opinion without any pressure. Early the
next morning he called me up, completely overwhelmed
by that incomparable work of genius, "Poem of the End."

---

*Osip Brik (1888–1945): Russian writer, playwright, and literary critic. Lily Brik
(1897–1978): his wife, Mayakovsky's "muse."

Later I heard him read it superbly at the Briks' (Lily and
Mayakovsky were in the Crimea). Kirsanov,* Aseyev's favorite pupil, got ink stains all over his fingers from copying
it all in one night. Aseyev also read "Pied Piper," just as beautifully, changing his voice for the different characters. We
talked about you until four in the morning. They dream of
having "Poem of the End" published in *LEF*.† I am not asking
your permission for this, because I am sure nothing will
come of it. I am sure Mayakovsky will not allow your name
to appear, even though everyone knows he would be delighted with the poem.

Is this analogous to your reading *Schmidt* to Svyatopolk-
Mirsky? Even on the same date (we burned the midnight oil
on the 28th–29th). But no, no, and again no, my angel, my
fate, my torturer, my incomparable poet! Such a suggestion
discredits us both. There can be no comparison.

Why did you read it to Svyatopolk-Mirsky? I don't mean
why did you read it to *him*, but why did you read *it*? I cringe
at the thought that you took *The Year 1905* seriously. At
times I let myself be carried away by you; nothing else can
explain that preposterous dedication. But I assure you that in
its strength, in the amount of energy expended on it, *1905* is
something between a formal commissioned work and *creative writing*. I do not presume to rate it as poetry.

I am offended by your concealed and suppressed pity.
But it is not worth mentioning. I haven't yet been paid for
1905; I will certainly finish it. It will not be dedicated to you
but "To the average reader and his patron"; or ". . . and his
hobbyhorse."

Again I ask you not to write to me and not to expect letters from me. Appreciate my not having said a word about

---

*Semyon Isaakovich Kirsanov (1906–72): Soviet poet.

†Journal published in Moscow from 1923 to 1925, succeeded by *Novy LEF* from 1927
to 1928. Mayakovsky was editor-in-chief of both.

the poem "about us." You have a rare imagination. Just an ordinary one would serve for reading and comprehending my
poem. I can bear it.

Yours entirely,

B.

Don't forget about your address. I kiss France for all she has
given me. You omitted Rilke from your explanation of why
you are moving back. Remember?

You asked about the articles "The Poet on Criticism" and
"Hero of Labor." Ehrenburg did not bring them with him.
Could you send them with someone else?

JULY 31, 1926

Rest assured, my incomparable one, that I love you to distraction. I was ill yesterday when I wrote that letter, but I will
repeat what I said in it. I cannot explain why and to what end.

But that is how it must be. If that for which I sacrifice
your voice, your letters, and my entire self (with the exception of my will), all of this encompassed by my adoration of
you—if this is not a private matter but one brought about by
the lofty forces of destiny, then it is Life's purpose, and *her*
purpose is to assert her oneness and see that it triumphs,
along with our own oneness. But if it is a private matter, then
I must face the fact that in my private life I have a duty, a
towering duty.

Today you were so frightened that you offended me. No,
no, you have never, never offended me! You could not offend
me, but there is one circumstance in which you could destroy
me, and that is if you ceased to be that exalted and enchanting friend given me by fate. When I left the Briks' place in
Taganka at five o'clock in the morning and walked through
empty Moscow streets, occasionally passing a cab driver or a
street-sweeper or a crowing cock, after our discussion of "Poem
of the End," in which everyone declared you to be "ours,"

i.e., Aseyev said it might have been written by Borya or Volodya* (which is wrong and silly, but don't be offended, be glad, because it shows the warmth and fellowship they felt for you, and was in no way an attempt to squeeze into boundaries a miracle, a wonder, a thing that knows no bounds; and besides, Aseyev was naming his dearest friends)—and again, as in the spring, I felt your presence beside me, felt it with my spine, my right temple, all of my right side, felt the tingling cold of your Valkyrie womanliness, felt the ringing, receding waves of tenderness your strength inspires in me.

There is only one thing I beg of you: never let me feel that my relations with Aseyev and Mayakovsky place a distance between you and me. As yet there is nothing to warrant my fears. Without understanding me, you may be affronted by my intimation of jealousy. The fault lies entirely with me, in my overweening desire that you become one of this fellowship of exceptional friends, individuals, and poets.

Aseyev said, "How can she live there?"—adding, strangely, "among those Khodaseviches."† The suggestion brought one of your letters to mind, and I told them how you despised Khodasevich and how disgusted you were when I attempted to defend him. I knew they would be attacking you on that score (they have no use for Khodasevich, they hate him), and so I spoke up, presenting matters in a somewhat different light. Good God! How delighted I was to hear them praise you to the skies and call me a fool and a pacifier.

Yesterday's request remains in full force. I beg you not to write to me. You know what torture it would be for me to get a letter from you and *not answer it*. Let mine be the last. I give you my blessing—you, Alya, Mur, and Sergei, and all who are near and dear to you. Don't be surprised by this im-

---

*That is, Boris Pasternak or Vladimir Mayakovsky.

†Vladislav Khodasevich (1886–1939): Russian lyric poet and literary critic who emigrated in 1922 and was one of the leading critics for the newspaper *Vozrozhdeniye*.

pulse, though it surprises even me for the moment, yet gives strength and purpose to our decision.

I end in tears. I embrace you.

Keep me informed of any change of address. Best wishes for your sojourn in Czechoslovakia!

"The Life and Work of the Back Stairs" is a fathomless title. Every word of it is full of promise, of lyrical and narrative possibilities. An enormous metaphor spoken airily.

Don't despise and don't ridicule me. There are some things about me you don't really understand. On the whole you may overrate me. You undoubtedly underrate certain of my serious aspects.

All nonsense—appraisals, judgments, underratings, overratings . . . Pay no attention.

———

In a letter of July 29, 1926, to his wife, Yevgenia (Zhenya), who had left with their little son for a month and a half in Germany, Pasternak revealed what breaking off his correspondence with Tsvetayeva meant to him and how he explained it.

I'm not trying to test your feelings by jealousy. I am at present absolutely alone. Marina asked me not to write to her any more after I told her about you and what I feel for you. This upsets you, too. It is indeed absurd. It seems I told her I love you above all else on earth. I don't know how it came about. But don't attach any significance to it, good or bad. People join our names together before we ourselves know where we are. People love us with the same sort of love before we become aware that we breathe the same air. That cannot be helped, cannot be changed. We address each other with the familiar pronoun *ty* and will continue to do so. In your absence I couldn't help telling her the things that

245

made her ask me to stop writing. I did not betray you, nor did I give you any cause for jealousy. On the whole, have I done anything intentionally, with an ulterior motive, or to spite you? I cannot see you separately from the forces constituting my *fate*. And I don't have two lives and two fates. I cannot sacrifice these forces and I cannot, for your sake, change my fate. I *want* you to be such a force, one of these forces. If you were, there would be no confusion, your integrity would triumph, and everything would fall into its proper place. But it would be inhuman even to think of *allowing* you, *unarmed* by a great idea or a *great feeling*, which is to say *not* one of the forces constituting my fate, to enter this circle, these lists. Through no fault of mine you are doomed to perpetual suffering. I do not want you, a person of great courage and strong will, to fight an unequal battle. You do not deserve defeat.

9

THE AILING Rilke was so lonely at Muzot that he eventually went to the health resort of Ragaz. There his friends Marie and Alexander von Thurn und Taxis, to whom he felt greatly indebted for their many kindnesses, were awaiting him. Although his cure did little to improve his health, he hid from everyone the seriousness of his illness. His last letters to Tsvetayeva were written from Ragaz, where he stayed until early September.

———

RILKE TO TSVETAYEVA

TEMPORARILY:
HÔTEL HOF-RAGAZ
RAGAZ (SUISSE)
JULY 28, 1926

You wonderful Marina,

As in your first letter, I admire in each of the ones that have followed your habit of precise seeking and finding, your indefatigable journey to what you mean, and, always, your being right. You are right, Marina (isn't that a rare thing with a woman, such a being-in-the-right in the most valid, the most carefree sense?). This having a right not *to* anything, hardly coming *from* anywhere; but from such pure self-sufficiency, out of the fullness and completeness of it all, you are right, and hence have forever a right to the infinite. Every time I write to you, I'd like to write like you, to speak my self in Marinian, by your equable, and withal so feeling, means. Your utterance, Marina, is like a star's reflection when it appears in the water, and is disturbed by the water, by the life of the water, by its fluid night; interrupted, canceled, and again admitted, and then deeper in the element, as if already familiar with this mirror world and, after each waning, back again and more deeply immersed! (You great star!) Do you know of the young Tycho Brahe's* trip home, made at a time when he wasn't really allowed to practice astronomy yet, but was on vacation from the University of Leipzig at an uncle's estate . . . and there it turned out that (despite Leipzig and jurisprudence!) he already knew the sky so exactly, so much by heart (pense: il savait le ciel par coeur!)[†] that a simple turning-up of his eye, more resting than searching, bestowed upon him the new star, in the constellation of the Lyre: his first discovery in starry nature. (And is it not, or am I mistaken, this very star, Alpha in Lyre, "visible de toute la Provence et des terres méditerranéennes,"[‡] which now seems destined to be named after Mistral[§]? Would that not be enough, by the way, to make us feel close to this era—that this is possible again, the poet flung beneath the stars: Tu diras à ta fille un jour, en t'arrêtant à Maillane: voici "Mistral," comme il est beau ce soir![ǁ] At last a "fame" beyond being on a street sign!)

But you, Marina, I did not find by the free-ranging eye; Boris placed the telescope in front of my sky for me. . . . First,

---

*Danish astronomer (1546–1601) who discovered a new star in the constellation Cassiopeia.

[†]Just think: he knew the sky by heart!

[‡]Visible from all of Provence and the Mediterranean regions.

[§]Frédéric Mistral (1830–1914): French Provençal poet who was a co-winner of the Nobel Prize for Literature in 1904.

[ǁ]You'll tell your daughter one day as you stop at Maillane: look, there is "Mistral," how beautiful it is tonight!

spaces rushed past my up-gazing eye and then, suddenly, you stood there in the middle of the field, pure and strong, where the rays of your first letter gathered you up for me.

The most recent of your letters has now been with me since July 9: how often I meant to write! But my life is so curiously heavy in me that I often cannot stir it from its place; gravity seems to be forming a new relationship to it—not since childhood have I been in such an immovable state of soul; but back then, the world was under the pull of gravity and would press on one who himself was like a wing wrenched off somewhere, from which feather upon little feather escaped into limbo; now I myself am that mass, and the world is like a sleep all around me, and summer is so curiously absent-minded, as though it was not thinking of its own affairs....

As you see, I am again away from Muzot: to see, here at Ragaz, my oldest friends and the only ones whom I considered still linked to me from Austrian times* (how much longer? for their age overtakes me by a great span...). And with them came, unexpectedly, a Russian woman friend of theirs†; a Russian—think how this struck home with me! Now they are all gone, but I'm staying on a little for the sake of the beautiful aquamarine-clear medicinal springs. And you?

RAINER

Car mon pis et mon mieux
Sont les plus déserts lieux:

This was your gift to me; I am writing it down in my notebook.

---

*Princess Maria von Thurn und Taxis and her husband, Alexander, were the owners of the château of Duino.

†Princess Gagarina, an acquaintance of Maria von Thurn und Taxis.

TSVETAYEVA TO RILKE

ST.-GILLES-SUR-VIE
AUGUST 2, 1926

Rainer, I received your letter on my name day, July 17/30,*
for I have a patron saint, if you please, although I consider
myself the first person to bear my name, as I considered you
the first holder of yours. The saint whose name was Rainer
had a different name, I'm sure. *You* are Rainer.

So, on my name day the loveliest gift—your letter. Quite
unexpected, as it is each time; I shall never get used to you
(or to myself!), or to the marveling, or to my own thinking
of you. You are what I'm going to dream about tonight, what
will dream *me* tonight. (Dreaming or being dreamed?) A
stranger, I, in someone else's dream. I never await you; I always awake you.

When somebody dreams of us together—that is when we
shall meet.

Rainer, another reason I want to come to you is the new
Me, the one who can arise only with you, in you. And then,
Rainer ("Rainer"—the leitmotif of this letter)—don't be cross
with me—it is *me* talking—I want to sleep with you, fall
asleep and sleep. That magnificent folk word, how deep, how
true, how unequivocal, how exactly what it says. Just—sleep.
And nothing more. No, one more thing: my head buried in
your left shoulder, my arm around your right one—and that's
all. No, another thing: and know right into the deepest sleep
that it is you. And more: how your heart sounds. And—kiss
heart.

Sometimes I think: I must exploit the chance that I am
still (after all!) body. Soon I'll have no more arms. And more
—it sounds like confession (what is confession? to boast of
one's blacknesses! Who could speak of his sufferings without

---

*By the Julian and Gregorian calendars, respectively.

feeling inspired, which is to say happy?!)—so, to keep it from sounding like confession: bodies are bored with me. They sense something and don't believe me (i.e., my body), although I do everything like everybody else. Too ... altruistic, possibly, too ... benevolent. Also trusting—*too much so*! Aliens are trusting, savages, who know of no custom or law. People from *here* do not trust! All this does not belong with love; love hears and feels only itself, very local and punctual—*that* I cannot imitate. And the great compassion, who knows whence, infinite goodness and—falsehood.

I feel older and older. Too serious—the children's game is not serious enough.

The mouth I have always felt as world: vaulted firmament, cave, ravine, shoal.* I have always translated the body into the soul (*dis*-bodied it!), have so gloried "physical" love—in order to be able to like it—that suddenly nothing was left of it. Engrossing myself in it, hollowed it out. Penetrating into it, ousted it. Nothing remained of it but myself: Soul (that is my name, which is why I marvel: name day!).

Love hates poets. He does not wish to be glorified ("himself glorious enough"); he believes himself an absolute, sole absolute. He doesn't trust us. In his heart of hearts he knows that he is not lordly (which is why he lords it so!); he knows that all lordliness is soul, and where soul begins, the body ends. Jealousy, Rainer, purest. The same thing as soul feels for body. But I am always jealous of the body: *so much celebrated*! The little episode of Francesca and Paolo —poor Dante!—who still thinks of Dante and Beatrice? I am jealous of the *human* comedy. Soul is never loved so much as body; at most it is praised. With a thousand souls they love the body. Who has ever courted damnation for the sake

---

Untiefe means "shallows, shoal," but Tsvetayeva may have construed the prefix *Un* to have its other meaning here, an intensifier, and intended to write "nethermost depths."

of a *soul*? And even if someone wanted to—impossible!
To love a soul unto damnation means being an angel. Of all
of hell we are cheated! (. . . *Trop pure—provoque un vent de
dédain!*[1])

Why do I tell you all this? From fear, perhaps—you might
take me for generally passionate (passion—bondage). "I love
you and want to sleep with you"—friendship is begrudged
this sort of brevity. But I say it in a different voice, almost
asleep, fast asleep. I sound quite different from passion. If you
took me to you, you would take to you *les plus déserts lieux*.
Everything that *never* sleeps would like to sleep its fill in
your arms. Right down into the soul (throat)—that's what the
kiss would be like. (Not firebrand: shoal.)

*Je ne plaide pas ma cause, je plaide la cause du plus ab-
solu des baisers.**

You are always traveling, you don't live anywhere, and you
encounter Russians who are not me. Listen, so you'll know:
In Rainerland I alone represent Russia.

Rainer, what are you, actually? Not a German, although all
German! Not a Czech, although born in Bohemia (N.B.: born
in a country that wasn't there yet—that is fitting); not an Austrian, for Austria *has been* and you *are becoming*! Isn't that
splendid? *You*—without country! "*Le grand poète tchécoslo-
vaque,*" as they said in the Parisian journals. Rainer, perhaps
you'll turn out to be a "Slovaque"? This makes me laugh!

Rainer, dusk is falling, I love you. A train is howling.
Trains are wolves, wolves are Russia. No train—all Russia is
howling for you. Rainer, don't be angry with me; angry or not,
tonight I'm sleeping with you. A rift in the darkness; because
it is stars I deduce: window. (The window is what I think of
when I think of you and me, not the bed.) Eyes wide open, for

*I am not pleading for myself, I am pleading on behalf of the most absolute of kisses.

outside it is still blacker than inside. My bed is a ship; we are going traveling.

> ... mais un jour on ne le vit plus.
> Le petit navire sans voiles,
> Lassé des océans maudits,
> Voguant au pays des étoiles—
> Avait gagné le paradis*

You don't have to answer—go on kissing.

M.

About being in the right (having right on one's side). "Even nature is unnatural" (Goethe)[2]; that's what you meant. I suppose! (Nature: right.) The déserts lieux were given me by Boris as a present and I'm giving them to you.

TSVETAYEVA TO RILKE

ST.-GILLES
AUGUST 14, 1926

Dear friend,

I wonder if you received my last letter. I'm asking you because I threw it onto a departing train.[†] The mailbox looked sinister enough: dust three fingers thick and sporting a huge prison lock. My toss was already completed when I noticed this, my hand was too fast; the letter will lie there, I suppose —until doomsday.

Approximately ten days ago. Contents? Letter *is* content,

---

* ... but one day it was seen no more./The little ship without sails,/Tired of oceans accursed,/Bobbing in the land of the stars—/Had come into Paradise. (Children's folk song from Lausanne.)

[†]Trains at this date often had mail cars with mailboxes on their sides.

therefore *hasn't* any, but, not to be too pedantic: something about sleeping, yours and mine (*et le lit—table évanouie . . .*[3]*). A bed—in order to see miracles, to divine things; a table—in order to do them, to bring them about. Bed: back; table: elbow. Man *is* bed and table, therefore doesn't need to *have* any.

(The other letter sounded quite different, and the train that . . . carries and buries it howled and whistled differently from a passenger train; if I could hear it, I would know at once whether the letter was still inside.)

Dear Rainer, Boris has stopped writing to me. In his last letter he wrote: All inside me that is not will is yours and is called you. —Will means his wife and his son, who are now abroad. When I learned about this second Abroad of his, I wrote: Two letters from abroad—don't do it! There are no two Abroads. Abroad and inland—yes. *I* am Abroad! I *am* and I will not share it.

Let his wife write to him and he to her. To sleep with her and write to me—all right; write to her and write to me, two envelopes, two addresses (in one France), to *become sisters* through the handwriting . . . him for a brother—yes, her for a sister—no.

That's how I am, Rainer, every human relationship an island, and always sunken—head, hide, and hair.

To me in the human being belong brow and some chest; heart I yield readily. Chest I begrudge. I need a vault to resound in; heart sounds muffled.

Rainer, write me a postcard, just two words: train letter received—or not received. Then I'll write you a long letter.

Rainer, this winter we must get together, somewhere in French Savoy, close to Switzerland, somewhere you have never been. (Or is there such a never? Doubt it.) In a tiny little town, Rainer. For as long as you like; for as briefly as you like. I write this quite simply because I know that you will

---

*And the bed—a vanished table (reference to a passage in Rilke's French verse).

not only love me very much but also take great joy in me. (Joy—attractive to you, too.)

Or in the autumn, Rainer. Or early in the year. Say yes, so I may have great joy from this day on, something to scan the future for (looking back to?).* Because it is very late and I am very tired, I embrace you.

MARINA

RILKE TO TSVETAYEVA

HÔTEL HOF-RAGAZ
RAGAZ (CANTON DE H. GALL)
SUISSE
AUGUST 19, 1926

The train, Marina, this train (with your last letter) of which you conceived a belated mistrust, steamed off breathlessly in my direction; the sinister mailbox was old, as camels and crocodiles are old, sheltered from its youth by being old: most dependable quality. Yes and yes and yes, Marina, all yeses to what you want and are, together as large as YES to life itself . . . : but contained in the latter there are, after all, all those ten thousand noes, the unforeseeable ones.

If I am less sure of its being vouchsafed to us to be like two layers, two strata, densely delicate, two halves of a nest—how much I would like to recall now the Russian for nest (forgotten)!—of the sleep nest, in which a great bird, a raptor of the spirit (no blinking!), settles . . . if I am less sure (than you) . . . (is it due to the oddly persistent affliction I am going through and often feel hardly likely to get over, so that I now expect the things to come to be not themselves but a precise and specific aid, an assistance made to measure?) . . . for all that, I am no less (no: all the more) in need of for once

_____
*Past is still ahead . . . [M. Ts.]⁴

restoring, up-hauling myself in just this way out of the depths, out of the well of wells. But fear in between of the many days until then, with their repetitions; fear (suddenly) of the contingencies, which know nothing of this and cannot be informed.

... Not into the winter! ...

"You don't need to answer" is how you closed your letter. *Could* not answer, perhaps: for who knows, Marina, didn't my answering come to pass *before* your asking? In Val-Mont that time I looked for it on the maps—*cette petite ville en Savoye**—and now you pronounce it! Move it out of time, take it for granted, as if it had already been. I thought as I was reading you—and right then there it was, your writing in the right margin—"Past is still ahead...." (Magical line, but in so anxious a context.)

Now forget, dear one, blindly trusting, what was asked and answered there; place it (whatever it may be allowed to become) under the protection, under the power of the joy you bring, which I need, which I may bring if you start off the bringing (which has already been done).

That Boris is keeping silent concerns and distresses me; so it actually was my advent, after all, that came to lodge itself athwart the great current of his outpouring to you? And although I understand what you say of the two "Abroads" (which preclude each other), I still find you stern, almost harsh toward him (and stern toward me, if you like, in that Russia must never and nowhere exist for me except through you!). Rebellious against any exclusion (which grows out of the love root and hardens into wood): do you recognize me like this, like this, *too*?

RAINER

---

*That little town in Savoy.

TSVETAYEVA TO RILKE

Rainer, just always say yes to all that I want—it won't turn
out so badly, after all. Rainer, if I say to you that I am your
Russia, I'm only saying (one more time) that I care for you.
Love lives on exceptions, segregations, exclusiveness. Love
lives on words and dies of deeds. Too intelligent, I, really
to try to be Russia for you! A manner of speaking. A manner
of loving.

Rainer, my name has changed: all that you are, all that *is*
you. (To *be* is to be lived. *Être vécu. Chose vecue.* Passive.)

Do you imagine that I believe in Savoy? Oh, yes, like
yourself, as in the kingdom of heaven. Some time . . . (how?
when?). What have I seen of life? Throughout my youth
(from 1917 on)—black toil. Moscow? Prague? Paris? St.-Gilles?
Same thing. Always stove, broom, money (none). Never any
time. No woman among your acquaintances and friends lives
like that, would be capable of living so. Not to sweep any
more—of that is my kingdom of heaven. Plain enough? Yes,
because my soil is poor enough! (Rainer, when I wrote in German *"fegen—Fegfeuer"**—that magnificent word—sweeping
here, purgatory there, swept right into the middle of purgatory, etc., *that's* how I write, from the word to the thing, re-
creating the words poetically. This is how you write, I think.)

So, dear one, don't be afraid, simply answer yes to every
"Give"—a beggar's comfort, innocent, without consequences.
Most of the time my begging hand drops away—along with
the gift—into the sand. What do I want from you? What I
want from all of poetry and from each line of a poem: the
truth of this moment. That's as far as truth goes. Never turns

---

* *Fegfeuer*, Luther's word for "purgatory," means literally "fire (*feuer*) to sweep (*fegen*) one clean."

to wood—always to ashes. The word, which for me already is the thing, is all I want. Actions? Consequences?

I know you, Rainer, as I know myself. The farther from me—the further *into* me. I live not in myself, but outside myself. I do not live in my lips, and he who kisses me misses *me*.

Savoy. (Pause for thought.) Train. Ticket. Place to stay. (Praise God, no visa!) And . . . faint distaste. Something prepared, won in battle . . . begged for. I want *you* to fall from heaven.

Rainer, quite seriously: if you want to see me, with your eyes, *you* must act—"In two weeks I'll be at such-and-such a place. Are you coming?" This must come from you. Like the date. Like the town. Look at the map. Perhaps it must be a large town? Give it some thought. Little towns are sometimes misleading. Oh, yes, one more thing: I haven't any money; the little I earn by my work (because of my "newness" printed only in the "newer" monthlies, of which in the emigration there are only two)—vanishes as soon as it is received. I wonder if you'll have enough for both of us. Rainer, as I write this I have to laugh: a strange sort of guest!

Well, then, dear one, when at some point you really want to, you write to me (a little beforehand, for I have to find somebody to stay with the children)—and I'll come. I am staying at St.-Gilles until October 1–15. Then to Paris, where I start from scratch: no money, no apartment, nothing. I'm not going back to Prague, the Czechs are angry with me for having written so much and so ardently about Germany and having been so firmly silent about Bohemia. And after all, having been subsidized by the Czechs for three and a half years (900 kronen monthly). So, some time between October 1 and 15, to Paris. We won't get together before November. But surely, it could also be somewhere in the South? (Meaning France.) Where, how, and when (from November on) you like. Placed into your hands. You can, after all . . . part them. I shall never love you more or less in any case.

I am looking forward to you *terribly*, as to a whole *totally* new realm.

About Boris. No, I was in the right. His answer was that of an Atlas liberated. (He, remember, carried a heaven with all its inhabitants! And, rid of his burden, he, too, sighed, it seems to me.) Now he is rid of me. Too good-natured, too compassionate, too patient. The blow had to come from me (nobody likes to terminate, to kill!). He already knew about the two Abroads. All I did was speak up, name things, break the spell. Now everything is all right, the realms separated: I in the innermost self—outermost foreign place—quite out of the world.

"Nest" in Russian is *gnezdó*, singular (nothing rhymes with it!), plural *gnëzda* (*e* soft in pronunciation, ë, almost *o*), rhymes with *zvëzdy*—stars.

How much longer are you staying in Ragaz and how do you feel? What is the last thing you've written?

Oh, yes, a big request. Make me a present of a Greek mythology (in German)—without philosophy, quite simple and detailed: myths. I think in my childhood I had a book by Stoll. My *Theseus* is coming out soon (Part I: "Theseus and Ariadne," dramatic poem). Now I'm starting on a "Phaedra" (the whole is meant as a triology: Ariadne—Phaedra—Helen) and I need a mythology. Aphrodite's hatred—that is the leit-motif. What a pity that you cannot read me! I before you— deaf mute (not deaf, really, but mute!).

Do give me the myths by Stoll, and with an inscription so that I'll *never* part from the book. Will you?

I take you in my arms.

M.

St. Gall—St. Gilles . . .*

---

*Ragaz is in the canton of St. Gall.

Tsvetayeva did not understand that Rilke was mortally ill; indeed, the seriousness of his illness was kept a secret even from those who were closest to him.

He went from Ragaz to Ouchy, near Lausanne. On the way he visited Paul Valéry on the border of Savoy and returned to Sierre at the beginning of October, where he put up at the Hôtel Bellevue. Yevgenia Chernosvitova, a Russian girl who had just graduated from the philology department of Lausanne University, became his secretary. Rilke told friends who were visiting him that her presence brought back memories and impressions of his early youth, and that at his request she was reading to him in Russian the memoirs of Sergei Volkonsky.*

Rilke did not answer Tsvetayeva's last letter. Taking his silence to mean she had lost him, she sent him a postcard (addressed to Muzot) with a view of the Paris suburb of Bellevue, to which she had moved from the Vendée in mid-September.

TSVETAYEVA TO RILKE

BELLEVUE (S. ET O.)
PRÈS DE PARIS
31, BOULEVARD VERD
NOVEMBER 7, 1926

Dear Rainer,

This is where I live.

—I wonder if you still love me?

MARINA

---

*See footnote on p. 139.

EPILOGUE

PASTERNAK worked intensely on *Lieutenant Schmidt*, not knowing whether Rilke and Tsvetayeva were still writing to each other and keeping up the friendship he had initiated. He was constantly tortured by the artificial situation he had created in failing to answer the letter in which Rilke had given him his blessing as a poet. This can be seen in his correspondence with his sister and her husband, who were then traveling in Switzerland:

I have received your short messages written en route. Thanks for remembering me. Glion, Territet—these, I believe, are the names of places where Rilke has lived or visited! My heart is full not of guilt, or shame, or remorse, but of grief. I have never responded, that is, have never sent a reply to his letter to me of early May! Everything has become too terribly mixed up.

In the middle of November, Leonid Pasternak unexpectedly received a letter and a small photograph from Rilke's secretary, Yevgenia Chernosvitova, in answer to his request of April 30 to know how much Rilke had changed in the fifteen years since they had last met.

———

YEVGENIA CHERNOSVITOVA TO
LEONID PASTERNAK

CHÂTEAU BELLEVUE, SIERRE
NOVEMBER 15, 1926

My esteemed Leonid Osipovich,

May I address you in this way? Only yesterday I learned your patronymic—Rainer Maria Rilke told it to me. He is your friend—and mine a little, too—and I am writing to you in the name of our common love of him and his great, pure, and profound poetry.

At the end of your letter, which he gave me to read, you spoke of the recent portraits of him you had seen, which did not satisfy you. A few weeks ago I took five or six photographs of him here in Sierre and am sending the one I consider best. Do you recognize Rainer Maria Rilke?

Your letter glows with the love you bear the poet, your admiration for him, and your joy in discovering that he is still alive. Anyone who reads it must be aware of your deep and sincere feeling. It has made me want to hold out my hand to you and share your joy. One can feel that it was written by a Russian to the poet who stands closer to Russia than any other contemporary European poet.

A few weeks ago I learned through Princess Gorchakova that Rainer Maria Rilke was looking for a secretary, and a Russian one at that! That is how fate directed me to him—a kind, gracious, wonderful fate!

Forgive me for writing so much in a first letter.

Monsieur Rilke has asked me to send you his regards, to thank you for your last letter, and to forgive him for his silence, the cause of which is a persistent, prolonged, and inexplicable ailment.

Most cordially,
YEVGENIA CHERNOSVITOVA

Leonid Pasternak sent this photograph and news of Rilke to his son in Moscow, asking that he return the photograph.

The year 1926 ended. One of the first pieces of news the new year brought was the following letter, which broke a long period of silence.

TSVETAYEVA TO PASTERNAK

BELLEVUE
DECEMBER 31, 1926

Boris,

Rainer Maria Rilke has died. I don't know the date—three days ago.* Some people came to invite me to a New Year's party and at the same time gave me this information.

His last letter to me (September 6) ended with the cry: "*Im Frühling? Mir ist lang. Eher! Eher!*"† (We had planned to meet.) He didn't answer my answer. Then I wrote him a single line from Bellevue: "*Rainer, was ist? Rainer, liebst Du mich noch?*"‡

Tell Svetlov of *Molodaya Gvardia* that his "Granada"§ is my favorite—I almost said it is the best poem that has been written in recent years. Yesenin hasn't done anything to equal it. But don't tell him that; let Yesenin sleep in peace.

---

*Rilke died on December 29.

†In the spring? Late for me. Sooner! Sooner! (Tsvetayeva is misquoting a sentence from Rilke's last letter to her [August 19]: "...Not into the winter!...")

‡Rainer, what is it? Rainer, do you love me still? (See Tsvetayeva's November 7 postcard to Rilke, also misquoted.)

§Mikhail Svetlov (1903–64): Soviet poet; his "Granada" was published in *Komsomolskaya Pravda*, August 29, 1926.

Will we ever see each other?

Happy New Era, Boris!—*His* Era!

M.

This news signaled the collapse of Pasternak's spiritual world, the destruction of his best hopes and plans. Without answering Tsvetayeva, he wrote to his sister:

> Zhonichka darling, Tsvetayeva wrote me that Rilke had died, but she did it in an offhand way as if the facts were known to everybody. How did it happen and what do you know about it? There is no need to tell you what I felt on reading it. I nurtured the hope of going to see him in Switzerland and lived by this hope.

The next day another letter came from Tsvetayeva.

TSVETAYEVA TO PASTERNAK

BELLEVUE

JANUARY 1, 1927

You are the first to whom
I have written this date.

Boris, he died December 30, not 31. Just one more of life's ironies. Life's last petty revenge on a poet.

Boris, we will never go and see Rilke. That city doesn't exist any more.

Boris, the cost of a Russian passport has been reduced (I read that last night). And last night (New Year's Eve) I dreamed about an ocean liner (I was on it) and a train. That means you will come to me and we will go together to London. Build your plans on London—on London, I tell you; I have long believed in London. Remember the birds on the ceiling and the blizzards on the other side of the Moscow River?

Never before have I sent for you; now the time has come. We will be alone in that enormous London. Your town and mine. We will go to the zoo. And to the Tower (now a barracks). In front of the Tower there is a steep little square, quite empty, only a single cat underneath a bench. We will sit there. Soldiers will be drilling on the big square.

How odd! Just after I had written you those lines about London I went into the kitchen and my neighbor (two families live here) said to me, "I just received a letter from . . ." (she mentioned a name I had never heard). "What's the postmark?" "London."

And earlier today, when I was taking Mur for a walk (New Year's Day, the streets are empty), I was amazed to see that the tops of the trees were *red*! Why? Young shoots (of immortality).

See, Boris?—If the three of us had remained alive, nothing would have come of it. I know myself: I couldn't have helped kissing his hands, couldn't have helped it even in front of you, even in front of myself, almost. I would have balked and kicked and struggled free, Boris, because, after all, it is still *this world*. Oh, Boris, Boris! How well I know the other one! From dreams, from the ambient air of dreams, from the density, the essentiality of dreams. And how little I know of this one, how much I dislike it, and how hurt I have been by it! But the other one—just fancy!—light, radiance, things illuminated quite *differently*, with your light and mine!

"*The other world*." As long as this idea remains, people will remain. But it is not about people I am thinking now.

About him. His last book was written in French: *Vergers*. He was weary of his native tongue:

> Tired of you, my foes, of you, my friends,
> And of the pliancy of Russian speech . . .
>
> 1916[1]

He was weary of his virtuosity, he wanted to learn all over again, so he seized upon the language least congenial to a poet—French (*poésie*)—and again he could do it, was doing it, was suddenly weary again. The trouble, it seems, lay not in the language but in the man. What he took to be a longing for French was a longing for the language of angels, the language of the other world. In *Vergers* he speaks in the language of angels.

See, he is an angel. I feel his presence always at my *right* shoulder (which is not *my* side).

I am happy, Boris, that the last word he heard from me was "Bellevue." His first word as he gazed down upon the earth.

It is terribly important that you come here.

In Tsvetayeva's notebooks there is a notation relating to the end of this letter:

—Rilke's death: December 29, 1926.

I'm glad that the last thing he heard from me was: *Belle-vue*. He, who so loved the landscapes of France. Bellevue —in the name of my little town is his entire first view of the earth from there. Now that is a Belle Vue![2]

Tsvetayeva was playing off the name of the town near Paris where she lived, a postcard of which she had sent Rilke

on November 7. In French Bellevue means "beautiful view."
In the same envelope Tsvetayeva put a letter she had written
to Rilke in German after his death.[3]

TSVETAYEVA TO RILKE

BELLEVUE
DECEMBER 31, 1926. 10 P.M.

The year ended in your death? The end? The beginning! You
yourself are the New Year. (Beloved, I know you are reading
this before I write it.) I am crying, Rainer, you are streaming
from my eyes!

Dear one, now that you are dead there is no death (or no
life!). What can I say? That little town in Savoy—when?
where? Rainer, what about that "nest" to keep our dreams
in? Now Russian is an open book to you, so you know that
the Russian word for "nest" is *gnezdó*. And you know so
many other things.

I don't want to reread your letter or I will want to join
you—there—and I dare not wish for such a thing. You know
what such a wish implies.

Rainer, I am always conscious of your presence at my
shoulder.

Did you ever think of me? Yes, of course you did.

Tomorrow is New Year's Day, Rainer. 1927. Seven is your
favorite number.* You were born in 1875 (newspaper date?).
Fifty-one years old?

How disconsolate I am!

Don't dare to grieve! At midnight tonight I will drink with
you (you know how I clink glasses—ever so lightly!).

Beloved, come to me often in my dreams. No, not that.

---

*See Rilke's letter of May 10.

Live in my dreams. Now you have a right to wish and to fulfill your wishes.

You and I never believed in our meeting here on earth, any more than we believed in life on this earth, isn't that so? You have gone before me (and that is better!), and to receive me well you have taken not a room, not a house, but a whole landscape. I kiss you . . . on the lips? on the temple? on the forehead? Of course on the lips, for real, as if alive.

Beloved, love me more and differently from others. Don't be angry with me. You must grow accustomed to me, to such a one as I am. What else?

No, you are not yet far away and high above, you are right here, with your head on my shoulder. You will never be far away: never inaccessibly high.

You are my darling grown-up boy.

Rainer, write to me! (A foolish request?)

Happy New Year and may you enjoy the heavenly landscape!

MARINA

Rainer, you are still on this earth; twenty-four hours have not yet passed.

Pasternak did not answer that letter, either. At the end of January he heard from his father, who enclosed a letter Chernosvitova had written in reply to his request to know the details of Rilke's illness and death.

JANUARY 19, 1927

The death of our dear Rainer Maria Rilke came so unexpectedly that I was prostrated at first. Only a few weeks before that I had received from his secretary a cordial letter and the photograph I sent you. (Incidentally, you don't have to return the photo. I asked her

for another and she has kindly sent it.) In her last letter
she informed me of the cause of his death: leukemia.
A few lines in your last letter (the one Zhenya brought)
revealed your despondency. I appreciate the extent of
your loss, but you must not let everything hang on this
("life has lost its meaning," etc.). That is going too far;
knowing you, I fear you will give yourself up to excessive grief and let yourself go. . . .

YEVGENIA CHERNOSVITOVA TO
LEONID PASTERNAK

BEAUVALLON, GOLF HOTEL
JANUARY 11, 1927

My esteemed Leonid Osipovich,

This time I have a terrible message. The illness (in viru-
lent form) developed with lightning speed even though it
lasted several weeks. We could not believe it when the end
came.

You ask what the illness was. In French it is called *"leu-
cémie."* It is the transformation of red blood corpuscles into
white ones, a pathological process that occurs suddenly and
unpredictably and is incurable. Doctors can do nothing to
stop the process, they can only try to relieve, if ever so
slightly, the patient's suffering. Poor Rainer Maria Rilke
suffered terribly, especially during the last days, in Sierre,
where we lived until November 31 [*sic*]. In the clinic ("Val-
Mont," above Montreux) they were able to reduce the pain
somewhat, and, thanks to the Heavenly Father, his end came
quietly. He is buried in a little cemetery in the mountains of
his beloved Valais, not far from the Château de Muzot,
where, in complete solitude, he spent so many quiet winters
and hot summers.

You know only too well what his loss means to us and to mankind. I cannot express in words what it means to me personally.

His *attitude* toward death and the future life was calm and full of faith. I firmly believe that his soul is here, with us, closer to us than in life.

As you see, I am writing from France, where *he* wanted me to be. At present I am living with Princesse de Bassiano, Rilke's friend, to whom he recommended me and who asked me to come and stay with her children for two months. My address is: Golf Hotel, Beauvallon par-St.-Maxime (Var).

I was able to read your last letter to our friend. I am sending you another copy of the photograph. He himself thought it the best, so I would rather send you another copy of the same one than send a worse likeness. May all of us who loved him be ennobled and drawn closer together by our common grief.

My greetings to you and your family, even though I have not met them. Tell your son Boris that R.M.R. loved him well, often spoke of him and you, and fondly recalled the times he spent with you.

Cordially,
Yevgenia Chernosvitova

P.S. Please be so kind as to give me the address of your son (the poet) in Moscow. Princesse de Bassiano publishes a journal in Paris called *Commerce*, in which some poems by your son (translated into French) were printed a few months ago. The princesse would like to send your son a remuneration but doesn't know how to do it: send it directly to him in Moscow, or through a bank, or perhaps through you? I will wait for your instructions in this matter.

———

A little later Tsvetayeva sent Pasternak a letter from Svyatopolk-Mirsky. On the envelope she wrote a brief note.

TSVETAYEVA TO PASTERNAK

JANUARY 12, 1927

Dear Boris,

I am forwarding a letter from Mirsky, to whom I did not give your address, and I beg you not to do so. The reason is superstitious (the Evil Eye and the like), but it is valid, take my word for it. If you feel uncomfortable about writing through me, about using my address (N.B.: the best thing would be: I jam your messages)—then give him the address of the Writers' Union or the Poets' Union or some other social organization. He yearns to have your private address and is so insistent that *he must not get it under any circumstances*. Moreover, 14 Volkhonka Street, Apt. 9, is *mine* and I don't mean to *share* it with anyone. When I see you I will tell you everything and you will understand.

At present it is enough to say that when he came to see me a few days ago I spread my hand over Rilke's picture in the newspaper. Your Volkhonka Street and Rilke's face are of the same order.

Don't betray me.

I embrace you and await your letter,

M.

I am deliberately writing on his letter so as to seal the desire (his to get your address; *yours* to give it to him).

In mid-January, Chernosvitova wrote Tsvetayeva that at last she was sending her the volume of Greek mythology that Rilke had ordered for her. She also sent her a photograph of Rilke (on the balcony at Muzot)—"his last gift." Tsvetayeva answered with a detailed letter, the text of which was reconstructed by Ariadna Efron from the notebooks.

TSVETAYEVA TO
YEVGENIA CHERNOSVITOVA

Dear friend,

I am answering while still under the shock of your letter.

I heard about Rilke's death on the 31st, New Year's Eve, from a chance acquaintance—heard it with my ears, with just my ears, which is to say it went past my ears. Comprehension came later, if the defiant, determined refusal to recognize a thing can be called "comprehending" it. Your letter found me in the middle of writing a difficult letter to him—an impossible one, because everything had to be said. Since the 31st of December I have lived with this letter; for its sake I dropped "Phaedra" (Part II of *Theseus*, conceived as a trilogy—but because of superstition...). I fear I will never finish this letter because when "the news" makes itself felt...I am also deterred by its openness (the letter's). An open letter from me to him. (You knew him and perhaps you will come to know me.) A letter that will be read by everybody—but him. On the other hand, perhaps he will write part of it, will prompt what is to be said. Would you like to know a certain thing about poetry? Every line is a collaboration with "higher forces," and a poet is doing *very well* if he acts as a good secretary. Have you ever considered the beauty of that word: secretary (from "secret")?

Rilke's role has changed only in that while he was alive

he collaborated with "a higher power" and now he himself is that power.

Please don't see this as Russian mysticism. We are talking about earthly things. The most divine inspiration isn't worth a fig if it isn't applied to earthly activity.

I am interested in knowing how you found out my address.

I only wrote him once from Bellevue—a postcard addressed to Muzot without any return address. He did not answer my last letter (from the Vendée). I sent it to Ragaz; do you know whether he ever got it? Another question: did he ever mention my name, and if he did—when and in what circumstances? Not so long ago I wrote to Boris Pasternak in Moscow, "I have lost Rilke at some turn in the road through the Alps. . . ."

This brings me to the most important thing. You lived beside him for two months, and he died only two weeks ago. Take upon yourself an enormous and heroic task: reconstruct those two months from the first second of your acquaintance, from the first impression—his appearance, his voice, etc. Get a special notebook and write down everything—at first haphazardly, every word, mannerism, trifle. When you begin to write consecutively everything will fall into place. It will be a sort of diary—two months late. Begin at once. If you have no time during the day, write at night. Don't succumb to the holy feeling of jealousy; renunciation (of self, of me, of mine) is more holy. Remember Eckermann's book, the only one of the many written about Goethe that gives us the live poet.

I am afraid I will cry when I receive the mythology book. So far I haven't shed a single tear—no time, no place (always people around), and, to be perfectly honest, no wish to cry. A wish *not* to cry. Crying is acceptance. As long as I don't cry he hasn't died.

I never saw him; for me this is a loss—in the spirit (does

273

that make sense?). For you it is a loss of what was; for me, of what was not. The loss of Savoy, to which I shall never go now; on December 31 it vanished from the earth along with all the Alps.... For some time I shall have no desire to look at a map—or at anything else.

To all of this add the fact that I do not belong to any church whatsoever.... [At this point the entries in Tsvetayeva's notebook break off.]

———

On February 5 Pasternak received from Tsvetayeva a description of Rilke's funeral taken from a French newspaper.

Two days earlier, Pasternak had written to Tsvetayeva again. The letter begins:

Dear friend,

I will write you this one chance letter, and then I will be silent again. But I cannot treat your endurance lightly. Snow was coming down in shaggy black flakes on the fogged windowpanes when the news of his death reached me. What is there to say? I became physically ill. It was as if I had fallen into space and hung there while life passed me by. For some days we did not hear or comprehend each other. Just at that time terrible cold set in—fierce, frenzied cold, raised to an almost cosmic degree. Can you imagine our orphaning in all of its *brutality*? No, I don't believe you can, and a very good thing: too great a feeling of helplessness is debasing. Yet all things have lost their value for me.

Well, let us live a long, long time, a defiantly long time; that is your duty and mine.

———

TSVETAYEVA TO PASTERNAK

Dear Boris,

Your letter is an excuse for a letter; that is, it was written with a high sense of decorum struggling against a secret reluctance to write. Secret? Not secret at all, once you say in the very first line, "... and then I will be silent again."

Such a letter does not break a silence, it emphasizes it, names it. I am not aware that there ever was such a letter. Therefore, everything is as it should be, and I am as I should be, stubbornly insisting that we continue a relationship underwritten by Rilke's death. His death authorizes my right to be with you—more than a right, a command signed by his own hand.

I did not feel the brutality. Your "orphaning in all of its *brutality*" echoes the first lines I wrote after hearing the news:

> The twenty-ninth, on Wednesday, a misty sky?
> A brilliant one? No contest, done!
> For orphaned were not only you and I
> That next to the last but one
> Of mornings ...

You will discover what I felt from a letter to him I finished yesterday (the 7th, his day) and began on the 31st (the day I got the news). Since it is deeply personal, please don't show it to anyone.[4] I consider it sacrilege to place Rilke's name next to Mayakovsky's, notwithstanding all (?) the love (?) I bear the latter. Sacrilege, I determined long ago, means hierarchical incongruity.

Boris, here is an important announcement that I have long wanted to make. The poem about you and me (the beginning of "Attempt at a Room") turned out to be a poem about him and me, *every line of it*. A most astonishing substitution took place: I wrote it at the peak of my concentration on him, but my mind and will were directed toward you. It turns out that I wrote too little not only about him—about him now (*after* December 29)—about his prescience, his divine insight. I simply told him, the live Rilke, whom I was expecting to see soon, why we had never met, why we had met in a *different* way. This explains the lovelessness, the detachment, the *rejection* felt in every line; even then it caused me strange discomfiture. The poem is called "Attempt at a Room" and my soul's rejection of it is felt in every line—yes, every single one. Read it attentively, deep into it. Verify it. I wrote three things this summer:

(1) "Instead of a Letter"* (to you), (2) "Attempt at a Room," and (3) "Stairs"—this last to free myself here, in time, from total absorption in him, but because of him, me, the life we still had, and (what turned out to be!) the death tomorrow was to bring, this proved to be futile. You have probably read "Stairs," because Asya has. Get it from her and correct the typographical errors.

And get the second issue of *Versty* from Zelinsky if he is still in Moscow, or else order it. It contains my *Theseus*, Part I, a tragedy. I began the second part this autumn but interrupted it to write the letter to Rilke, which I finished only last night (in deep depression).

Thanks for admiring Mur.† Flattering (to my heart). Oh, yes, in your letter you speak of "phantom sound," and in *Theseus*

---

*The original title of "From the Seaside," dated May 1926. For the other two poems, see footnote on p. 219.

†During the summer of 1926 Ilya Ehrenburg had brought to Moscow and shown to Pasternak a photograph of Tsvetayeva's son; in his letter to her of February 3, 1927, Pasternak called Mur "Napoleonid," a nickname Tsvetayeva repeated thereafter with pride.

I have: "The phantom, joyous sound of play." What force the word "phantom" acquires with a sound accompaniment, what force is exerted by a phantom sound; have you considered it?

The last stage on your path to him is to write him a letter—an open one, of course—to teach the critic* to observe rank, and the prince, courtesy. (Note on rank: where a poet and a critic are involved, there can be no secrets from the poet. I never mention names, but in this instance ours obviously fit.) It goes without saying that I will not read your open letter.

   Oh, yes; here is the most important thing. Last night (February 8) I had my first dream of him in which "not everything about him was a dream"; indeed, *nothing* was. I had been unable to sleep, I read, then for some reason decided to sleep with the light on. Scarcely had I closed my eyes when Alya (we sleep together, and sometimes Mur sleeps with us) said, "There's a silver head between us." Silver is metal, so I understood her to mean not silver but gray. We were in a big hall. The floor was bristling with candlesticks and candelabra. I was wearing a long dress and had to avoid catching my skirts on them as I ran through the hall. The dance of the candlesticks. I wove in and out among them. Many people were wearing black. I recognized Rudolf Steiner[†] (I had seen him once in Prague) and guessed that I was at a meeting of devotees. I went up to a gentleman sitting in an armchair off to one side. I looked into his face. He said with a smile, "Rainer Maria Rilke." I replied, somewhat flippantly and reproachfully, *"Ich weiss!"*[‡] I withdrew, came back again, looking about me: everyone was dancing. I waited until he had finished talking, or, rather, listening to what someone

---

*Prince Svyatopolk-Mirsky.

[†]Founder of anthroposophy (1861–1925).

[‡]I know!

was telling him (I recall that it was an ecstatic elderly lady in a brown dress); then I took his hand and led him away. More about the hall: it was brightly lighted, not at all gloomy, and all the people were lively, even though their faces were grave. The men were wearing frock coats as they used to do, and the women, mostly elderly, were in dark gowns. There were more men than women. And some priests of uncertain persuasion.

We went into another room, a drawing room. Friends; acquaintances. General conversation. In a far corner stood a young man; next to him—the one we are talking about. On my knees I held an iron pot with something boiling in it. I threw a chip into the pot (symbolic of a ship and the sea). "Look! And after this people dare to set out to sea!" He: "Oh, but I love the sea, my sea, the Geneva sea." (I to myself: "How pointed, how personal, how like Rilke!") Then: "The Geneva sea, of course, but I hate real seas, especially the ocean. At St.-Gilles..." And he, *mit Nachdruck**: "*Everything* is wonderful at St.-Gilles," clearly identifying St.-Gilles and life (as he did, by the way, once before, in one of his letters; "St.-Gilles-sur-vie—survit").† I: "How can you not understand my poetry when you speak Russian so beautifully?" He: "Now." (When you read "A Letter" you will appreciate the naïveté of my question and the explicitness of his answer.) While still speaking to him (he with his head half turned to me): "Your acquaintance..." without naming him, without revealing him. In a word, I visited with Rilke and he with me.

Conclusion: If it is possible to have such a calm, fearless, natural, noncorporeal feeling for "the dead," then this is a fact, and this is what we will experience in the other world.

---

*Emphatically.

†For the exact quote, see Rilke's letter of May 10, 1926.

What, then, are we afraid of? Of being afraid. I was *not* afraid. On the contrary, for the first time in my life I rejoiced to see the dead. And one other thing: awareness of the body's disintegration (when there is such an awareness) is probably related to the (approximate) length of time disintegration takes, yet Rudolf Steiner, for instance, died two years ago, and he is not dead at all, in no way, and never will be.

I accept this dream as a gift from Rilke, as was the whole of yesterday (the 7th, his date), which gave me solutions for *all* (about 30) of the impossible, the seemingly unsolvable problems in "A Letter." The answers all came to me at once, without the least effort.

I know from experience that there are frustrating, intractable, impossible lines in a poem to which you become *tone-deaf.* And lo and behold! I coped with 24 such lines in one day! Never before has this happened.

I live with him and by him. I am deeply concerned about the distance between our heavens—his and mine. Mine can be no higher than the third, whereas his, I fear, is the last, which means I will have to come back many, many times and he not more than once. All my labors and concerns are now concentrated on one thing: not to miss that once (his last).

The brutality of orphaning. Against a background of what? The tenderness of fatherhood, of sonship?

This is the first time the best *for me* and the best *on this earth* have coincided. Is it not but natural that he should have gone? How do *you* regard life? For you his death is not in the natural order of things. For me his life is not in the natural order of things, is in a different order, is itself a different order.

Ah, but here is the main thing. How could you have made the focal point of your letter the temporary divergence of our ways—yours and mine—for an hour, a year, ten years—instead of the lasting separation from him for all of our lives, for all of this world. In a word, you began with the last line of your last letter instead of with the first line of mine (of the 31st). Your letter is a continuation. Isn't that strange? Can there be any continuance now? Can't you see, Boris, that the divergence of our ways or any other personal thing in our lifetime has now been reduced to nothing. Then, he "hoped," "wanted," "resolved"; now: all is over.

Or perhaps you did it intentionally? The unconscious fear of suffering? Then remember his *Leid*,* recall the sound of the word, and transfer it to me, who after *such* a loss remains invulnerable to anything except another such loss. What I want to say is, Don't be afraid to be silent, don't be afraid to write, none of that matters as long as you are alive.

Did you receive the description of his funeral? I learned a little about his death: he died in the morning, quietly, I am told, without a word, with three sighs, as if he was unaware of dying (oh, I believe that!). Soon I shall see the Russian girl who was his secretary for the last two months. Oh, yes—two weeks later I received a gift from him—a German mythology published in 1875—the year of his birth. The last book he read was Paul Valéry† (remember my dream?).

We are terribly crowded here—two families in one apartment, sharing the kitchen, the three of us in one room; I am never alone; I am miserable.

Who of the Russian poets (we have none here) mourns him? Did you give my regards to the author of "Granada"? (I forget his name.)

---

* Suffering.

† *L'Âme et la danse* (The Soul and the Dance).

> Oh yes, a new song,
> Oh yes, a new mood.
> No need, guys, to brood
> For lack of a song.
>
> No need to, no need to,
> No need, friends, to pine!
> Granada, Granada, Granada of mine.*

The émigré press is harassing *Versty*. Lots of people don't even speak to us. Khodasevich especially. If you are interested I will write you more about it.

———

At this point Tsvetayeva for the first time actually discussed "Attempt at a Room," though she had referred to it in her letters throughout the summer. She sent the poem to Pasternak in her next letter, and he received it on February 20, 1927. Two days later he wrote that he recognized certain details taken from their correspondence in the spring. No doubt he was alluding, among other things, to the dream about Marina he had described in his letter of April 20, 1926: "a bright, immaculate hotel without bedbugs and away from everyday life."

> Both in the dream and in the wall, floor, and ceiling analogies of existence, that is, in the anthropomorphic similarity of the air and hour—you were Tsvetayeva, that is, you were the language found by everything to which the poet addresses himself his whole life without the hope of receiving an answer.

———

*Tsvetayeva was misquoting the last lines of Mikhail Svetlov's "Granada."

Tsvetayeva, having suffered in silence as she waited four months for Rilke's reply, accepted his death as the culmination of all the misery resulting from the postponement of their meeting. The belief that Rilke had not wanted to meet her now gave way to the fateful recognition that he could never meet her: "Then, he 'hoped,' 'wanted,' 'resolved'; now: all is over."

With her characteristic tendency to pit this world against the other, and to reject this world in favor of that other, Tsvetayeva adopted a spiritual outlook apparently based on the anthroposophical conception of the reincarnation of the soul. This gave her the hope of yet meeting Rilke.

Since Tsvetayeva thought that Rilke's death had brought him closer to her, she felt no "brutality of orphaning." Her loss had been anticipated and, to some extent, already suffered, as she expressed it in her letter to Chernosvitova of January 15, 1927. The same theme occurred in her prose work "Your Death": "For you were never a part of my life, Rainer, despite Savoy, L'Auberge des Trois Rois, etc. What was part of it? Your going to be, your becoming. *Ob ich an die Savoye glaub? Ja, wie an das Himmelreich, nicht minder, doch nicht anders.** Surely you remember that?"[5] At the same time, she interpreted Rilke's death as giving her the right and even "his own personal command" to realize her union with Pasternak. Recalling the spring, when she had "diverted" his visit to her, she wrote on January 1, 1927, "I never before called you, now the time has come."

Tsvetayeva explained their former misunderstanding, the moment when their paths "diverged," in the fewest possible words: "You see, Boris?—The three of us together, alive, noth-

---

* "Do I believe in Savoy? Yes, as I believe in the kingdom of heaven, not less but no differently." Tsvetayeva was paraphrasing her own letter of August 22, 1926.

ing would have come of it." In verifying a copy of this letter typed by Alexei Kruchyonykh in 1944, Pasternak drew a circle around the words "the three of us together." Such an attitude on Tsvetayeva's part explained to Pasternak why he was excluded from the Rilke-Tsvetayeva correspondence: three bilateral relationships might have been possible, but not one three-sided one.

On February 5, 1928, Tsvetayeva wrote to Leonid Pasternak, "Boris and I intended to go see Rilke together, and we have not abandoned the idea—the grass will not grow over the path leading to his grave; we will not be the first or the last to go there."

In his February letter to Tsvetayeva, Pasternak juxtaposed the names of Rilke and Mayakovsky. He placed Tsvetayeva in the same category. In the spring of 1926 he had written his sister about "Poem of the End": "I have been so deeply affected only by Scriabin, Rilke, Mayakovsky, Cohen." This list was later reflected in the chapters of his autobiographical work *Safe Conduct*. In February 1927 Tsvetayeva found the juxtaposition of Rilke and Mayakovsky blasphemous, a "hierarchical incongruity," though later (in her 1932 essay "The Poet and Time") she paired them in terms of their attitudes toward the contemporary world. For Tsvetayeva, both poets were important for their "timeliness" and both were indispensable to their time.

Tsvetayeva's immediate response to Rilke's death was the poem "A New Year's," and she wrote Pasternak about it, calling it a "Letter." Pasternak received the poem a year later, along with another, "From the Seaside," when Anastasia brought it to him from Paris. "A New Year's" is a kind of requiem, a "lament" for Rilke. The poem sheds light on the real events reflected in Rilke's and Tsvetayeva's last letters. However, reality has been entirely transformed by art. As

Tsvetayeva wrote: "I do not like life itself: for me it begins to be significant, that is, to acquire meaning and weight, when it is transformed, i.e., in art."[6]

On reading "A New Year's," Pasternak wrote to Tsvetayeva:

> What can I say to you, Marina! It is inexpressibly good! I read it the way I once read Blok; the way I read it is the way I once wrote my best work. Terribly heartfelt and sad and transparent. Expression, growing and developing, as always in your work, lives through the coincidence of significance and passion, cognition and emotion.

A NEW YEAR'S[*]

Happy New Year—new world—new home—new roof!
First good wishes to your new abode
(Piously mistermed a welling, lush one[†]—
Belly mush), a place of roar and rushing,
Like a Cavern of the Winds, forsaken.
Your first letter from your newly vacant
Country, where, alone, I eat my heart out,
While to you it is by now a part of
Some star. . . . By the rules of rear-guard battle
Your beloved becomes a never-was, past's chattel,
Where before she was out-of-this-world.
Shall I tell you of . . . yours? How I heard?
Earth shook not below nor avalanche aloft, this

---

[*]The noun one expects to follow this adjectival phrase, *pismo* (letter), *poslaniye* (message), or *stikhotvoreniye* (poem), is not supplied.

[†]A disdainful allusion to the Russian Orthodox burial service, which has the priest chant solace to the mourners: "His/her soul now reposes at the place of fruitfulness, the site of abundance." Tsvetayeva maliciously echoes the phrase with a rhyming one that evokes a complacent, jelly-bellied bourgeoisie.

Man came in—just anyone—(the one I love is
You). "A grave event, indeed, of tragic moment;
Marked by *Novosti* and *Dni** ... You'll comment?"
"Where did ...?" "In the Alps." (Spruce fronds in
    window;
Bed sheet.) "You don't see the press, I think? Oh,
For your piece, then ..." "No." "But ..." "Once for all."
(Loud:) "Too hard for me." (Inside: I? sell out Christ?)
"At that health resort." (Your rented paradise.)
"When?" "Last night; the day before ... I don't recall...."
Coming to the Alcazar?" "I can't."
(Loud:) "My family." (Play Judas? That I shan't.)

Happy Year Ahead (as of tomorrow's nearing)!—
Want to know what *I* did, right after hearing ...?
Tsk ... that came out wrong. My fault of old.
Keeping life and death in quotes, tales told
Consciously by way of idle chatter.
Nothing of my doing, yet some matter
Came to pass that worked without a shadow
Or an echo!
        Now—how did you travel?
How was torn—but not to pieces—your
Heart? As though on Orlov pacers whom
Eagles could not pass (you said!)[†] your breath of
Life was sucked away—or was it better,
Gentler? Heights and depths he pays no heed
Who rides truly Russian eagle steeds.
We have ties of blood to the nether world:
You have been to Russia, saw that world

---

*Émigré Russian newspapers.

[†]Meaning race horses from Court Orlov's famous stables. His name is the same as, and derived from, the possessive adjective of *oryol* (eagle). Evidently Rilke had hit upon this artless pun.

While on this one. What a deft desertion!
I pronounce both "life" and "death" with a cautious
Smile—and you will touch it with your own!
I enounce both "life" and "death" with a starred
Footnote (oh, the night I wake for here:
Leaving this cerebral hemisphere
For a starry one!).

        Dear friend, please don't forget
What I tell you now: if Russian letters
And not German tumbled from my pen,
This is not to signal that by then
Nothing mattered, dead man's (beggar's) lot
Being to eat what comes, unblinking—but rather that
Ours, the nether world, at age thirteen I learned in
Novodevichye,* was omni-, not a-lingual.

Here I ask, then, not without dismay:
Do you ask no longer how to say
"Nest" in Russian? Well, the only rhyme on *gnëzda*
(Covering all kinds of nests) is *zvëzdy*.

I disgress? But when the very idea
Of disgressing from you can't appear!
Every impulse, each *Du Lieber* thought
Leads inside you—and what sense is wrought
(German be more kin to me than Russian,
Next to angel tongues) asserts that room
Is not where you're not, save in the tomb.
All that it was not, and all it was—
"Can it be that no one feels . . . a real . . . ?"†

---

*The convent school Tsvetayeva attended.

†Rilke's voice interrupts Tsvetayeva with a simple earthly plaint: "Isn't anybody (missing) me at all?" She answers, in gently teasing irony, with a picture-postcard inquiry.

What's the place like, Rainer? How do you feel?
Positively, absolutely first
Eye encounter of the universe
(And of course, subsumed within the latter,
Of the poet) and the last with the planet,
Granted you once fully, and never afresh,
Not of bard and barrow, spirit and flesh
(Which to sever would offend the two),
But of you with you, you with the very you,
And—no favors for the seed of Zeus—
Not of Castor-you or Pollux-you,
You-marmoreal with you-who-burgeon,
Is this parting or meeting—but a converging
Eye to eye: both meeting and departing
First of kind.

           How you surveyed then, starting
With your own hand (trace of inkstain on it)
From your ump-(how much?)-teen-mile-high summit
Or unending, for unstarting, height
Poised above the crystal dish of light,
Mediterranean and other silver.
All as it was not, all as it will be
With me, too, beyond the suburb's brow.
All as it was not, and all as it is now,
(Like to one on leave for an out-of-phase
Extra week!)—where else is there to gaze,
Elbow propped upon your box-seat rail,
From *this* world if not at *that* one; from *that* same
Where but at the long-suffering *this*.
Bellevue is where I live. A little place
Made of nests and branches. Quoting the guide:
"Bellevue. Stronghold commanding a splendid sight
Of all Paris; seat of the Gauls' Chimera . . . "
Over Paris—that's the nearer—but there's one farther;
Elbows propped upon the red plush margin,

Epilogue

How absurd it must to you appear,
Or must *they* to me, from those boundless spheres
These our Bellevues and Belvederes!

Rushing this and that way. Personal, urgent things.
New Year's almost here. What for, with whom to clink
Toasts across the board? What in? A cotton flake
For foam. Why? So it's striking twelve: And where's my
    stake
In this, what would I do at a New Year's shindy,
"Rainer's dead" a scanding phrase within me;
If *you* could, an eye like yours, just set,
Then life is not life and death not death.
This means (darkly now, when we meet I'll learn it)
That there's neither life nor death, but a third thing,
Which is new. For its sake ('27's straw
Spread for parting '26's withdrawal*—
What high joy to end and start with you!)
Should I raise my glass, then, to your glass
'Way across a board the eye can't pass,
Toasting this? No—not that tavern chime:
I to *you*, whose fusion yields the rhyme,
That third thing.

                    My glance across the table
Finds your cross. How many out-town places,
How much out-town space! To whom else flowers,
Waving, a bush? Those places peculiarly ours,
No one else's! Each sheaf, every single leaf!
Spots which are just yours-with-me (yours-with-
    yourself's).
(Need I say I'd even go to a Party bash
If with you?) So many places! And months—a rash!

---

*An allusion to the custom of spreading straw on the roadway outside a dying man's
house to muffle the traffic noise.

Think in weeks! And faubourgs in a squall,
Bare of people! Mornings! And what all
Nightingales have not even started, surely!

So cooped up, my sight must function poorly;
You, up where you are, must clearly see:
Nothing ever came of you and me,
Such a pure and simple nothing-on-earth,
Tailor-made to just our size and girth,
That there was no need for altering.
Nothing but—look for no offbeat thing
(He who straggles off the beat is wrong!),
But for something that had (which? how long?)
Join some harmony!
                    The eternal song:
Nothing, in some trait of it, is something,
Anything—if only from afar, a shade's
Shadow! What though it's that hour, that day,
That house—even the doomed, to scaffold driven,
That—that mouth—by memory are given!
Or did they dispose too shrewdly here?
Out of all of *that*, the nether *world* alone
Did we own, as we ourselves are mere
Glints of self, who for all *this*, took all *that* world!

Here's to that least built-up subdivision,
To your new place, Rainer, your new world!
To cognition's utmost margin hurled,
On new hearing, Rainer, your new vision!

All to you was irksome,
Friend and passion, too.
Here's to new sound, Echo!
Sound, to echo new!

Wondering, on the school bench, times past counting:
What would rivers there be like? And mountains?
Are views finer—free of tourist blight?
Eden's hilly, Rainer, am I right?
Thund'rous? Not for widows' bland pretensions—
Eden II, above the first's dimension?

Eden—terraced? Take the Tatra chain:
Eden *must* be amphitatra-shaped,
Yes! (On someone is the curtain drawn. . . .)
Rainer, I was right, no? God's a *growing*
Baobab tree? Not any Roi Soleil.
Not just one God? Over Him holds sway
Another?

        How is writing at your spa?
You and verse are *there*, of course: you *are*
Verse! Is writing hard in the other land?
With no desk for elbow, brow for hand,
Cheek for palm?

        Please write, by the usual code!
Happy in a novel rhyming mode?
For, interpreting the word aright,
What is Rhyme but (here a swarming flight of
New rhymes settle) Death?

        Gone: mastered his tongue.
Whole arrays of senses, assonances rung,
New!

      Here's till we meet! To our acquaintance!
Meet—who knows; but fuse in one joint cadence.
With self-provinces unknown to me—
With my whole self, Rainer, all the sea!

Let's not miss each other—drop a card;
Here's to your new sound-recording art!

Stairs in Heaven, downward the Host is pointing...
Here is, Rainer, to your new anointing!

With my hand I shelter it from damp.
Past the Rhone and the Rarogne's banks,
Right across that plain and sheer expanse,
This to Rainer—Maria—Rilke's hands.

Bellevue
February 7, 1927

———

On February 21, 1927, Tsvetayeva informed her Czech friend Anna Tesková that she had begun a new piece—later to be called "Your Death"—dedicated to Rilke:

> I have finished the letter to Rilke—a poem. Now I am writing "prose" (I put it in quotes because it is such a high-sounding word)—that is to say, I am merely putting down the pre-sounds and post-sounds of his death as they vibrate within me. His death was spoiled for me: Ariadna's old governess died just before he did, and my little Russian friend Vanya died just afterward (all within three weeks!). Actually there is only *one* death (and one resurrection). I did not choose the leitmotif of the piece; two lines from Rilke volunteered themselves:

> > *denn Dir liegt nichts an den Fragenden:*
> > *Sanften Gesichtes*
> > > *siehst Du den Fragenden zu.**

———

*Tsvetayeva misquoted the last line of this verse, repeating *Fragenden* (questioners) in place of the correct *Tragenden* (bearers of burdens). The lines, from an untitled poem in Book II of Rilke's *Book of Hours*, actually read: "For questioners mean nothing to you./With a tender face/you regard the ones who bear their loads."

His death will change me greatly (inwardly).[7]

For Pasternak, the news of Rilke's death and the break in his correspondence with Tsvetayeva had made work on *Lieutenant Schmidt* difficult. Sending Tsvetayeva the second part of the poem on February 9, 1927, Pasternak wrote:[8]

> All the work is recent. Summer and fall were empty and fruitless. But, of course, I read, thought, and sketches piled up. Everything really came together at Christmas. The night of the first was particularly wonderful. I didn't go anywhere for New Year's. Zhenya met the New Year with Aseyev, Mayak[ovsky], and the whole Lef group. That night the second part of the poem came together as a whole.

Tsvetayeva received the second part of *Lieutenant Schmidt* in February and the concluding chapters in May. They didn't change her opinion of the poem. In her notebooks there is a draft of her reply:

> On B. P[asternak]'s L[ieutenant] Sch[midt]. The victory of a person who is not you, who doesn't exist in you. The victory of *all* over *one*. Sch[midt] complains. Sch[midt] drools. Sch[midt] is a whiner. Spittle and snot.
> Sch[midt]'s letters—are *1905* slang in rhyme.[8]

A year later Pasternak described the end of work on the poem and his plans for the future:

> In February 1926 I found out that the great German poet, my beloved teacher, Rainer Maria Rilke, knew of my existence, and this gave me an excuse to write to him, for which I am grateful. At about the same time I

got a hold of a copy of Marina Tsvetayeva's "Poem of the End," a lyrical work of rare depth and strength, the most extraordinary since Mayakovsky's "Man" and Yesenin's "Pugachev." Both these events possessed such concentrated force, that without them I would not have finished work on *1905*. I promised myself that on finishing *Lieutenant Schmidt* I would go and see the German poet; the anticipation of this visit supported me, and spurred me on. But my dream was never to be realized: he died in December of that year, when I had yet to finish the last part of the poem; it is highly probable that his death is reflected in the mood of the final pages. After *Schmidt* my one purpose was to write about our unexampled lyric poet and the unique world that he, like any true poet, creates in his work. But as I wrote, in the logical process of fulfilling my task, the article turned into an autobiographical fragment about how my views on art were formed and from what roots they sprang. I have not yet thought of a title for the book, which I dedicate to his memory. I haven't finished it yet.[9]

Pasternak wrote to his sister Josephine in October 1927: "Under the title 'An Article on the Poet' I want to write about Rilke, not as a special case, but as a law."[10] He collected materials about Rilke, asked for the *Duino Elegies*, which he had not read, and for Rilke's letters, monographs, and Paul Valéry's article on the poet. He was particularly interested in Rilke's French friends Valéry, André Gide, and Léon-Paul Fargue.

Safe Conduct, as this work was soon to be called, was dedicated to Rilke's memory and begins with a description of a ten-year-old schoolboy's unforgettable, chance encounter with the young Rilke at Kursk Station in Moscow in May 1900.

I am not writing my biography. I am drawing on it, when another's requires it. Together with its main protagonist I think that only heroes are deserving of genuine life chronicles, and the history of a poet in this form is completely unthinkable. It would have to be collected from inessentials that bear witness to concessions to pity and coercion. The poet gives voluntarily such a steep incline to his whole life, that it can't exist in the biographical vertical where we expect to encounter it. It can't be found under his name and must be looked for under someone else's, in the biographical columns of his followers. The more closed the creative individual, the more collective, without the least bit of allegory, is its story. The subconscious region of a genius cannot be measured. It consists of everything happening with his readers, who he does not know. I am not giving my memoirs to Rilke's memory, on the contrary, I myself received them from him as a gift.[11]

As an enamored reader Pasternak felt himself to be merely an imprint of "the main protagonist" of his biography, the follower of an immortal example. The main question of his life—what is "art in general, art as whole, in other words—in relationship to poetry"—Pasternak approached from Rilke's point of view, as though he were seeing through his eyes.

I will answer it neither theoretically, nor in a fairly general sense, but much of what I will say will be an answer to it, which I can give for myself and for my poet.

The affinity to Rilke's creative philosophy expressed in *Safe Conduct* provoked harsh criticism in Russia; Pasternak was accused of subjective idealism, which at the time was equivalent to being accused of counterrevolutionary activity. Published in censored form in 1931, the book was later removed from libraries and reprints were forbidden.

In the spring of 1927 it became clear that there could be no question of a trip abroad. Pasternak wrote to his friend Raisa Lomonosova, explaining that he needed to remain in Russia to finish his work. Pasternak had given Tsvetayeva the gift of Rilke's correspondence; now he shared Lomonosova's friendship and help with her as well. But the impossibility of meeting provoked a desperate letter from Tsvetayeva.[12]

TSVETAYEVA TO PASTERNAK

MAY 11, 1927

Boris! Did you ever think that there is an entire, enormous, marvelous world forbidden to poems, in which such enormous laws are revealed—were revealed. Just now, walking along the street, I thought: isn't it strange that a man, who gives drink, falls to a woman as to a spring. The drink-giver drinks! *The truth* of this reversal (inversion). Further: isn't giving drink—the only way to live? Learning together—that's what I would call it, that's what it is called. Boris, nothing is knowable together (everything—is forgotten), neither honor, nor God, nor a tree. Only your *body, which is closed to you (there is no entrance).* Think about it: the strangeness. An entire area of the soul, which I (you) cannot enter alone, I CANNOT ENTER ALONE. And it's not God who is needed, but a human being. Becoming through another person. *Sesam, öffne dich auf!**

I think that if I were with a person I loved a lot—no, a lot is too little, I also loved the hero of that long poem a lot—no, with someone like a Columbus, for instance—directed inward like me—I would say, I would find out, confirm, affirm, rediscover, an entire range of extraordinary things—

---

*Open Sesame!

indescribable only because they have not been described. A sudden insight, that there is a whole self (not a better half), a second self, another self, an earthly self, whom I don't know, though I was living for something, yes, despite the "Poem of the End." That was the stupefaction . . . of being loved (no one had ever dared to love me like that, like any other woman!), enchantment *with another's* enchantment, breathlessness with another's breathlessness—an echo in the mountains—(the "Poem of the Mountain"). Infection and inflection—the strongest type of psychic responsiveness to have found earthly words.

Boris, it is frightening to say this, but I have never been a body, neither in love, nor in motherhood, just a reflection, something through, in translation from (or into!). It seems strange to write this to you, a person I don't know (I don't mean you personally) and especially a thousand leagues away. I rarely thought about this you—only in scalding flashes— never dwelling on it. And over the past year . . . you've so completely become Rilke's younger brother, I won't finish the thought from superstition.

But today? And there's such burning regret that it isn't to be, not to be! An entire world (which could have been revealed) will sink to the bottom! (And it could have exploded.) An entire world won't rise to the surface. I would have found such pure words: (of course the reader would think that I'm speaking of the Heavenly Kingdom, just as now, thanks to Boris and Rilke, I am convinced of [the truth] of this poem at least:
    an entire was, was)

As though bearing a mountain in my skirts—
My whole body hurts!
I recognize love by the pain
My whole body's length.

As though a field in me had been rent
For the least deluge.
I recognize love by the distance
Of everything nearest.

As though a lair had been dug inside me,
To the core, the tar.
I recognize love by the vein
Moaning my body's

Length. Fanning out like a mane,
Sudden gust, a Hun:
I recognize love by the crack
Of all the truest

Throat strings; rust in the throat
Crevices. Live salt.
I recognize love by the cleft,
No, by the trill,
My whole body's length![13]

Boris, you were already in this underwater world in *My Sister, Life*—the fiery purity, the fiery purge of that book! At that time, when I wrote (badly, for that matter), I hid it like a secret. But you didn't hide it in the night, you handed it round the circle of the day, [introduced] trees and clouds into it. You gave it away, you crucified it. Everyone overlooked this in your book. I'm not talking about *Liebeslieder*, I'm talking about certain lines. There are identical lines—they possess resultant force.

You know what marvelous lines there are for my discoveries and yours. What a treasure trove of likenesses (correspondences).

The other world, Boris, is night, morning, day, evening and night with you, *it is around the clock!* And then . . .

Don't misunderstand me: I live not to write poems, I write poems in order to live. (Who would make writing poems an end in itself?) I write not because I know, but *in order to know*. Until I've written about a thing (have looked at it), it doesn't exist. My way of knowing is through expression—there's the knowledge, right from under the pen. Until I've written a thing, I don't think about it. (You're the same, you know.) The pen channels experiences of what is extant, but dormant. Just as the Sybil doesn't know until the words come. The Sybil knows immediately. The word is the background of the thing in us. The word is the path to the thing, *and not the other way around*. (If it were the other way around, we would need words, not things, and the ultimate goal—is the thing.)

I need you, Boris, like an abyss, a bottomless pit, so that there's some place to throw and not hear the depths. (Wells in ancient castles. A stone. One, two, three, four, seven, eleven ... There it is.) So that there is a place whence to love. I cannot love a non-poet (THAT WAY). Neither can you. After all, my secret dream, and yours, too, is to become a beggar. But what sort of beggars, when (whether you like it or not), the sublime is present in you. Understand [the value] of your defeat, my defeat, if it happens. Not by a divinity, not by just anyone; by an equal (a co-divinity or a co-anyone in another world!). The dream of equality—is a dream of defeat by an equal. Equality—as competition. . . .

I will, of course, love you more than anyone ever will, but not by my own scale. By my own scale (with all myself—myself in someone else, in everything) is too little. Somehow I draw things into love that make it not happen, disperse it, break it asunder. (For others it develops twice: as development (gradualness) and as de-envelopment (decay) and then it returns to me in unraveled tufts from everywhere around the circle of severance: from the sky, from the trees, from hands stretching up beneath the feet (on the right and the left) (hands of the earth—that is, through the grass). (The other person loves me, I love—everything. The other person loves me —I love everyone. It may be *in him* but nevertheless EVERY-THING and EVERYONE).

But what does this have to do with you? There, on the border of the other world with one foot already in it, we cannot inform God which way we're leaning—isn't this the very miracle of the other world, that here we cannot help but! I cannot imagine myself different and I know that on the first visit—different is what I will become. A different I—is you. Just appear . . .

*   *   *

And returning to the first half of the letter.
   —But perhaps—it is indeed God???

*   *   *

M.

————

By this time, Tsvetayeva's independent position in the Russian émigré community had acquired all the features of a tragedy. The poor state of Sergei Efron's health, which prevented him from earning a regular living, the poet's growing isolation in literary circles, her infrequent publications and ever rarer readings, gave Tsvetayeva no chance of breaking out of poverty.

Pasternak's often expressed desire to help Tsvetayeva in any way possible led him to get involved in the fall of 1927, and a new theme appeared in the poets' correspondence: Anastasia's trip to visit Maxim Gorky in Sorrento and her sister in Paris.

Anastasia's account of Marina's situation concerned Gorky and he offered to intercede. Tsvetayeva sent him her books and wrote asking if he would arrange for a Russian edition of her new collection, *After Russia*. "The thing would be returned to its womb," she wrote. "Here no one needs it, but people still remember me in Russia."

But Pasternak, on hearing from Anastasia of Gorky's plan to help, immediately sensed danger. Tsvetayeva risked being completely and definitively ostracized from émigré circles; her reputation would be ruined. Gorky himself would be put in an awkward political position in the eyes of his Soviet supporters for his connection to this White émigré. With characteristic openness and directness, Pasternak now asked Gorky to relinquish this burden, promising to take it on himself. In an October 13 letter, written the day after Anastasia arrived in Moscow, Pasternak wrote:

> In the knot of facts, which you so generously touched on this summer ... important and dear to me is the enormous gift of Marina Tsvetayeva and her unfortunate, impossibly tangled fate.
>
> The role and lot of M.Ts. are such that if you asked what I intended to *write* or do, I would answer: anything at all that could help her, and raise and return to Russia this great human being, who perhaps has not known how to put her gift on an equal footing with destiny, or, rather, the other way around.[14]

Pasternak had in mind making Tsvetayeva's poetry available to Russian readers—and thus providing her with a further source of income. Gorky, however, misunderstood, imagining he wanted to arrange her return to Russia. "This," he wrote to Pasternak, "is hardly possible." Tsvetayeva's poems about the White Army were of course the problem. But Gorky did search for a discreet, indirect way to send her money, though he was clearly nervous about discussing the subject in writing. (He almost certainly knew that his letters were being read.) He also expressed an extreme dislike of Tsvetayeva's poems.[15]

In his next letter, on October 27, having decided to act directly, Pasternak wrote:

Permit me to speak quite openly. I know that this is—to some extent—a secret, which I have a right to know, but which I should not touch. But how can I get out of this circle while still observing all the degrees of convention and not violating anyone's interests! And so, I'm breaking it.

I'm speaking about the new example of your responsiveness, about money for M.Ts. My request contains nothing but the desire for simplicity and goodwill. You will make me happy if you will understand and act accordingly. Here it is. I beg you to reject the idea of any monetary help to her, neither you nor M.Ts. will be able to escape the inevitable difficulties that will result. There is no urgent need of this at the moment. I have been able to take some action, perhaps I will be able to do so again sometime.[16]

Here Pasternak refers to a money transfer to Tsvetayeva through his sister Josephine on October 3. Soon he was able to set up further help through Lomonosova, compensating her transfers with equivalent sums paid to her friends and relatives in Russia.

Gorky suddenly broke off his exchange of letters with Pasternak, asking him not to write again. To Anastasia he conveyed his irritation that she had given away the "secret" of his charity.

In his work of this period, Pasternak is preoccupied with the theme of the tragic separation of people by borders. This is especially true of his novel *Spektorsky*. Corresponding with Gorky about Tsvetayeva, Pasternak said he meant to write in order to "wrench this enormous gift from the vise of a false and insufferable fate and return it to Russia," and he repeated this in a letter to Tsvetayeva herself. Six months later Pasternak inscribed his *Two Books*, which had just been published, to an admirer:

> Dear reader, the best poet of our generation is Marina Tsvetayeva. Not every role in emigration is voluntary, nor is every role here at home. May 10, 1929. B. Pasternak.

In the spring of 1929 circumstances gave Pasternak a new opportunity to immerse himself in the world of his father's old friendship with Rilke. The publisher Insel Verlag approached Leonid Pasternak with a request to provide Rilke's letters to him for publication, so Leonid wrote Boris, asking him to send the letters to Berlin. Struck by their richness and depth, Boris wrote to his father asking permission to keep copies of the correspondence.

> Today I will sit down to copy Rilke's letters. Oh, there are no words to express this. How guilty I feel that up till now, when I felt this with incredible pain, to the point of tears, I didn't realize how guilty I am before you ... and not before the memory of R[ilke] or literature. But I am so afraid that they will be lost (and afraid for you that you will be deprived of them) that I can't just send them.[17]

The day before he received the package of Rilke's letters from his son in Moscow, Leonid Pasternak happened to meet Clara Rilke while visiting another artist. He was overcome by a rush of memories and touched; eventually he would give her originals of the letters. In sending Rilke's letters to his father, on March 15, 1929, Boris had already remarked that he would find in them

much that will be dear to the widow, there is her correspondence and [...] signs of his care for her. I know
some things and can guess at much else. Besides which,
it all painfully resembles everything of mine, down to
the last details.[18]

Here Pasternak was comparing his own difficulties with
his artist wife to those, twenty years before, of Rilke in his
marriage to the sculptor Clara.

Pasternak wrote to his father on March 26, 1929:

I may translate one of his things, and in that case information that she [Clara Rilke] could probably give
would be most essential [...] If you like, ask yourself
who was Wolf Graf von Kalckreuth, to whom the
"Requiem" is dedicated. By the spirit of the poem it
should be a poet of naked emotion, the opposite of
Rilke, with, it's true, a colorful biography and with passions that end in suicide. [...] And so, the information
has to be reliable.[19]

On May 21, 1929, the poet's father copied out a letter received from Clara Rilke and sent it to his son.

————

CLARA RILKE TO LEONID PASTERNAK

You ask about the Count Wolf von Kalckreuth, and I will
willingly tell you what I know. I didn't know him myself, but
one of his close friends told me of him soon after his death.
He was, as follows from the "Requiem," an extraordinarily
talented man; after his death a volume of his poems was published. It is likely that he suffered from the extreme instability of his nature, one part of which lifted him to the heights

of spiritual concerns, the other of which caused him to suffer from depression. The commencement of military service, which his father expected would have a calming and strengthening effect, only served to deepen his depression, which led to the fateful end described in the "Requiem."

That is more or less what I heard at the time; to what extent it corresponds to reality, I cannot say. Later on I met his parents and sisters and became friends with the whole family. His father is the artist Leopold Kalckreuth, now deceased.[20]

The first part of *Safe Conduct* appeared in the journal *Zvezda* in August 1929. Pasternak's translation of the "Requiem for Wolf Graf von Kalckreuth," translated that spring, was published as an addendum to it. Over the summer of 1929 Pasternak translated a second requiem.

He wrote to his sister on July 15:

Rilke's requiem "Für eine Freundin" is very good, do you know it, Zhonichka? In its laconic quality and clarity, it is perhaps the strongest and most moral of everything said with a socialistic note in art of the last, pre-war period. The petit-bourgeois attitude is unmasked without naming it, *par défaut*, without challenge, in organizations where it doesn't have access anyway. And like everything great, the thesis of this requiem, if one were to draw a conclusion from it—lies in the absurd, in an even bolder absurd than *The Kreutzer Sonata*.[21]

Safe Conduct was finished in 1931, and the manuscript ends with a letter to Rilke—the very letter that Pasternak was not able to write him during his lifetime.

If you were alive, this is the letter I would send you today. I have just finished writing *Safe Conduct*, dedicated to your memory. Last evening I was asked to
come to the VOKS* offices about a matter concerning
you. They had received a request from the German
compilers of a posthumous collection of your letters
that I send them the note in which you warmly pressed
my hand and gave my work your blessing. I did not answer that note. I was counting on seeing you soon. But
my wife and son went abroad in my place.

It was not easy for me to leave unacknowledged a
gift as precious as your kind words. But I feared that,
content with corresponding with you, I would never
reach you in person. And I had to see you. Until that
time came I would not write to you. When I put myself
in your place (imagining your wonder at my silence), I
comforted myself with the knowledge that Tsvetayeva
was writing to you, and while I could not be a substitute for Tsvetayeva, she could be a substitute for me.

At that time I had a family. Sinfully I embarked on a
venture for which I had none of the requirements; I
drew another life into it with me and she and I conceived a third life.

Here Pasternak digressed to describe the two women—the
one who was then his wife and the one who was soon to become his wife.

A smile gave roundness to the young artist's chin and
poured its light upon her eyes and cheeks. When she
smiled she would narrow her eyes as against the sun,
but not with an intense gaze, rather with a hazy nar-
rowing like that of people who are frail or nearsighted.

---

*All-Union Society for Cultural Relations with Foreign Countries.

As the light of her smile rose to the beautiful broad brow, causing the whole image to waver between round and oval, one was reminded of the Italian Renaissance. Irradiated by this smile, she was very like the portrait of a woman by Ghirlandaio. At such moments one could not tear one's eyes from her face. Since her beauty depended upon such illumination, she could be attractive only when she was happy.

Some may say that all faces are like this. Not so. I know others. I know a face that is as striking and moving in grief as in joy and becomes only more lovely in circumstances that would make another's beauty fade.

Whether this woman is mounting the heights or plunging into the depths, her frightening fascination remains the same; she has much less need of anything earthly than the earth has need of her, for she is femininity itself, a rough-hewn, indestructible monolith of pride extracted whole from the quarry of creativity. Since a woman's character and disposition are revealed most truly in her appearance, the second woman, whose life, honor, passions, and inner essence are perceived independently of lighting, has less reason to fear life's vicissitudes than the first one.

Well, then, thus I lived as a family man. How well I remember that day! My wife was not at home. She was working in a studio at the art academy and would not be back until evening. In the hall stood our dining table, which had not been cleared since morning. I was sitting at it playing pensively with some cold potatoes in a frying pan, while outside the window snow was coming down in scattered flakes that seemed to hesitate in their fall, as if troubled by doubts. The day, noticeably longer now that winter was turning to spring, hung like a picture in the blurred silver windowpane.

Just then the doorbell rang. I opened the door and

was handed a letter with a foreign stamp. It was from my father. I read it eagerly.

That morning I had read "Poem of the End" for the first time, in one of those handwritten copies that are circulated in Moscow; the giver had no notion of how much the author meant to me and how many letters had passed between us and were at that moment on the way. But until that day I had not been acquainted with this poem or with "The Pied Piper," which I received later. Having read the poem that very morning, I was still dazed by its overwhelming dramatic force, and it was in this emotional state that I read Father's announcement of your fiftieth birthday and of the pleasure you expressed in receiving his letter of congratulation. Suddenly I came upon a then-inexplicable postscript to Father's letter saying that in some strange way you had come to know my poetry. I pushed my chair away from the table and got up. This, then, was the second time in one day that I had been shaken to the very foundations. I went to the window and wept.

I could not have been more astonished had I been told that I was read in heaven. Not only had I never considered the possibility of such a thing in the more than twenty years of my worship of you as a poet, but I had supposed it to be out of the question. Now my conception of my life and the course it was to take were suddenly changed. The angle whose two sides were moving farther apart with every year, and were meant never to meet, suddenly snapped together. And when? In the most unpropitious hour of the most unpropitious day!

Out in the yard the pale, murmurous shadows of a late-February twilight were gathering. For the first time it occurred to me that you were a human being, and as such I could write to you and tell you what a superhuman role you had played in my life. Until that moment such an idea had never crossed my mind. Now it took deep root in it. Soon after that I wrote to you.

I would be afraid to see that letter now; I don't remember what I said. The easiest thing in the world would have been to tell you what a transcendent being you are. If, however, I spoke of myself—that is, of our times—I could hardly have done justice to a theme still germinating within me.

I could not have adequately told you about those first days of all revolutions when the Desmoulinses* leap up on tables and incite mobs to violence with toasts to the thin air. I saw them do it. Reality, like a natural daughter, ran half naked out of her prison cell and, illegitimate and dowerless, defiantly planted herself in front of legitimate history. I saw a summer on this earth that seemed not to recognize itself, a summer as pristinely natural as a revelation. I wrote a book about it in which I recorded all the elusive and incongruous aspects of revolution that the mind is capable of comprehending.[22]

The years after Rilke's death saw a decline in the intensity of Tsvetayeva's poetic productivity, and she turned more and more to prose. Still haunted by Rilke's image, she corresponded with those who had been close to him, including Yevgenia Chernosvitova, Nanny Wunderly-Volkart, and Ruth Sieber-Rilke. She translated into Russian seven letters written by Rilke to the young poet Franz Xaver Kappus and wrote an introduction to them.

"Rainer, you have bound me to all who have lost you," Tsvetayeva exclaimed in the essay "Your Death," and this

---

*Camille Desmoulins (1760–94): French revolutionary.

was not an empty phrase. From 1930 to 1933, Tsvetayeva corresponded with Wunderly-Volkart, evincing a lively interest in everything related to Rilke's life and death.

She complained to Wunderly-Volkart on April 2, 1930:

> I don't know anything at all about his death. How did he leave? Did he know? Who was with him? What were his last words?
>
> I know only what was printed in the papers.
>
> And I didn't have anyone to ask, I didn't know anyone—that's how alone I was with him.

From the letters to Wunderly-Volkart we also learn that between 1927 and 1930 Tsvetayeva met with Chernosvitova, who "told me a lot about him" (in a July 5, 1930, letter) and who showed Tsvetayeva a piece of paper with Rilke's "will" printed on it. Tsvetayeva was very disappointed by her conversation with Chernosvitova: Rilke's former secretary impressed her as a superficial individual who was trying to interpret as "fate" her rather chance, brief acquaintance with the great poet.

"I met with her only once and left without regrets," Tsvetayeva wrote on October 17, 1930.

Tsvetayeva constantly mentions Rilke in her letters and literary essays of the early 1930s ("The Poet and Time," "Art in the Light of Conscience," and "The Epic and Lyric of Contemporary Russia").

In the West at the end of the 1920s a great deal began to be published on Rilke: books, articles, memoirs by his contemporaries. The poet's rich epistolary legacy was being collected and prepared for publication. Having read some of Rilke's correspondences, Tsvetayeva nurtured several ideas related to her beloved poet's life. One of them she shared in a letter to Nanny Wunderly-Volkart on January 12, 1932.

First and foremost I would like to select everything from
R.'s letters that relates to Russia—and translate them.
R. M. Rilke et la Russie or *La Russie de R. M. Rilke*—
that sounds more profound, truly profound. (His Russia,
as *his* death: everything and only that which doesn't belong to anyone, belongs *to him*. *His* wife—no, *his*
child—no, *his* Russia—yes.) Do I have the right to make
such a selection (and—the French translation)? *La
Russie fut le grand évenement de son être—et de son
devenir**—that's the way my introduction would begin.
My French would be exactly like *his* German. [. . .]

This shouldn't turn into a book, that is, the time
hasn't yet come for a book, after all in later volumes
Russia will be spoken of more than once (more than
once—things will be redolent of Russia). For the moment it could appear in some good journal. And eventually become a book, that book—of Rilke on Russia,
which he wanted to write. And in the end wrote. It
just needs to be compiled, that's all—and there you'd
have it!

Now: Rilke on Russia, not Rilke and Russia—*Russia
in* Rilke, that's the way I see it.

Rilke's Russia, translated by a Russian poet into his
second poetic language—French. I think that he would
have been (will be) pleased.

Tsvetayeva's ideas were never realized. Her desire to un-
dertake a serious work in memory of Rilke and his love for
Russia met with little interest among the German poet's
friends and publishers. After 1933, Tsvetayeva's connections
with Rilke's circle were broken off. For her own part, she
carefully guarded the "secret" of her relationship with him,
cherishing her memories of their 1926 correspondence.

---

*Russia was the great event of his being and of his becoming.

Tsvetayeva only rarely expressed her feelings, most often in her letters to Boris Pasternak.

In April 1929 Pasternak published two poems to Tsvetayeva in the journal *Krasnaya nov'*, continuing their poetic dialogue. In mid-December 1931, speaking in a discussion organized by the All-Russian Writers Union, Pasternak said that "some things haven't been destroyed by the Revolution," and that "time exists for man, not man for time." Reading these words in a report published in *Literaturnaya Gazeta*, Tsvetayeva concluded the programmatic article "The Poet and Time" she was then writing with the following paragraph:

> Boris Pasternak—there, I—here, across all expanses and prohibitions, external and internal (Boris Pasternak—with the Revolution, I—with no one), Pasternak and I, without consulting, are thinking about the same thing and saying the same thing.
>
> This is what it means to be contemporary.

Nonetheless, the epistolary romance of Tsvetayeva and Pasternak gradually receded into the past. On June 7, 1928, Tsvetayeva wrote down an excerpt of a letter to Pasternak in her notebook:

> B[oris], our current letters—are the letters of the despairing: of people who've made their peace. At first, dates were set, names of towns—at least in 1922 and 1925. The dates disappeared from our correspondence, we became ashamed—what!—simply—to lie. After all, you know perfectly well—what I know perfectly well. Along with the dates, the hurry disappeared (*not* the other way around!) the urgency of one another. We don't expect anything. O B[oris], B[oris], it's true. We are

just living, and all *that* (*the two of us!*) is off to the side. No, having been ahead of us, it became—all around us, it dissolved.

You have gradually become for me (and I for you) simply a friend to whom I complain: it hurts—lick my wounds. (It used to be: it hurts—burn it out!)[23]

On December 31, 1929, Tsvetayeva wrote:

Boris, I'm afraid of all words with you, that's the reason for my not-writing. After all, we have nothing but words, we're doomed to them. Everything that everyone else has—without words, through the air, that warm cloud *from* and to—for us is through words, voiceless, without the correction of the voice [. . .] Each of our letters—is the last. One is the last until we meet, the other the last forever. Perhaps because we write so seldom, each time—everything is anew. The soul feeds off life—here the soul feeds off the soul, self-engorgement, hopelessness.

And another thing, Boris, it seems I'm afraid of the pain, of this simple knife, which turns. The last pain? Yes, it seems it was back then, in Vendée, when you decided to not-write and tears actually fell into the sand—into the actual sand of the dunes. (Tears about R[ilke] didn't fall down, but up, a regular Thames at low tide.)

Since then there has been nothing in my life. More simply put: I have not loved anyone—in years—years—years. [. . .]: But I realize this *now*, on my surface I have simply petrified. [. . .]

Boris, I smothered you, covering you with the scattered cinders of winters' fires and the sea sand (Mur's) of years. Only now, when the pain's about to hit—do I understand how much I have forgotten you (myself).

You are buried in me—like a treasure of the Rhine—for the time being.[24]

On January 25, 1930, she wrote:

We were not destined to become the crux of one another's lives, at the Last Judgment it is *not* for me that you'll answer (what power in: not destined! What faith! I know God only through what does not happen).

Neither were the two poets destined, as Tsvetayeva had once dreamed, to visit Rilke's grave together in Switzerland. He was buried in Rarogne, not far from Muzot, next to a church wall, from which there is an astonishing view of the Rhone river valley. Tsvetayeva carefully preserved a photograph of the grave, sent to her by Salomeya Andronikova, with Rilke's letters. On the back of the photograph is a letter from Andronikova.

SALOMEYA ANDRONIKOVA TO TSVETAYEVA

SEPTEMBER 2, 1931

Dear Marina,

I've just returned from a trip to Switzerland and found your letter. I beg you to forgive me. I'm sending this right away.

I thought about you during my trip, as you see: I was at Rilke's grave and I'm sending you a picture of the church where he is buried, the grave and flowers on the grave, which I picked for You. [...]

For the moment I send you a kiss.

SALOMEYA

Tsvetayeva and Pasternak's long-awaited meeting finally took place in Paris, in June 1935 at the International Congress in Defense of Culture.

Ten years later, on November 26, 1945, Pasternak made the following notes at the request of Alexei Kruchyonykh, for his archive on Russian poets and poetry.

In '22–'23 (the winter) I was in Berlin, and Tsvetayeva was in Prague. That time I went back home without seeing her. In subsequent years I planned to go abroad on several occasions, in particular quite decisively and seriously at the beginning of 1926, after the connection established by me and Tsvetayeva with R. M. Rilke not long before his death.

But nothing came of all these proposed trips, and I saw Marina Ivanovna abroad only in Paris in June 1935, at the antifascist congress, where I arrived ill (I had had insomnia for six months and was almost on the edge of a mental breakdown).

At that time I met with M. I. and her family every day.[25]

This unexpected, but by now psychologically anticlimactic meeting, took place because an ill and unwilling Pasternak had been ordered to Paris by the Kremlin. He arrived on June 23, 1935, and five days later, on June 28, Marina Tsvetayeva left with her son for Favier in the south of France. She termed her visit with Pasternak a "non-meeting." Sergei Efron and twenty-three-year-old Ariadna remained in Paris and Pasternak spent time with them, trying, through his stories of life in Moscow, to dispel their enthusiasm for Soviet Russia and their desire to return. They met for another week until July 4, when the Soviet delegation, avoiding fascist

Germany, returned to Moscow in a roundabout way by sea through London and Leningrad.

This event, like the many encounters Tsvetayeva and Pasternak had in Moscow between 1939 and 1941, belongs to an entirely different historical era, when lyric poetry had withered under the Terror and the threat of World War II.

On August 8, 1941, Pasternak escorted Marina Ivanovna and her son Mur to the train station when they were evacuated from Moscow. Two months later he met with Mur, who returned to Moscow soon after his mother's suicide.

Pasternak told Zoya Maslennikova in 1959:

Mur was handsome, spoiled, an unusually precocious boy for his age. He was probably unhappy in Elabuga. And one time Marina said to him:

"Mur, I'm in your way, but I don't want to be, the obstacle needs to be removed."

Mur answered:

"That bears thinking about," and he went out for a walk.

When he returned, his mother had hanged herself.

Mur left for Chistopol, but he was anxious to get to Moscow. He brought a trunk with him, stuffed with his mother's manuscripts. He sold a number of things and lived off this. He left the manuscripts with the symbolist poet Sadovsky, who lived in Novodevichy Monastery.[26]

In Kruchyonykh's album there is a note from Pasternak after he saw Mur in Moscow:

OCTOBER 12

How do you like this whole thing, Alyosha. We always had a feeling this might happen. Who could [live] after all of this.

BORYA[27]

In the words "after all of this" one can imagine Mur's story of the arrest of his father and sister, and his mother's anxiety about them.

Just before being evacuated from Moscow, Pasternak handed over a folder with Tsvetayeva's letters to him to two young women working in the Scriabin Museum. Two days later he left for Chistopol where his family was waiting. Wandering the streets of this provincial town where Tsvetayeva arrived three days before her death, he planned the poem "In Memory of Marina Tsvetayeva," which was written later, in Moscow, at the end of 1943.

Tsvetayeva's letters were lost during the war. Kruchyonykh was partly at fault, since they had been turned over to him to be copied for inclusion in his Tsvetayeva archive. Kruchyonykh told Pasternak of the loss, and received in return a gift—the postcards with Wenzel Hollar's* engravings of London during the Great Fire which Tsvetayeva had once sent to him.

> To Alyosha's collection as a memento: today, November 26, 1945, in the morning, almost simultaneously, or one after the other,
>
> 1) I was brought myself in English prose from London;
>
> 2) Kruchyonykh informed me of the loss of what I cherish most, Marina's many letters to me. I'm writing this on one of the postcards with an engraving of London by Hollar from the series given to me and sent to me from London by Marina in April 1926, when she was there, and where I went nine years later for a few days on the way back from the antifascist congress in Paris.
>
> For safekeeping to Alyosha.[28]

---

*Bohemian engraver (1606–77).

The loss of Tsvetayeva's letters was a terrible blow to Pasternak, adding to the innumerable losses of recent years: of friends, parents, stepson, his father's paintings, his own papers, his apartment in Moscow. He saw it as a symbol of the fateful road of loss that he was condemned to travel for life.

In 1948, Ariadna Efron was in exile after being released from the camps, and she planned to travel to Elabuga to look for her mother's grave.

Pasternak wrote on May 21, 1948, to V. D. Avdeyev in Chistopol:

> Tsvetayeva's daughter asked Nikolai Aseyev in a letter whether it is known exactly where Marina Ivanovna was buried in Elabuga. At one time I asked Lozinsky, who lived in Elabuga, about this, and he couldn't tell me anything. Perhaps given your proximity to Elabuga (maybe you know people there) you know something about this.
>
> If someone had told me ten years ago (she was still in Paris then, I was against this move), that she would end up like this and that I would be asking where she was buried and no one knew, I would have thought this insulting and unthinkable nonsense.[29]

This tragic note ends our account of the relations and correspondence of these three great European poets. One theme stands out clearly: the limits of lyrical expression and the fate of lyric poetry as a whole.

Many biographical details remain outside the bounds of this book; we have presented the materials at hand, for that "Luminous Judgment" Marina Tsvetayeva hoped would come.

MARINA TSVETAYEVA: TWO ESSAYS ON RAINER MARIA RILKE

Translated from the Russian by Jamey Gambrell

YOUR DEATH

Every death, even the most out of the extraordinary, I mean yours, Rainer, inevitably falls in line with other deaths, between the last prior to it and the first after.

No one has ever stood at a graveside without the thought: "Whom did I stand by last? Whom will I stand by next?" In this way a certain link is established between your dead, your own *personal* dead, a bond which exists only in a given consciousness and is different in each one. Thus, in my consciousness you appeared before the Unknown between A and B; for someone else who lost you, between C and D, and so on. And the sum of our recognitions is your surroundings.

Now, as to the nature of this bond. In the worst case, most frequently, the link is superficial, local, ordinal, to say it all—quotidian, to put it more *all-ly*—cemeterial, dependent upon the location of numbers and graves. A meaningless link and thus not a bond.

An example. In life there was no link between X and Y. Neither is there in death, unless you count death itself, in which case—life too is a bond. Too little to establish their kinship. That sort of grave falls out of our sepulchral line, the line closes to two graves that have meaning for us. By this process of selection the line of our deaths and our death is created. When I speak of a bond, I have in mind only these deaths, which compose our own death.

Each death returns us into every other death. Each of the dead returns to us all who went before him, and returns us—to them. If others were not to die, we would sooner or later

321

forget those who died before. Thus, from grave to grave—a round-robin warrant of our faithfulness to the dead. A sort of posthumous coexistence in the memory: in the line of one's own graves. Because all of our dead, whether they lie in Novodevichy Cemetery in Moscow, or in Tunis, or somewhere else, for us, for each of us, they lie in one cemetery—inside us—with time, they all lie in one fraternal grave. Ours. Many in one, and one buried in many. There, where your first grave and your last meet—on your own gravestone—the line closes to a circle. Not only the earth (life), but death, too, is round.

Through the kiss of our lips, kissed hands become kin, and touch each other. Through their kissed hands, the lips that kiss become kin and reach for each other. A round-robin of immortality.

Thus, Rainer, you have bound me to all who have lost you, as I in return have bound you to all those I've lost, and closest of all to two.

As on waves, death carries us on hills of graves—to Life.

Rainer, your death has split in my life, stratified into three. One death prepared yours in me, the other concluded it. One is a fore-tone, the other an after-tone. Stepping back a bit in time—a tri-tone. Your death, Rainer, and I am already speaking from the future—was given to me as a triunity.

MADEMOISELLE JEANNE ROBERT

"Well, Alya, how did it go at Mademoiselle's?"

"Wonderful, Mama! But the most wonderful thing was that we came, because if we hadn't there would have been only two of the children, two girls—one grownup and the other one a kindergartener. And she would have gotten everything ready for nothing. And you know—I was so surprised—she has a wonderful apartment: a marble staircase, carpeted, and polished banisters, and some sort of bronze bells. . . . It's even fun to walk up a staircase like that, though not for her, I guess, since it's on the seventh floor, French style, and she's about seventy.

"Inside it's wonderful: paintings, mirrors, and souvenirs on the mantelpiece and everywhere—all kinds of them, embroidered, knitted, all with inscriptions from her pupils. And books, Mama! Whole walls of them. Mostly about Roland, the *Quatre fils d'Aymon*—that kind of stuff. But the most wonderful thing is that she has two grand pianos in one room. It's just because she's so poor that it's wonderful. If it was a rich man's house, well then, it would make sense. Just a lot of everything: napkins, knives. . . . So he up and bought himself two pianos at once, and will buy two more. But at Mademoiselle's it doesn't make any sense. And it's completely clear—from love. (Mama, I just had a strange thought: what if she grows into a giant at night and plays on both of them with no trouble at all? All alone, both of them at the same time—with four hands?)

"And it's terribly cold. Two fireplaces were going, but it was just like outside."

"Tell everything in order. From the very beginning when you arrived."

"As soon as we arrived Lelik and I were given a huge old book on Paris to look at. Then the bell started ringing and different former students started showing up in fur coats, from seventeen to forty years old. And a few mothers. Mademoiselle looked all worried, and kept running to the kitchen with cups, and I helped her a little. Oh, and Mama, how wonderful that I didn't exchange that box after all—remember, you said: The candies are important, and not the box. No Mama, the box *was* important—for Christmas. Candy in a box—is a present; just candy—is just candy. And the box will always be there—for letters, ribbons, or anything. She was so pleased and wanted to pass them around, but I convinced her to save them for her trip, because tomorrow she's going to the country to her sisters. Lelik brought her apples and oranges, and he tried unsuccessfully to buy her hard candies at the store. He said that ten francs worth would have been a whole lot. But his mother wouldn't let him. She passed out the oranges and kept the apples—probably for her sisters. So she'll go with gifts.

"Mama, she's probably very poor, more than we thought, probably everything goes for the apartment and her sisters —because the only refreshments were *petit-beurres*. And a choice of cocoa or tea. Some young cousin of hers, also in a fur coat, helped her. But she was wearing her eternal black dress, with the same velvet collar and the little brooch with Joan of Arc on it—the silver one, remember? She probably thinks, like you do, that it isn't right for the hostess to be dressed up since it's *her* home, but maybe she doesn't have anything else to wear, I, at least, haven't ever seen her in anything but that black dress. . . ."

"So then what happened?"

"Then some fat creature I took for a little girl joined us, but the little girl turned out to have on powder and lipstick, and so I didn't know what to think. Anyway, we decided to entertain it (the creature) with a game of Truth, and did such a good job that it disappeared after five minutes, probably because the little girl—the kindergartener—called her a *boule de graisse*,* and then *boule de viande*[†]—and of course we kept up with her. And then it got dark and Mademoiselle pointed out the Eiffel Tower, which was just as near or as far as from our windows. As it always looks from everywhere.

"Mama, I was dreadfully hungry, but I restrained myself

---

*Butterball.

[†]Meatball.

and only ate one *petit-beurre*. And Lelik ate one. And the little girl ate all the rest.

"Then we started to get ready to go home, but Mademoiselle wouldn't let us go for anything, because we hadn't danced yet. Lelik and I thought we were going to watch, but then it turned out that we were supposed to dance ourselves."

"What did you dance?"

"Just what they showed me. Mademoiselle dances well, very gracefully, though of course, old dances. When Lelik saw that we weren't dancing the Hungarian he started frowning and announced that he was dizzy. But she danced with him a bit anyway. She danced with everyone and got very tired. Oh yes! The most important thing. Over the sofa in the living room is a portrait of Mademoiselle—when she was young. She's lying on the grass reading a book, and there are apples near her. She's wearing a pink dress with ruffles—and is very pretty. And thin, too, only now it's from old age, and then it was from youth. —And her nose grew. Her sister painted it—not the crazy one, the other one—who's a bit touched and doesn't like the dust to be taken out of her room. She sweeps it under the rug and keeps it. But it's a wonderful painting."

"How was it when you left?"

"Oh, just fine. We kissed and I thanked her, and she thanked me. She was very pleased with your book, but I don't think she looked at the inscription—I think she thought it was just something for her to read. But then just think, tomorrow in the train she'll realize and be even more pleased. When we said good-bye I invited her to our Christmas tree again and she said that she would definitely come. What are we going to give her—gloves or stationery?"

———

Gloves or stationery? As bad luck would have it, as ever, there was no money for the once and forever!—for the last gift.

Or perhaps a notebook? There are quite inexpensive ones. Or maybe—one is so loathe to go out at the last pre-Christmas-tree moment—nothing? We just—invited her for the tree. Why should there be presents anyway? After all, you only give presents to children.... But the crudeness of the self-persuasion and the artificiality of the arguments made it clear—a present was necessary. Only what should it be: gloves or stationery?

The gloves, it turned out, had already been purchased by the little boy's mother: "They're warm and sturdy, because hers, poor thing, are all worn. After visiting her—in this cold —I just keep wanting to give her something warm. I hope she won't be offended." (Offended—by Russians! A beggar might as well have given her the gift.)

The presence of the gloves confirmed the stationery. "From five to six francs, no more than seven or eight, at the very most, ten. Something not too bright, for a middle-aged woman." ("Middle-aged," when she was just about to return to dust; "woman" when she was—Mlle Jeanne Robert!)

*Très distingué—parfaitement distingué—tout ce qu'il y a de plus distingué—on ne peut plus distingué....**

(6 Frs ... 9 Frs cinquante ... 12 Frs cinquante ... 18 Frs.)

The boxes stack up with a light cardboard crackling. One —is too loud; the next—too skimpy looking; the third—too boring; the fourth—expensive; the fifth—expensive; the sixth —expensive. And, as always, with the exclamation: "*Ah, il y en a encore une que j'oublie*"†—the last one is the very thing. (As if testing the precision of our taste, a small temptation by the salesman....)

Light blue. Rag. With little flowers in the same light blue on the cover, so simple they aren't trite. Without pinked edges, or those supposedly English rough edges. A lot. Reasonable.

---

*Very refined—refined in every respect—most refined—the most refined there is....

†Oh yes, I forgot one.

"*Rien de plus pratique et de plus distingué. Et pas cher du tout, Madame, quarante feuilles et quarante enveloppes. Un bon cas de profiter.*"*

At home, still in the doorway: "Alya! We have a present for Mademoiselle."

À Mademoiselle Jeanne Robert pour notre Noël russe[†]—*Ariane.* It is not a store-bought box which lies under the Christmas tree next to the pink package d'Olegue (Lelik)—because it is no longer nameless. Soon—the tree; soon—Mademoiselle. She was in Russia once, but has she been to a Russian Christmas tree since that time (fifty years ago)? And the anxious finding of the Christmas tree—at the last minute in a flower shop near the station—we didn't manage to renew the invitation, and so she's coming, not for the tree, but for an ordinary Thursday lesson, the first after her (French) vacation. She's coming to teach and will come upon the tree. "And Lelik, don't say anything, it's better not to let on, just bring her— or say that we're having our lessons downstairs—because there's no heat upstairs." For the children, Mademoiselle coming for the tree eclipses the tree itself. (Just as for angels waiting to receive a righteous man who knows not what awaits him, heaven is eclipsed by his coming.)

"She should be here any minute. It's ten of? Oh, another whole ten minutes."

"She should be here now. What time is it? She's never late."

"Maybe she only got back today, and that's why she's a bit late? Are you absolutely sure" (the children to each other) "that the first lesson is today?" "She said the 5th." "But the

---

*You can't get anything more practical or more refined. And not at all expensive, Madame, forty sheets and forty envelopes. A good buy.

[†]To Mademoiselle Jeanne Robert for our Russian Christmas.

5th was yesterday, why didn't she come yesterday? She told me Thursday." "She told me the 5th. But today's Thursday and so she'll be coming any minute now."

Only her two gifts remained under the tree.

———

The days came and went, Mademoiselle didn't. At first this alarmed everyone, then we got used to—alarm. The non-arrival of Mademoiselle, and she didn't arrive time after time, gradually became the refrain of the day for all the inhabitants of the house, small and large. That is, it became a thing which gradually lost its content from one time to the next. (The independent life of a refrain, outside of its significance.) Just as at the beginning we were surprised at Mademoiselle's not coming, now we would have been just as surprised—had she come. Surprise simply shifted from the point of departure to the point of application. It was surprising from *over there*. (Thus, Rainer, just as we were surprised that such a man could live, now—that he could die.)

People aren't very attentive to verb forms—*font du sort sans le savoir.** From the personal first—second—third counted times that "Mademoiselle didn't come" to the chronic, "Mademoiselle doesn't come anymore," what a road and what work. Mademoiselle simply took up residence in the absence into which she had (for us) accidentally fallen. There was not a lunch or dinner where one of the adults or children, between courses, in a tone now tinged with sedimentary surprise, did not state—"Mademoiselle hasn't come." And immediately—as though that were all we'd been waiting for, in unison along the beaten track of echo: Maybe she's sick? But she would have written. Maybe her sister is sick? But she would have written in that case, too. Maybe she's so alone that there's no one to

———

*They seal someone's fate without realizing it.

help her write? But then there wouldn't be anyone to wait on her either. Maybe. . . .

Ill somewhere, Mademoiselle festered.

They were all sober people—(the grandmother, aunt, uncle, the boy's mother, the girl's parents) people who had lived through a lot—some in Soviet Russia, some in the White Army, all in emigration, and most important of all—they were people with that wounded pride by which exiles can be recognized, people who had devoted their lives to their chil-dren, substituting their children's future (and what a future it would be!) for their own failed, overstrained present, people of time (the eternal lack of it) and for this reason—*in every way*—merciless with children's time, people who monitored children's time. And this time—thicker than water, a child's time —was passing, and the children, not without a bit of confusion —for they were good children—idled about, relatively speaking, of course—especially in the case of the girl who looked after her little brother and for whom lessons were a rest. Lessons were repeated and forgotten once again, books were laid out and again fitted onto shelves. Mademoiselle wasn't coming.

The house relaxed somehow, softened, no one—within the limits of the house—hurried to do anything. Put the milk out, because Mademoiselle will come. . . . Clear the table, because Mademoiselle will come. . . . You ought to wash your hair, but Mademoiselle will be here any minute. . . . Bring some coal up from the cellar, or else Mademoiselle will come and. . . .

The house was cold, only two rooms were heated—and Mademoiselle rearranged everything with her comings. If this is the classroom, then that is the dining room, and the sewing room is somewhere else and so on. But even this nomadic existence passed.

It gradually became clear that tiny unheard and unseen Mademoiselle (she used to come up the back stairs quietly and—often, "Has Mademoiselle been?" "Yes, she's already left.") was the backbone and mover of this big, complex co-existence of two families, of this willful—for it was, after all, Russian—household.

What did these people who had placed all their hopes in their children do? Six adults in all. Nothing at all. "We have to write to Mademoiselle." —At first assertively, then more and more questioningly, more knowing that it would never be done. More futilely. Hopelessly. Mademoiselle hadn't gone away, she'd gone astray. She hadn't gone astray, but vanished.

The first to say it, it seems, was the girl's mother—but as a riddle. It happened this way. The girl's mother was taking a knife out of the cabinet (one of two knives) and was standing with her back to the boy's aunt, who was clanking scissors on the big dining room table. Therefore the following question was addressed to her back.

"So no one's gone to see the French woman?"

"To see the French woman—it's so far away!"

"It's not too far for her, but for us—too far?" The malice in the aunt's tone was tempered by the triumph of the witticism.

"It's not too far for her, but for us it's too far," affirmed the girl's mother, freezing at the formulation.

"But still, we should, it's only right"—the aunt nagged, distressed by the failure of her wit and, in my view, insufficiently shocked by the unheard (in that form) coarseness of the response.

"But still, we should, it's only right."

"At some point, yes . . ." but these words were not heard since they were mumbled.

So it was actually the grandmother who said it first.

"Either she's very ill, or she's gone"—said the grandmother, with the quiet sadness of the old who are resigned to the whole thing, and know it inside out.

But "she's gone" still isn't quite "she . . ." And so it was the little boy's mother who said it first after all, the evening of that same day, after French dinner, that is Russian supper.

"If we haven't heard from her by now, she's either very ill —or she's dead."

And—the house came to life.

The resonance of death, have you ever thought about it, Rainer? In a house where after a long, demanding, devastating illness, someone finally passes on. Now, it would seem—is the time for peace, and when, if not at that moment—peace. Nothing of the kind! It's only the beginning.

A house where someone is dying is quiet. A house where someone has died is loud. The former sleeps—a death potion poured into all its nooks and crannies. Death is in every crevice. It's the hole in every crack in the floor. The former is flooded with the potion of death—the latter sprinkled with the potion of life. When the vial filled with the potion of life is smashed to smithereens, in every sliver, though it may wound—there is life. There's no crying in the house of the dying, and should you cry—you'll hide. In a house where someone has died—sobs. The first sound—tears.

*Lebenstrieb** of death, Rainer, have you thought about it? Then, the feet were run ragged, now the hands are busy, but of the two—hands and feet—it's the *hands* that are quiet and the *feet* that are loud. And what is quieter than—two hands filled with water, for example? But their very fullness—how, with what, from whence? For it was today at five o'clock that he relinquished his needs, departed "from all grief, anger, and need"—his prayer finally arrived! They'll answer me (not you, Rainer, others): him—no, his body—yes. Enough of that! Doesn't every survivor know deep down that the priest, the undertaker, and the photographer—are only an excuse for our fingers which are itching to get to work, are our affirmation, our conventionalized "I exist"—our full consent to live. We

---

*Life force.

don't cling to the dead, we cling to the undertaker! In our hurry to photograph the dead there is less the desire to preserve—than the desire to replace—the living features—with a photograph (the memory of the dead—is living torment)—or than there is the certainty of forgetting sooner or later. The photographic print—is our subscription to oblivion. To keep? To bury deep!

Delineating. Wooing. Move something, rearrange. With trifling snippets, cares, repair the old patterns of life. The barbarity of these cares. Almost like facing *alles geschehen—nichts geschehen.* * (And my words to you, Rainer, but differently: *Nichts kann dem geschehen, der geschah.*† In Russian: It doesn't happen to the one who happened.)

The taming of the unknown. The domestication of death, as once—love. The usual inability to find the right tone. Our —till the hour of death—*awkwardness* in love.

... There is another, simpler explanation of this posthumous burst of paganism. Death inhabits the house of the dying, there is no death in the house of the dead. Death leaves the house before the body, before the doctor, and even before the soul. Death is the first to leave the house. Hence the sigh of relief, despite grief. "Finally!" What? Not the person himself, who was loved—but death. Whence the celebration of its departure: for simpler people, the funeral feast—gorging and drinking at wakes (he can't eat or drink—so we will eat and drink!); and for us who came later, the gorging and drinking is, I keep wanting to say, recollective—the telling and repeating of the smallest details—to the point of stupefaction—to muteness—to well-wornness. There—eating away; here—the talking away of the dead. The thunderousness of a house after death. That's what I'm talking about.

And the first genuine quiet (that endless midday July bum-

---

*The greatest of events [vs.] the most trivial.

†Nothing can happen to the one who happened.

blebee buzzzz in the ears) sounds in the house only after the carrying-out. When there is no longer anything to carry on about. But visits to the cemetery do remain.

And while we wander along the paths, we read the inscriptions, entrust the grave to the caretaker, and select our own future death, taking advantage of its absence....

Thus do former owners, hearing that newcomers have moved into their country house, come and stand awhile, wander around and about....

And so, the house awoke. Since it so obviously awoke, it became clear that it had been asleep: the house, along with the grandmother, the uncle, the aunt, the boy's mother, the father and mother of the little girl, the girl herself, the boy himself, all its inhabitants, had been sleeping as if spellbound for three weeks.

In the way the house came to life, it became clear: she was dead.

"Mama, I'll write to Mademoiselle now."

THE LETTER

Chère Mademoiselle,

C'est en vain que nous vous attendons depuis longtemps. Chaque lundi et mercredi, jeudi et samedi nous vous attendons et vous ne venez jamais. Mes leçons sont écrites et apprises, celles d'Olègue aussi. Avez-vous oublié notre invitation pour l'arbre de Noël? Je crois que oui, parce que vous n'êtes pas venue chez nous l'avant-dernier jeudi quand nous avons notre fête. J'ai reçu beaucoup de livres: Poèmes de Ronsard, Oeuvre de Marot, Fabliaux, le Roman du Renard, le Roman de la Rose, et surtout la Chanson de Roland. Deux cadeaux vous attendent, d'Olègue et de moi. Ecrivez-nous chère Mademoiselle, quand vous pourrez venir chez nous. Nous vous embrassons. *

ARIANE.

"That evening she was so tired, so exhausted. I kept wanting to say to her, 'Why did you do all this? And those dances on top of it all. . . . Let us all go home, you sit down in the armchair near the fire, get warm and rest.' But she simply wouldn't let us go without the dances, the picture books, refreshments, dances—to complete the evening. And those ladies in the fur coats, dragging in bit by bit for who knows what reason, making her whole apartment cold—and it was so cold already. You can't imagine how cold it was. It's cold here, but the-e-re. I couldn't get warm all evening."

The boy's mother and I climbed the "polished marble" slowly. The staircase slowly led us from landing to landing. At the very top in front of a big black door—we stopped. It was clear there was no farther to go. There were two doors, the left-hand and the right. Mademoiselle lived be-hind the right one. In silence, we knocked. In silence, we knocked again. More silence. More knocking. Our knocks thinned out. They became few and the intervals further between. The knocks themselves remained on the surface of the door, not penetrating to the world on the other side, or, having pene-

------

*Dear Mademoiselle,

   For a long time we've waited for you in vain. We wait for you every Monday and Wednesday, Thursday and Saturday, and you never come. I've written my lessons out and learned them, Oleg too. Have you forgotten our Christmas tree invitation? I think so, because you didn't come to our house Thursday before last, which is when we have our celebration. I received a lot of books: Ronsard's poems, Marot's works, the Fabliaux, *Le Roman de Renard, Le Roman de la Rose,* and especially *La Chanson de Roland.* There are two presents waiting for you, one from Oleg and one from me. Write to us, dear Mademoiselle, and tell us when you can come to us. Hugs and kisses.

trated, were swallowed up by what was behind the door, by all the behind-the-door emptiness (by that in-the-other-worldness). The door didn't answer. The door kept its silence.

"Let's go to the concierge—we could stand here for an hour —we can ask, perhaps she knows something"—not whispering (like anything out of the ordinary, it wakes people) but with that special half-voice used around sleeping people, and others.

"Maybe we should knock on this door?"

The door on the left echoed and surrendered itself, revealing at first a kerosene lamp and then the middle-aged face of a woman.

"Excuse us Madame, but do you know anything about Mlle Jeanne Robert? We knocked, but no one answers. It seems there's no one home. Our children study with her."

"Come in, come in, I'm so glad to talk about her. We've been neighbors for twenty-eight years."

The lamp yielded, and, turning around itself, led the way. The lamp, whose duty was *es an den Tag bringen.* * The old woman, and the two of us, followed.

"Please sit down. I don't quite understand, you say—your children?"

"Yes, our children study with her. We're foreigners. Our children study French and other subjects with her. We live in Bellevue."

"Oh, so that's it. *Je sais qu'elle prenait toujours le petit tram de Meudon.* † She was going to you then? A lovely place —Bellevue—we go there every Sunday."

"That's right. And now it's been a month since we've heard anything from her. She was supposed to come to our Russian Christmas tree, because Russian Christmas is after yours, thirteen days difference.... We have gifts for her..." (as if trying to conjure and conquer the unknown with realities).

---

* To bring to light.

† I know she always took the little tram from Meudon.

"So you invited her to your Christmas tree? How kind of you."

"Yes, and she didn't come, and we've been expecting her now for the last two weeks. My daughter wrote to her" (thoroughly disregarding the fact that the letter, written only that morning, could in no case, even the most alive, have expected to receive an answer by this time—so far away was this morning from now) "my daughter wrote to her and received no reply. What is wrong with her?"

"*Mais elle est morte!—Et vous ne l'avez pas su?*"*

"The 23rd, *l'avant-veille de Noël.*† The evening before she ran all about, up and down, *rien que son petit châle sur les épaules. 'Mais vous allez prendre froid, Jeanne, voyons!' Et je lui tirais les manches sur les mains.*‡ She kept buying things. The next day she was supposed to go to her sisters."

"But the evening before, the 22nd, our children, and this lady, the mother of the little boy, visited her. Yes, yes, it was the 22nd. She invited all her pupils, she danced. . . ."

"I didn't know anything about that. When, what time was it?"

"About four, and they left around seven. She was very excited. She wouldn't let them go without dancing. The next day? I don't understand anything."

"Yes, the 23rd, in the morning. From a hernia—a malignant tumor. Well, she never wanted to wear a truss, because then she would have had to go to the doctor, and they—well, you understand me—she didn't want to. A long-standing her-

---

*But she's dead!—And you didn't know?

†Two days before Christmas.

‡With just her little shawl about her shoulders. 'But you'll catch cold, Jeanne!' And I pulled her sleeves down over her hands.

nia. You mean, coming here, you didn't know anything? Then please forgive me—*de vous l'avoir annoncé si brutalement.*"*

"Then it's been a month since she died?"

"A month, today in fact. You say that she danced? Perhaps that's what did it. Dances—with a hernia. And no bandage...."

"But how did she die? Was anyone with her?"

"No one, she was completely alone. About three o'clock her cousin dropped by—she sometimes helped her *dans son petit ménage,*† and Jeanne had given her the key the night before—she knocked, no one answered, so she went in and she saw her. She was lying across the bed, completely dressed in her hat and gloves, obviously ready to go to a lesson—she still had one lesson to give before leaving—the last one. *Cette pauvre Jeanne!* Sixty-four years old—*c'est pourtant pas vieux.*‡ Neighbors for twenty-eight years. *On était amis, on se disait Jeanne, Suzanne....*§ And all these misfortunes! Perhaps you know? Her sister..."

"She has a nervous condition."

"Yes and it happened suddenly, no one expected it.... And Jeanne had to... *une fille si intelligente, si courageuse,*‖ to work not just for two, but for three, because the third sister is with the other, the sick one, in the country—*c'est elle qui la garde*#—and what can you earn in the country, especially as an artist, because the third sister is an artist, a good artist. *Cela a été le grand coup de sa vie. Elle aurait pu se marier, être heureuse, mais....***

---

*For having told you so bluntly.

†With her light housekeeping.

‡That's not old, after all.

§We were friends, we called each other Jeanne and Suzanne.

‖Such a smart, plucky girl.

#She's the one that looks after her.

**That was the great blow of her life. She could have gotten married and been happy, but...

"But even so . . . *on a eu de beaux jours ensemble! On faisait la fête.** My husband and son-in-law are musicians, Jeanne was a musician too. Did you see the two grand pianos in her room? One was for her, the other for her students. She was actually a music teacher you know. And so they played music together. Jeanne—on piano, my husband—on the violin, my son-in-law —on the flute. By the way, do you have any friends who would like to study music? Just in case, I'll give you a card."

> So and so
> —Violin and flute—
> Professeur à l'Opéra

Mlle Jeanne Robert, traveling to the Russian girl Alya, not asking whether to Villette or Bellevue. Mlle Jeanne Robert, knowing neither rain nor snow. Mlle Jeanne Robert, charging seven francs in 1926 as she did in 1925 for an hour lesson which lasted two, taking into account not the "fall of the franc," but the falling of the franc onto our—*intelligence russe*[†] —heads. Mlle Jeanne Robert, hesitating to accept her monthly envelope containing money—"But don't you need it now?" and *"Cela ne presse pas."*[‡] Mlle Jeanne Robert, traveling not by train, but by streetcar, and not to Bellevue, but to Meudon, to save us, *intelligence russe*, 1.60 francs four times a week, Mlle Jeanne Robert, who at the sight of a cup of coffee and a piece of bread, would protest, "Oh, but why?" and would invariably drink the coffee, and, by the beggars' code of honor— leave the bread untouched, Mlle Jeanne Robert, singing

---

*We had some happy days together. We had a good time.

[†]Russian intelligentsia.

[‡]There's no hurry.

V siélé novom Vanka jyl...*

to the year-old son of an emigrant so that he wouldn't forget Russia and coining the name Mur, from Amour, Mlle Jeanne Robert, who last year not only came to my Russian poetry reading, but was the first to come—

"Un moment j'ai cru entendre une marche. Etait-ce peut-être une poesie sur la guerre? On croyait entendre marcher les troupes, sonner les trompettes, galoper les chevaux... C'est que je suis musicienne, moi... C'était beau, beau!"†

Mlle Jeanne Robert, confusing a lesson date for the first time: one on Wednesday (the 5th), the other on the 6th (Thursday).

Mlle Jeanne Robert who didn't wait for her new gloves after all—

Rainer Maria Rilke, are you pleased with—Jeanne Robert?

And, addressing to you the words you once directed to another—

> *denn Dir liegt nichts an den Fragenden,*
> *sanften Gesichtes*
> *siehst Du den Tragenden zu.*‡

P.S. I happened to find out that the last book you read was called *L'Âme et la Danse.*§

That is, all the last Jeanne Robert.

---

*In the village Vanya lived...

†For a minute I thought I heard a march. Maybe it was a poem about the war? You could hear the troops marching, the bugles blowing, the horses galloping... It's because I'm a musician... It was beautiful, beautiful!

‡See note on page 291.

§*The Soul and the Dance* by Paul Valéry.

VANYA

The Russian boy Vanya died. I first heard of him from his sister at the ocean this summer. I was sitting on the sand, playing with my one-and-a-half-year-old son. "I have a brother," my acquaintance suddenly said, "about as developed as your son. Papa, Mama, uncles, thank you, please. . . ."

"How old is he?"

"Thirteen."

"Mentally retarded?"

"Yes, and a very good boy, very kind. His name is Vanya."

"That's a good name, the most Russian, and the rarest, no one names children that nowadays," I said, limiting my judgment to the name.

The next I heard about Vanya was from a close friend who had just that evening dropped in with Vanya's sister to see Vanya's mother.

"As I was going there I was a bit scared: How do you act with someone like that? Do you play? Strange, somehow it feels like a false position. But he reassured me immediately: as soon as he saw me—his face lit up and he smiled and said, 'Uncle, uncle!' "

"How big is he?"

"Big, normal size. And he isn't at all as unaware as I feared. The nanny started getting things ready for dinner. "Vanechka, set the table"—and he set it, only he mixed up the plates, put down small ones instead of the big ones. And the nanny says reproachfully, "What's wrong with you Vanechka? Why these plates, are you crazy or something?" —The nanny is wonderful, she's devoted her whole life to him. They live together, the mother, the nanny, and Vanya. They live for him.

"I'm chatting with his mother about something and all of

a sudden, 'Uncle, uncle!'—I look around: he had walked up ever so quietly from behind and was staring at me. And such a good, kind smile. I really understand how he could be a joy. There really is a light emanating from him."

A bit of time passed. And then one day, a rumor started circulating that Vanya was sick. Pneumonia.

The rumor moved in. It blew in from Meudon. The breeze traveled from the red brick house I vaguely knew to be Vanya's. It traveled in two directions—to his sister in Clamar, and to me in Bellevue. The illness settled in. Chained to his bed, Vanya traveled.

The days passed. The wind continued to blow from Meudon. Soon the illness of the unseen Vanya became usual, taken for granted, in the order of things—that destroy order.

"How is your brother doing?"

"Bad, the temperature won't go down, we give him camphor all the time. . . ."

I knew of camphor from the last minutes of my father's life and for me—it spelled death.

"Sit a little longer. . . ."

"I can't, I have to go to Mama, my brother's awful poorly."

I thought about the mother and the nanny, not with sympathy, a vicarious substitute, but with the unsubstitutive empathy of pain. But I thought of them only occasionally.

Absorbed in your death Rainer, that is, associating it with every other death I have endured in life thus far: the proud death of my mother, the highly moving death of my father, many other various deaths—associating or juxtaposing?—I, of course, was on my guard against Vanya's camphor.

Two rooms and a kitchen. A little bed. (Maybe it was big, but since he called him "Uncle," it had to be small.) The nanny's despair, regulated by daily cares and church-going. (What sort of despair was the mother's?) The horror of the fact that this is Meudon and not Moscow (in Moscow we would have . . .). The horror of the unauthorized, uncontrollable

thought of a foreign cemetery. . . . We brought him to Meudon
. . . if it hadn't been Meudon. . . . If we hadn't taken him to the
store that day . . . if. . . .

"How's your brother doing?"

"He's gentle, so good, he lies in bed just like a little boy—
it's touching. . . ."

The last thing I know of Vanya's life is that he ate caviar.

"I ate caviar today. They gave some to my brother, he
didn't finish it and so I did. He didn't want to eat anything,
and then suddenly took a fancy to caviar. . . . We were all
so pleased. . . ."

Caviar reminded me of my mother's pre-death champagne
—she didn't want anything, and then suddenly fancied champagne. Caviar too—spelled death.

"Will you be at such and such a place tomorrow?"

"Well, I don't know, if I don't stay with Mama. My brother's
awful sickly, anything could happen. . . ."

About two days after the caviar one of the inhabitants of
our house, coming in from outside:

"The G——kovsky boy died after all."

———

"Two rooms and a kitchen." The little bed isn't visible, nothing can be seen but backs. The funeral service goes on without light. I stand on the threshold between the foyer and the
first room. The coffin seems to be a thousand miles away, unattainable.

The bell rings, more and more new people come to say
farewell.

The priest exists, creating a void around himself. A priestly
void, sacred. A circle of emptiness created by the inhuman. A
traveling circle. There was room for no one—now—for everyone. The elasticity of the vessel, or the condensability of the
contents? A refusal of the vital in the name of that surplus.

Refusal of oneself and of everyone else in the name of that one alone. And room for everyone. Only refuse—and there will be plenty of everything. "I would suggest you hire these singers" (says—the priest). "But why not the ones who. . . ." "It would be better to have these. . . ." "What, do they sing better?" There is an urgency in the inquiring voice which frightens me, I don't want to hear the answer.

"But I heard that these sing better. . . ."

"They sing well, yes" (Here! Here it comes!) "but . . . very dear, whereas the others. . . ."

In the half darkness I kiss the mother and nanny who pass by.

"You came on foot? Are you tired? Sit down a bit. . . ."

Without tears, with kindness.

(Oh, the beautiful reticence of Russian grief!)

Why didn't I go up to him? A false shame, false fear of tears upon first sight of him. The fear of shame and the shame of that fear. I want everyone to leave, so that right there, standing over him, I could tell the two of them about you, Rainer, about everything I know through you. I know that at that moment, I, *remaining*, was for them, remaining behind, indispensable. That my place . . . was irreplaceable. And faintheartedly, formally saying my farewell, I leave.

———

"Dearest Vanya!"

—the sound of something not heard, but disclosed, as once to my inner-mouth's inside "Gray-haired dawn" came Blok's "Gray-haired dawn"—

Dearest Vanya!

If you could see us all gathered here, the church overflowing, you would probably ask "What holiday is it?" And we would answer: "It's your holiday, Vanya. We're celebrating you."

Yes, Vanya, it is in your honor that we've gathered here in this church today, this church in which you occupied the humblest place. Your place is the most important one today. I can see you now, right here, to the left in the corner—your habitual, modest place. I see you praying and crossing yourself, I see your bright face, and your smile. . . . You were a regular and faithful church-goer—I don't remember a single service at which you were not present. It's true you didn't always pray with the words of the prayer, you forgot them sometimes, but then you prayed with your own words, with only one word: Little Lord! Little Lord!

And how you loved this Little Lord, how you believed in Him.

When you became very ill you asked me to come. I was told that I was summoned to the house by your own wish. I'll never forget how, before you gave your confession, raising yourself just a bit, you signaled weakly with your hand for all present to leave the room. Only your near and dear were there—and what could your sins have been? But you knew that the secret of confession occurs alone with the priest, and in this your sensitive heart proved you to be a faithful son of the church.

You didn't say much to me, but after the absolution, with what happiness, with what light in your face you again raised your hand, this time calling your loved ones back into the room.

Dearest Vanya, if only you could see us all—surrounding your little coffin—from your heights, yes and you do see from those heights—seeing our tears, our grief, what would you say to us Vanya, would you want to return here again? No, Vanya, neither you, nor anyone who has beheld *that* beauty would ever wish to return to earth, and the only words you would speak would be words of gratitude. Gratitude to your parents who surrounded you with such love, and especially to your nanny—with whom you were one. Thank you, mournful old nanny.

Pray for us.

———

The mother stood at the head of the bed and—or did I imagine it?—each time someone approached, she uncovered her son's face, pulled something up, which then fell back over him. Over and over again for each person. Why? Wouldn't it have been easier. . . .

It didn't matter what was easier, what mattered was that the mother was showing him to the world—to everyone, for the last time, to each person individually. After the "Look, you haven't seen him yet" of birth—the "Look, you won't see him again" of burial. Revealing, she concealed (the face in herself) revealing again, she again concealed—deeper and deeper—until she hid him away altogether, from everyone, under the coffin cover, until she hid him away—from the whole earth, in the earth, forever.

The mother was taking her son back into the womb.

In this gesture there was also a simple maternal bond.

———

Something else. Not flesh, not stone, not wax, not metal—something else. From everything seen—the unseen. The face in front of me never existed. What is here doesn't exist. Is of some other substance.

The distinctive features: incomparableness and the impossibility of acclimation. Can't be torn away. Can't become accustomed. A purely external (and thus significant) impenetrability. Inseparability. Incorruptibility. You can't cut it with a knife, can't cleave it with an ax. The face of the deceased is not a mask, but an elemental cast.

All ends have come together. A focus.

Once and forever.

Closest of all, of course, is wax, but still—wax doesn't come close.

What reply to the body that lies here? *Refusal.*

———

I look at the hand and I know—it can't be raised. How much life weighs we know—but this isn't life, it's death. The hand isn't filled with lead, but with death. The pure weight of death. All of death in every finger. One would have to raise all of death. That's why it can't be raised.

This—is with the eyes, while beneath the lips:

First of all: kisses won't get through. Not the lips (life) on the brow (death), but the brow (death) on the lips (life). Not, I warm—but, he chills. Impenetrability? Heat-resistance. Heat-resistance? Cold-radiation. I shall stand here and warm, and he'll lie there and chill. Such cold doesn't exist in nature. Nor this density. Because this doesn't exist in nature at all. In another nature.

Heatable: metal, wax, stone, everything. Everything responds. Grows warm.

The brow—refuses.

———

Vanya G——v—I reinstate you back to life.

Firstly, the narrowness. Narrow cheek bones, narrow lips, narrow shoulders, narrow hands. Narrow, and therefore—not crowded. Not crowded, therefore—joyous.

The lightness of the hair on the brow and, passing over the qualities existent in the nonexistent, the tender, stern adolescent face which at this moment I read backward: into life.

———

That's all Rainer. What about your death?

On this I'll tell you (tell myself) that it never existed in my life, because, Rainer, in spite of *Savoye, L'Auberge des Trois Rois*, etc., you never existed in my life. There was: it will be, it has remained. —*Ob ich an die Savoye glaub? Ja, wie an Himmelreich, nicht minder, doch nicht anders.* * You surely remember this.

I'll also tell you that not for one moment have I felt you to be dead—and myself alive. (Not for one moment have I felt you: momentarily.) If you are dead—I, too, am dead; if I am alive —you, too, are alive—isn't it all the same, whatever we call it?

But I'll tell you one more thing, Rainer—not only did you not exist in my life—you didn't exist in life at all. Yes, Rainer, despite you and *life*: you—books, you—countries, despite you —the local emptiness at all points of the globe, despite your universal absence, half the map empty of you—you were never in life.

There was—and this is, from my lips, the greatest *titre de noblesse*† (I'm not speaking to you but to everyone)—a specter, that is, the greatest indulgence the soul grants the eyes (our craving for the real). An enduring, uninterrupted, patient specter, who gave us, the living, life and blood. We wanted to see you—we did. We wanted your books—you wrote them. We wanted you—you were. He, I, another, all of us, the whole earth, our whole troubled time, to which you were indispensable. "In Rilke's time. . . ."

———

*Do I believe in the Savoy? Yes, as I believe in the Kingdom of Heaven, not less, but no differently.

†Title of nobility.

A clairvoyant? No. You yourself were spirit. We were the clairvoyants. If you had walked into my room a year ago, my heart would have stood as still as if you walked in now—more, really—now, less than a year ago, because that sort of entrance would be . . . more natural.

> Three walls, ceiling and floor
> Everything's ready
> Now—Appear!

I wrote this to you last summer. Wasn't it really on everyone's behalf? We conjured you up on earth with our will, that is, with all the tragic lack of it, all our will-lessness, with all our prayers about *all* your will, we conjured you up on earth, and held you there—for a time.

You were the will and conscience of your time, despite Edison, Lenin, et al., *from* Edison, Lenin, et al.—its only leader. Not a responsible monarch, but a monarch of Responsibility. (Thus we [time] once gave ourselves over, with all our questions, to Goethe, made him—whether he wanted it or not—our response. We made you—our responsibility. That's why you both gave back: Goethe—light; you—blood.)

"*Und Körper nur noch aus Galanterie, um das Unsichtbare nicht zu erschrecken*"*—was what you said about the last years (as it turned out—days) of your body. A sick *or* a healthy man's—whose words are these? Not a human's at all.

Remember your Malte, how everyone followed him along all the streets of Paris, almost loafing about, entreating not everything of him, but him, all of him. And so we followed you—for a time. Remember Malte, who transmitted his will through the wall to his neighbor, on whom he had never laid eyes. His neighbor hadn't asked either. But Malte—heard that cry! "*Wer ist dein Nächster? Der dich am nothwendigsten*

---

*And still a body only out of courtesy, so as not to frighten the invisible.

braucht" *—an exegesis of the neighbor, at a Protestant lesson on scripture, which has remained definitive for me.

We were all your neighbors.

With admissions, confessions, penitence, questions, aspirations, prostrations, affections, we loved you down—wore sores on your hands. All the blood flowed out through them.

Blood. The word has been spoken.

Your *Blutzersetzung* (decomposition of the blood)—which I didn't understand at first—how could it be: he was the first after the Old Testament to say *blood*, having said blood *in such a way*, simply *having told of blood*!—this isn't an article and I won't try and prove anything—it was *he* who died from this *Blutzersetzung*, the impoverishment of blood. What irony! Not irony at all, but my first, in the heat of the moment, lack of foresight.

He bled good blood for the salvation of our bad blood. Simply, transfused his blood into ours.

Stop.

I know that the medical illness from which you died is treated by blood transfusions, that is, some next of kin, who wishes to save the person, gives blood. Then the illness— ends. Your illness—began with the transfusion of blood—yours —into all of us. The world was sick, you were its next of kin. What will then save the transfuser!

Poetry doesn't have anything to do with it. "An unnecessary irritation, creating bad blood for nothing"—is what people say. The limit of this "unnecessary" and "for nothing" —is the final spoiling of the blood, that is, death. Your death.

While I cannot forgive life for the humiliating approximateness of its dates—the 29th of December instead of the 31st, moreover, the eve of your beloved nineteen hundred and *twenty-seven*, I am grateful to it, life, for the precision of form and appellation . . .

---

*Who is your neighbor? The one who needs you most.

Rainer Maria Rilke, and every doctor will confirm this, died from decomposition of the blood.

Having transfused his own.

————

And all the same, Rainer, despite the magnificence of your death, your right- and left-hand bedfellows in me are and will remain:

Mlle Jeanne Robert, teacher of the French language and Vanya G——v, an aggrieved Russian boy and—sweeping aside the surnames and even their first letters—simply

Jeanne—(all of that France)
and
Vanya—(all Russia).

I chose neither the definitiveness of the names, nor the perfection of the proximity.

————

Rainer Maria Rilke, at rest on the cliff of Rarogne
above the Rhône—all alone—
rests in me, his loving Russian admirer,
between Vanya and Jeanne—John and Joan.

—Bellevue, February 27, 1927

A FEW OF RAINER
MARIA RILKE'S LETTERS

I DON'T feel like writing an article about Rilke. I don't feel like talking about him, thereby removing and estranging him, making him a third person, a thing one talks about, outside of me. (As long as a thing is in me, it is—me, as soon as a thing is outside, it is—it, but not you, *you* are once again —*me*.)

I feel like talking—to him (more precisely—into him) as I have already talked in "A New Year's Letter" and "Your Death," as I will again talk, will never stop talking whether aloud or to myself. What do I care that others hear, I'm not talking to them, I'm talking to him. Not to them about him, to him—speaking him himself. For he is that very thing I want to tell him, that very he, my he, the he of my love, existing nowhere outside of it.

I want to talk with him as well—this was, and is finished, for even counting dreams, dreams—are rarely dialogues, are almost always monologues—of our longing for a thing, or of the thing's longing for us. Reciprocal dreams don't exist. Either I call someone into my dream, or someone enters my dream. One's company, not two. (Let's recall all those visitations from the other world, faced with which we are in life (not counting Hamlet, since that's—literature) struck speechless. And all of our invocations to appear, to which no one responds. "I'll show up when I can," the way we say: "I'll see it when it shows up," something like the old-fashioned "by occasion." A bond preserved only inside and which breaks with the slightest attempt at realization. A conversation over a

351

line that's been cut. (The only proof of death.) And—even if dialogues—then two arrangements of one longing.

In a word, the conversation: question and answer (in this case—an answer and an answer), mine with Rilke, is finished, and perhaps—it's the only thing that is finished.

But most importantly, I want him to talk—to me. This could be in dreams and through books. Dreams are many and books are many—undreamed dreams and Rilke's unpublished letters. Counting the echo—it's enough to last a lifetime.

On posthumous letters. I'm grateful to those who gave me the opportunity to read them, but I won't hear their gratitude, and as to the nature of my own gratitude—I shall remain silent. (The exception—the "unknown" woman who relates, that is creates, something which would not have existed *in words* without her—her own Rilke, yet another Rilke.)

Would they have done this yesterday? More weighty evidence than "would"—is that they didn't do it. Then why are they doing this today? What happened between yesterday and today to inspire and authorize them to make Rilke's letters public? —Death? —So they actually believed in it, recognized it? Yes, they recognized it, and having recognized it, made use of it. Reasons are not the point—we'll assume they're the most virtuous. —"To share." —But why is it that yesterday, during his lifetime, you didn't share, but guarded, preserved?

"It would have bothered Rilke." —And today? What, for God's sake, is the difference? How is it that a thing which yesterday would have been—almost a betrayal of trust, is considered today, in regard to the same person, virtually a "sacred duty"?

A thing is either bad or good, the day—has no meaning, the fact of death—has no meaning, for Rilke—it has no meaning and never had any. Did he publish the letters of his friends the day after their death?

What matters is not the reason, but the season. Fifty years

from now, when all of this will have passed, will have *completely* passed, and the bodies will have decayed and the inks will have faded, when the addressee will have long since gone to the sender (me—that's the first letter that will reach its destination!), when Rilke's letters will have become simply Rilke's letters—not to me—to everyone, when I myself have dissolved into everything, and—oh, this most of all!—when I will no longer need Rilke's letters, because I will have—all of Rilke.—

One should not publish without permission. Without permission, that is—before its time. As long as the addressee is here, and the sender there, there can be no answer. His answer to my question will be—the time has come. "May I?" Be my guest. But no sooner than—God alone knows.

They'll tell me (and if they don't—I'll tell myself, for we are our own worst (best) opponents—the most keen-sighted and merciless): "But Rilke himself was in favor of publishing his letters, in which he lived as fully as in his verse . . ."

Rilke—yes, and you? Permission to publish—very well, but permission for the desire? ("Permit me to feel like . . .") And, even if it was Rilke's own wish—how could it have become yours? And even if it's the simple fulfillment of his wishes, even if, moreover, against your own—where is love? For love not only obeys—it dictates, not only gives away, but defends.

So, should Rilke permit me a thousand times—it's my job to refuse. And should Rilke ask me for the thousandth time —it's my job to refuse. For the will of my love is higher than his will over me, otherwise it would not be love: that which is greater than everything. (I take the worst case for myself: Rilke's reiterated, insistent request which of course never was, was—a slip of the tongue—if it was at all.) So, having inquired—is there permission for desire?—I maintain: there is permission for nondesire, not given to me—by Rilke, but taken—from Rilke—by my love. —Permit me not only not to publish your letters, but not to want to either.

And, from myself to others: Where is love? Or are you so much spirit that you don't begrudge a piece of paper? Whence this catastrophic love, as of yestereve, for thy neighbor—"to share"—a love which wasn't there yesterday, since you didn't share yesterday, a love which yesterday was surpassed by love for Rilke—since you didn't "share" then. Isn't there an element of impunity in this haste also—"he won't see" (the elder—the deceased—God) and isn't what I'm talking about not only an acknowledgment of death, but also a nonacknowledgment of immortality (of presence)?

Loving a person, how is it possible to give him away to everyone, "to the first comer, the most unworthy."* How can you stand this—the translation of his handwriting into lineo- or monotype, from that paper—onto this paper?

Where is jealousy, *sacred* after death?

The point is not other ears, which don't interfere if only because they don't hear, they don't hear the right thing, they hear what they want to, but the directionality of my speech—from him (since about him!), the bare fact of the detour of speech, outside of its content. For: not only abuse betrays, praise also betrays—the trust of him who put his faith in you, who accorded you the honor of being himself—in your presence. Not only—his trust, and your trust—of him (our feelings are not in us, we are in them), but betrayal of mutual trust, which is mystery, which is love.

Every mother, failing to resist the temptation to share with others, outsiders, some profound or endearing word of her child, and later clothing the cautioning clutching of her heart in the troubled words: "It was wrong... Why?... I shouldn't have...," suffers the torments of betrayal. He told me (in my presence), and I—told everyone. Though he said something good (and I repeated that good), I—am a traitor. For betrayal lies not in the reason, but outside the reason,

---

*Quotation marks from the future. [M. Ts.]

in the simple fact of conveyal. To convey—is to betray, just as in this case (the publication of Rilke's letters)—to give is to betray.

A painful accompaniment to our every syllable, a painful echo, with this difference, that it precedes sound—this is the heart. An echo in reverse. Not a reverberation, not a resounding, but a pre-sounding. My mouth is still closed and I already repent—for I know that I'll open my mouth—and disclose a secret. The disclosing of a secret is just the dis-closing of the mouth. Who among us has not experienced this: "like falling down a hill . . ."

Thus, Joan of Arc lo-o-o-ng did not speak at home of the miracle of voices.

There was a secret. The secret is no more. There was a union. The union dissolved. Through the breach broken by the printing press, all have entered.

The only striking exception, and I don't believe in them, for every exception, exclusion from—is an inclusion in (it is impossible to exclude oneself into a void), is—an inescapable falling into another law—("the law isn't written for him"—yes, because at the moment it's being written by him)—and so, the only striking exception (exclusion), that is to say, the beginning of a new law—is the famous *Briefwechsel** of Bettina Brentano.

For just a moment, let us believe in the "exception," and—

First of all: Bettina was not giving just letters, but a correspondence, not one voice, but two. If betrayal—then full and complete.

Secondly: in the correspondence with Goethe (*Goethes Briefwechsel mit einem Kinde*[†]), Bettina, by her own admission, is erecting a monument to him. A monument to an elder, deigning to write to a child, to the Goethe that she evoked,

---

*Correspondence.

[†]*Goethe's Correspondence with a Child.*

that she created, that she alone knew. —Psyche, playing at the feet, not of Eros, but of Zeus; Zeus, leaning over not Semele, but Psyche. —To exalt him within the means of her own (childish—she thought) powers. To exalt him again, in yet another way. If we remember Goethe the Secret Counselor—we'll understand Bettina.

Nor should we forget that the last guest of the dying Goethe was Bettina's oldest son, and that Bettina gave away her remotest past—almost posthumously.

In another book: Gunderode (correspondence with a woman friend)—the same monument, there—to old age and glory, here—to youth and shadow. To long life. To an early death. To revive immortality. To immortalize early death. That same duty of love. To exalt. To erect.

Thirdly: Bettina published the correspondence with her near ones during their lifetime—the correspondence with her brother, for example (Clemens Brentanos Jugendkranz), or with her young friend, for example—when she was already an old woman (Julius Pamphilius), which already removes any shadow of posthumous betrayal from her.

And—all these instances taken together—in publishing the letters of her friends, Bettina speaks through them for the speechless. No one knew this Goethe, no one knew this Gunderode, and this Clemens (presently a gloomy religious fanatic)—*had been forgotten*, there was no such Julius Pamphilius at all, he was completely inspired by Bettina, and stayed around in the air only just as long as she held him there.

But Rilke, such as he is in his letters—everyone knew, for no other Rilke—a "famous" Rilke, a "domestic" Rilke, a "man of letters" Rilke, a "society" Rilke, ever existed. There was one Rilke, that is, everything, except the above-mentioned, in one. What can be added to everything? Yet another—everything?

Fourthly: total absence of the idea of sharing. Total absence of the idea of the other (a third presence). A vital absence, because for Bettina even a second is too much. *Ich will keine Gegenliebe!**—after such a challenge, thrown in Goethe's face, that is, in the face of love itself, dare we suspect her of the softhearted desire to "share"—with just anyone—the beloved she didn't even share with the beloved?

Love cannot abide a third person. Bettina cannot abide a second. For her, Goethe—is an impediment. To love—alone. To love—by herself. To take upon herself the entire mountain of love and to carry it herself. So that it wouldn't be lightened. So that it wouldn't be lessened.

What is the opposite of sharing? Giving away! In the "*Goethes Briefwechsel mit einem Kinde*," Bettina gives away her undivided (and only for that reason unrequited) love—in its entirety—not to somebody, but in Thy name. She gives it away, just as she (herself!) once took it. Just as entirely as she once defended it.

Thus are treasures thrown into the fire.

No thought of others. No thought of herself. Thou, thou, thou. And—o miracle!—a monument to whom? To the *Kind*, and not to Goethe. To the lover, not the beloved. A monument to Bettina, who was not understood by Goethe. To Bettina, who was not understood by Bettina. To Bettina, understood by the Future: R. M. Rilke.

Boast, brag, praise, laud, eulogize. Let's begin at the end. Let's begin at the beginning of Bettina. "Every breath doth praise the Lord." Bettina praised the Lord—with her every breath. Some recent commentator on Bettina: "Bettina never found God because she never searched for him." Because from birth she had found him. Does one search for the forest—in the forest?

And if Bettina never called God "God"—he doesn't care, for he knows it isn't his name—he doesn't have a name—and is called by this name, too. And in her every "Thou," wasn't

---

*I don't want requital!

there more than any person could contain? And wasn't Goethe, with his brushings-off and his refusings, dispatching her directly to God? If she did get there sometimes, then—*he* didn't dispatch her. "I am not God"—was all Goethe could say to Bettina. Rilke would have said: "God—is not me."

Goethe returned Bettina to Bettina.

Rilke would have sent Bettina—further on.

Bettina's every breath—is a eulogy. "*Loben sollen wir*"*— did Bettina say this, or was it Rilke?

Bettina's letters (not Goethe's to her)—this is one of Rilke's favorite books, as Bettina herself is one of his favorite, if not the most dearly loved, of beloved beings to him.

Moreover—Bettina was the first. And, as the first—she paid for it. Between the reception of her "*Briefwechsel mit einem Kinde*" and the reception of Rilke's currently appearing correspondence—lies an abyss as wide as a whole century and as deep as a whole new human consciousness. Bettina knew what she was doing, otherwise she wouldn't have prefaced her step with the cry: "*Dies Buch ist für die Guten und nicht für die Bösen!*"†—and she went ahead in spite of it. The present addressees also know what they're doing—and that's why they're doing it.

Nothing sets an example. Bettina doesn't either. Bettina is irrevocably and irrepeatably right according to that cruel *law of exceptionality*, into which she stepped at birth.

And, ending up face-to-face with Rilke: Perhaps he wrote for everyone? —Perhaps. —But there will always be an "everyone," not a particular everyone—but a future everyone. And those distant ones will hear Rilke, with his God-descendant, better. Rilke is that which is yet to come true—over centuries. The seven letters I have lying in a box at home (doing

---

*We ought to praise.

†This book is for the good, not for the bad!

the very same thing he is doing, not he, but his body, just as the letters—are not thought, but the body of thought)—these seven letters, lying at home in a box, with his pictures and his last elegy, I am giving to those who will come after me—not, I will give—I am giving now. When they're born—they'll receive them. And when they are born—I will have already passed.

This will be the day of the resurrection of his thought in flesh. Let them sleep until it's time, until—not the Last, but—the Luminous Judgment. Thus, true to both duty and jealousy, I will not betray and will not conceal.

And today I want Rilke to speak—through me. In the vernacular, this is known as translation. (How much better the Germans put it—*nachdichten*! Following in the poet's path, paving anew the entire road which he paved. For let *nach* be—(to follow after), but—*dichten*!* is that which is always anew.) *Nachdichten*—to pave anew the road along instantaneously vanishing traces. But translation has another meaning. To translate not only *into* (the Russian language, for example), but also *across* (a river). I translate Rilke into the Russian tongue, as he will some day translate me to the other world.

By the hand—across the river. An article about Rilke is all the more useless because he didn't write articles about others, and didn't read ones about himself. He wouldn't have read (and will not read) mine either. Rilke and articles (in Germany they even write dissertations on him)—is absurd. To reveal essence is impossible, approaching from outside. Essence is only revealed by essence, from within—inward—not investigation, but absorption. Mutual absorption. Allow the thing to absorb you and—thereby—absorb it. As one river

---

*To sing, to tell, to compose, create?—it doesn't exist in Russian. [M. Ts.]

flows into another. The point where the waters merge—but it isn't ever a point because—the meeting of the waters—is a meeting without parting, for the Rhine—takes the Main into itself, as the Main does the Rhine. And only the Main knows the truth of the Rhine (its own truth, Mainian, just as the Moselle—knows the Mosellian; the whole truth of the Rhine —of Rilke—is not given to us to know). Like a hand in a hand, yes, but even more: like a river in a river.

Absorbing, I am absorbed.

Every—*approach*—is a retreat.

Rilke—is a myth, the beginning of a new myth of God— the descendant. It's early yet to be investigating—allow it to happen.

A book about Rilke—yes, sometime, approaching old age (the age along with youth, particularly dear to Rilke) when I will have caught up with him a bit. Not a book of articles, a book of genesis—but of his genesis, of genesis in him.

For those individuals touched by these letters, and who may not know German (there is no good translation of his poetry into Russian), I refer them to his book *Les Cahiers de Malte Laurids Brigge* (in the excellent translation by Maurice Betz, checked by Rilke himself) and to the small book of verse, *Vergers*, written just before his death, in the French original.

—*Meudon, February 1929*

NOTES

INTRODUCTION

1. Marina Tsvetayeva, "Neskolko pisem Rainera Mariya Rilke" (Several Letters from Rainer Maria Rilke), *Volya Rossii* (Paris), no. 2 (1929), pp. 26–27, 31.

2. Boris Pasternak, "Lyudi i polozheniya" (People and Circumstances), *Novy mir* (Moscow), no. 1 (1967), p. 233.

3. In 1943–44 the poet Alexei Kruchyonykh (1886–1968) assembled a collection of typewritten manuscripts entitled *Vstrechi s Marinoi Tsvetayevoi* (Meetings with Marina Tsvetayeva), which included copies of some of Tsvetayeva's letters to Pasternak, poems dedicated by Pasternak to Tsvetayeva, book inscriptions, poems written by Tsvetayeva in her youth, and various observations by Tsvetayeva, all with Kruchyonykh's running commentary.

4. Boris Pasternak Archives, Moscow. Henceforth no reference will be given for material from the Pasternak archives, either in Moscow or in Oxford.

5. Tsvetayeva, "Neskolko pisem," pp. 31–32.

6. Letter (in French) from Boris Pasternak to Michel Aucouturier of February 4, 1959, in *Cahiers du monde russe et soviétique* (Paris) XV, nos. 1–2 (1974), p. 232.

7. Marina Tsvetayeva, *Pisma k Anne Teskovoi* (Letters to Anna Tesková) (Prague, 1969), p. 52.

8. Rainer Maria Rilke and Lou Andreas-Salomé, *Briefwechsel* (Zurich, 1952), pp. 109–10.

9. Letter to Leopold von Schlözer of January 21, 1920, in *Briefe*, by Rainer Maria Rilke (Frankfurt am Main, 1980), p. 617.

10. Letter "To a Young Friend" of March 17, 1926, *ibid.*, p. 929.

11. Letter of February 15, 1923, in *Rilke vivant*, by Maurice Betz (Paris, 1935), p. 46.

12. Manuscript Section of the Moscow State University Library, S. N. Schill Collection, no. 1004.

13. *Wiadomości literackie* (Warsaw), no. 46 (November 16, 1924).

14. S. N. Schill Collection.

15. Rainer Maria Rilke, *Briefe und Tagebücher aus der Frühzeit* (Leipzig, 1931), p. 66.

16. *Ibid.*, pp. 14–15.

17. "Letters of Rainer Maria Rilke to Hélène," *Oxford Slavonic Papers* IX (1960), p. 160.

18. *Ibid.*, p. 156 (letter of June 9, 1899).

19. *Ibid.*, p. 159 (letter of July 27, 1899).

20. Rainer Maria Rilke, *Briefe aus den Jahren 1892 bis 1904* (Leipzig, 1939), pp. 75 ff.

21. S. N. Schill Collection.

22. Rainer Maria Rilke, *Tagebücher aus der Frühzeit* (Leipzig, 1942), p. 232.

23. S. Brutzer, "Rilkes russische Reisen," unpublished dissertation, Königsberg, 1934, p. 6.

24. Rilke, *Briefe und Tagebücher aus der Frühzeit*, p. 37.

25. S. N. Schill Collection.

26. Heinrich Vogeler, *Erinnerungen*, ed. Erich Weinert (Berlin, 1952), p. 100.

27. Manuscript Section of the State Museum of Russian Art in Leningrad, Collection 137, no. 1953.

28. Lou Andreas-Salomé, *Rainer Maria Rilke* (Leipzig, 1928), p. 90.

29. Manuscript Section of the Institute for Russian Literature (Pushkin House), Collection 619, no. 19.

30. *Ibid.*, no. 4.

31. Manuscript Section of the Central State Archives for Literature and Art, Collection 459, I, no. 3958.

32. Rainer Maria Rilke and Lou Andreas-Salomé, *Briefwechsel* (Frankfurt am Main, 1975), p. 116.

33. Rainer Maria Rilke, *Auguste Rodin*, in *Werkausgabe* (Frankfurt am Main, 1965), 5, p. 141 (originally published in 1903).

34. Marina Tsvetayeva, "Poet i vremya" (The Poet and His Times), *Volya Rossii* (Paris), nos. 1–3 (1932), pp. 18–19.

35. Rainer Maria Rilke, *Briefe an Nanny Wunderly-Volkart* (Frankfurt am Main, 1977), 2, p. 1047–48.

36. Leonid Osipovich Pasternak, *Zapisi raznykh let* (Notes Written over the Years) (Moscow, 1975), p. 146.

37. *Ibid.*, p. 148.

38. Boris Pasternak, *Okhrannaya gramota* (Safe Conduct) (Leningrad, 1931), pp. 5–6.

39. Leonid Pasternak, *Zapisi raznykh let*, p. 150.

40. Eleven Rilke letters from 1899 to 1906, and one from 1926, are extant. At the request of Clara Westhoff-Rilke, eleven were sent to the Rilke archives in 1928; only one, written in Russian and dated February 13, 1901, remains in Moscow.

41. Marina Tsvetayeva, "Svetovoi liven" (Torrents of Light), *Epopeya* (Berlin), no. 2 (1922), pp. 10–33.

42. Pasternak, "Lyudi i polozheniya," p. 232.

43. *Ibid.*

44. Handwritten annotation in the copy of the journal *Cahiers de l'étoile*, no. 10 (1929) (which included Tsvetayeva's essay on Rilke),

sent to Nanny Wunderly-Volkart, quoted in *Rainer Maria Rilke: Katalog der Ausstellung des deutschen Literaturarchivs* (Marbach/Neckar, 1975), p. 333.

45. Marina Tsvetayeva, "O Germanii" (On Germany) (exerpts from her diary of 1919), in *Nesobrannyye proizvedeniya* (Uncollected Works) (Munich, 1971), p. 469.

46. Anastasia Tsvetayeva, *Vospominaniya* (Memoirs), 2nd ed. (Moscow, 1974), p. 15.

47. *Ibid.*, p. 173.

48. Tsvetayeva, *Pisma k Anne Teskovoi*, p. 48.

49. *Novy mir* (Moscow), no. 4 (1969), p. 204.

50. Pasternak, *Okhrannaya gramota*, p. 112.

51. Pasternak, "Lyudi i polozheniya," p. 219.

52. Tsvetayeva, *Pisma k Anne Teskovoi*, p. 57.

53. Letter to Vera Bunina of May 4, 1926, in *Neizdannyye pisma* (Unpublished Letters) (Paris, 1972), p. 399.

54. Letter of May 23, 1938, in *Pisma k Anne Teskovoi*, p. 159.

55. Marina Tsvetayeva, "Zhivoye o zhivom" (Live Talk About Live Things), in *Maksimilian Voloshin—khudozhnik* (Maximilian Voloshin—Artist) (Moscow, 1976), p. 143.

56. Marina Tsvetayeva, *Posle Rossii* (After Russia) (Paris, 1928), p. 11.

57. Marina Tsvetayeva, "Pisma k A. Shteigeru" (Letters to Anatoly Steiger), *Opyty*, no. 5 (1955), p. 47.

58. Tsvetayeva, *Posle Rossii*, p. 74.

59. Tsvetayeva, "Pisma k A. Shteigeru," p. 59.

60. Anastasia Tsvetayeva, *Vospominaniya*, p. 77.

61. Letter of September 16, 1926, in Marina Tsvetayeva, *Neizdannyye pisma*, p. 230.

62. Letter to Yuri Ivask of April 8, 1934, in *Russki literaturny arkhiv* (New York, 1956), pp. 214–15.

CHAPTER 1

1. Ariadna Efron, "Stranitsy vospominanii" (Pages of Recollections), *Zvezda* (Moscow), no. 6 (1975), p. 163.

2. *Ibid.*, p. 165.

3. Letter to the biologist Selma Ruoff of May 12, 1956, in *Voprosy literatury* (Moscow), no. 9 (1972), pp. 170–71.

CHAPTER 2

1. Marina Tsvetayeva, *Pisma k Anne Teskovoi* (Prague, 1969), p. 91.

CHAPTER 4

1. Poem 14 from the cycle "Podruga" (My Friend) (1915), in *Neizdannoye* (Unpublished Work) by Marina Tsvetayeva (Paris, 1976), p. 74.

2. Letter to Selma Ruoff of May 12, 1956, in *Voprosy literatury*, no. 9 (1972), p. 171.

3. First published in *Novy mir*, nos. 8–9 (1926).

4. These lines are from Pasternak's poem "Lofty Malady." In the second line, "world" is Tsvetayeva's substitution for Pasternak's "age."

5. The first lines of the chapter "Mutiny at Sea" from Pasternak's poem *The Year 1905*.

6. From Pushkin's poem "To the Sea." See Tsvetayeva's reference to it in the questionnaire she filled out, p. 77.

7. From Tsvetayeva's poem "Eurydice's Gift to Orpheus," in *Izbrannyye proizvedeniya* (Selected Works), p. 231.

8. From the poem "The hair at my temples is graying . . . ," in *Izbrannyye proizvedeniya*, p. 273.

9. The cycle of poems called "The Two" consists of three poems, whose last lines Tsvetayeva gave here: *Izbrannyye proizvedeniya*, pp. 258–60.

CHAPTER 5

1. Translated by A. Karelsky, published in *Novyye stikhotvoreniya* (New Poems), by Rainer Maria Rilke, pp. 321–23.

CHAPTER 6

1. Ariadna Efron, "Stranitsy vospominanii," *Zvezda*, no. 6 (1975), p. 165.

2. Marina Tsvetayeva, *Pisma k Anne Teskovoi* (Prague, 1969), p. 145.

3. A line from Rilke's poem "Ich bin auf der Welt zu allein," included in his *Book of Hours*.

4. A free paraphrase of the last two lines of Rilke's poem "Herbst" from *The Book of Images*: "*Und doch ist Einer, welcher dieses Fallen unendlich sanft in seinen Händen hält...*"

CHAPTER 7

1. Vladimir Mayakovsky, "Don't hurry to blame the poets..." *Krasnaya nov* (Red Virgin Soil), no. 4 (1926), pp. 223–24.

2. A version of two lines from the unfinished poem "Time is not a heavy burden..." (May 1924), with an epigraph taken from Boris Pasternak's "I live with your picture..."

3. Lines from Pasternak's poem "A Thunderstorm—instantaneous forever..."

4. From Rilke's poem "Nul ne sait, combien ce qu'il refuse," *Vergers* (1926), p. 14.

5. From the poem "Eau qui se presse, qui court," *Vergers*, p. 22.

6. From the poem "Puisque tout passe, faisons," *Vergers*, p. 40.

7. From Tsvetayeva's poem cycle "Poets," in *Izbrannyye proizvedeniya*, pp. 231–32.

8. First line of the poem in *Vergers*, p. 25.

9. From the second poem of the cycle "Printemps," *Vergers*, p. 47.

10. From the poem "Le Drapeau," *Vergers*, pp. 52–53.

11. From the poem "Au ciel, plein d'attention," *Vergers*, pp. 82–83.

CHAPTER 8

1. Ariadna Efron, "Stranitsy vospominanii," *Zvezda*, no. 6 (1975), p. 165.

2. Marina Tsvetayeva, *Neizdannyye pisma* (Paris, 1972), p. 140.

CHAPTER 9

1. From Rilke's poem "Combien le pape au fond de son faste," in *Vergers* (1926), p. 27. Exact quotation: "... *Trop pure, la cathédrale provoque un vent de dédain*" (Too pure, the cathedral provokes a wind of contempt).

2. From Goethe's 1782 article on nature: "And that which is most unnatural is also part of nature."

3. Last line of Rilke's poem "Combien a-t-on fait aux fleurs," in *Vergers*, pp. 12–13.

4. More exactly, "*Vergangenes steht noch bevor...*," a line from Rilke's poem "Ich bin derselbe noch, der kniete" (*Book of Hours*).

EPILOGUE

1. From Rilke's poem "Above the blue of Moscow woods" in the cycle *Poems About Moscow*, in *Izbrannyye proizvedeniya*, p. 82.

2. Marina Tsvetayeva, *Svodnyye tetradi* (Moscow, 1997), p. 544.

3. Since the original is lost, the following is based on a Russian translation that was preserved, edited, and corrected according to entries in Tsvetayeva's notebook.

4. This refers to "A New Year's," originally entitled "A Letter," published in *Versty*, no. 3 (1928), pp. 7–18.

5. Marina Tsvetayeva, "Your Death," in *Volya Rossii*, nos. 5–6 (1927), p. 25.

6. Marina Tsvetayeva, *Pisma k Anne Teskovoi* (Prague, 1969), p. 37.

7. *Ibid.*, p. 49.

8. Tsvetayeva, *Svodnyye tetradi*, p. 544.

9. Boris Pasternak, in *Chitatel i pisatel* (Reader and Writer), nos. 4–5 (1928).

10. Stanford, Book I, p.148.

11. Boris Pasternak, *Sobraniye sochinenii v piati tomakh* (Moscow, 1990–1992), vol. 4 , p. 159.

12. The initial copy of this letter was made by E. A. Krasheninnikova on October 19, 1941.

13. This poem, entitled "Signs" (*Primety*) and dated November 29, 1924, was first published in the Parisian Russian émigré newspaper *Posledniye novosti*, no. 1737, December 20, 1925. Tsvetayeva included it in her collection *After Russia*.

14. Pasternak, *Sobraniye sochinenii*, vol. 5, p. 217.

15. *Gorkii i sovetskie pisateli* (Moscow, 1963), pp. 301–2 (October 19, 1927).

16. Pasternak, *Sobraniye sochinenii*, vol. 5, p. 220.

17. Boris Pasternak, *Pisma k roditeliam i syostram* (Letters to His Parents and Sisters) (Stanford, 1988), Book I, p. 214.

18. *Ibid.*, p. 220.

19. *Ibid.*, p. 222.

20. *Ibid.*, p. 227–28.

21. *Ibid.*, p. 240. The reference is to Leo Tolstoy's story.

22. Pasternak, *Sobraniye sochinenii*, vol. 4, pp. 786–87.

23. Tsvetayeva, *Svodnyye tetradi*, pp. 388–89.

24. Pasternak, *Sobraniye sochinenii*, pp. 275–76.

25. Manuscript Section of RGALI, Russian State Archives for Literature and Art, Moscow, Collection 1334, I, no. 798.

26. Zoya Maslennikova, *A Portrait of Boris Pasternak* (Moscow, 1995), p. 69.

27. RGALI, Collection 1334, I, no. 798.

28. RGALI, Collection 379, I, no. 104.

29. *Literaturnaya ucheba*, no. 6 (1988), p. 116.

INDEX

369

Index

OTHER NEW YORK REVIEW BOOKS CLASSICS*

For a complete list of titles, visit www.nyrb.com or write to:
Catalog Requests, NYRB, 1755 Broadway, New York, NY 10009-3780